MODERN LEGAL STUDIES

GRIEVANCES, REMEDIES AND THE STATE

AUSTRALIA AND NEW ZEALAND
The Law Book Company Ltd.
Sydney : Melbourne : Perth

CANADA AND U.S.A.
The Carswell Company Ltd.
Agincourt, Ontario

INDIA
N. M. Tripathi Private Ltd.
Bombay
and
Eastern Law House Private Ltd.
Calcutta and Delhi
M.P.P. House
Bangalore

ISRAEL
Steimatzky's Agency Ltd.
Jerusalem : Tel Aviv : Haifa

MALAYSIA : SINGAPORE : BRUNEI
Malayan Law Journal (Pte.) Ltd.
Singapore

PAKISTAN
Pakistan Law House
Karachi

MODERN LEGAL STUDIES

GRIEVANCES, REMEDIES AND THE STATE

by

PATRICK BIRKINSHAW, LL.B.
Lecturer at the Faculty of Law,
University of Hull

LONDON
SWEET & MAXWELL
1985

Published in 1985 by
Sweet & Maxwell Limited of
11 New Fetter Lane, London.
Computerset by Promenade Graphics Ltd., Cheltenham.
Printed in Great Britain by
Robert Hartnoll (1985) Limited, Bodmin, Cornwall

British Library Cataloguing in Publication Data

Birkinshaw, Patrick
 Grievances, remedies and the state.—(Modern legal studies)
 1. Abuse of administrative power—Great Britain
 2. Ombudsman—Great Britain
 I. Title   II. Series
 354.41009'1   KD4900

 ISBN 0-421-32600-X
 ISBN 0-421-32610-7 Pbk

PREFACE

This book has had a long gestation period. The idea developed while I was working with Norman Lewis on local government in the late 1970s. It seemed to me then, and now, that neither lawyers nor researchers in other disciplines had explored adequately the internal processes of governmental institutions and the way they respond to complaints, complainants or allow informal opportunities for consultation or even participation in decision-making; or, most cherished of all, simply leave organisations or interests to regulate their own affairs within the framework of the general law. The plan was to examine a section of the institutions of the contemporary British State, to establish what they did in relation to grievances from the public affected by their administration, and to study what connections there were between these informal practices and the more formal procedures for complaint resolution or dispute settlement culminating with Ombudsmen and Courts of Law. In other words, I was inverting the traditional approach which begins with the courts and, sometimes, works "down" as it were. As such, the idea was ambitious, possibly over-ambitious. There was a necessity for much original empirical field-work; in government departments, (comprising interviews and visits between 1982 and 1984), local authorities, with nationalised industry consumer councils, health authorities and public corporations etc. I did not want simply to go and examine and report. I wanted also to explain how these processes tied in with a representative—democratic model of government, and how our public institutions operated when set beside the ideals which our system of government and law are supposed to foster; and to ask what was there about the ideals which needed developing, advancing or strengthening and was this possible given political, economic and cultural constraints? A phrase of Roberto Unger's—the dialectic interplay between the organisation of power and its legitimation—seemed to sum up what I had in mind.

This is a study of public institutions. This is not to deny the importance of individuals. Far from it. Rather it is an acknowledgment of the fact that the institutions of the State, comprising individual politicians and officials, and their operations, set the political climate in which our lives, rights and liberties flourish; or otherwise.

On the acknowledgments side, my debt is embarrassing. First and foremost to my wife, Jane, who typed, and re-typed, and re-typed most of the manuscript, the tables and index. Literally

v

countless civil servants, local government officials, public officials and appointees have shown enormous forbearance and assistance. My thanks to all of them. Tony Prosser, Ian Harden, Chris Himsworth, Tony Bradley, Richard Thomas and Ray Smith all read chapters and made helpful criticisms and suggestions. Patrick McAuslan provided encouragement and much constructive advice. Norman Lewis has as tutor, colleague and friend more responsibility than anyone else for stimulating my interest in the present subject and making me realise the limits of my knowledge of the field. The shortcomings, oversights and errors in the work are mine alone. I have been able to refer to developments up to December 31, 1984. Finally, I would like to thank my colleagues in the Faculty of Law at Hull for covering for me while on study leave and Pat Wilson, Melanie Bucknell and Joan Wilson who typed various sections of the book.

Notice of *R.* v. *H.M. Treasury*, *ex p.* Smedley [1985] 1 All E.R. 589 (*vires* of Treasury decision expressed in delegated legislation, even in draft, are justiciable, page 18) and Tribunals and Inquiries (F.C.C) Order 1984, S.I. 1984 No. 1247 (Foreign Compensation Commission now under supervision of the Council on Tribunals, page 31) came too late to incorporate in the text.

Hull University
March 1985.

CONTENTS

OTHER BOOKS IN THE SERIES

ABBREVIATIONS USED IN THE TEXT

Agricultural Dwelling-House Advisory Committee	ADHAC
Central Electricity Generating Board	C.E.G.B.
Civil Aviation Authority	C.A.A.
Commission for Local Administration	C.L.A.
Commission for Racial Equality	C.R.E.
Comptroller and Auditor General	C. and A.G.
Department of Education and Science	D.E.S.
Department of the Environment	D.o.E.
Department of Transport	D.T.
Electricity Council	E.C.
Housing Corporation	H.C.
National Consumer Council	N.C.C.
National Federation of Housing Associations	N.F.H.A.
Nationalised Industries	N.I.s
Nationalised Industry Consumer Councils	NICCs
Outer Circle Policy Unit	O.C.P.U.
Parliamentary Commissioner for Administration	P.C.A.
Society of Local Authority Chief Executives	SOLACE

TABLE OF CASES

TABLE OF STATUTES

Chapter 1

INTRODUCTION

This book seeks to discuss, in terms of our contemporary constitutional apparatus, some of the less well charted opportunities
which exist for individuals and groups to make complaints to and
about governmental institutions. It will also examine the extent to
which opportunities are available for participation by individuals
and groups in the decision-making processes of governmental
institutions. As such the examination will take us beyond the existence of statutory devices for review or appeal, judicial, internal or
otherwise, reconsideration of a decision or complaint-handling,
and will look at non-statutory practices both of a formal and
non-formal nature. It is hoped that the examination will tell us
something of value about the constitutional map of power in the
contemporary British State, by which is included central government, local government, the whole range of quasi-government,
the police—in short the *loci* of official power. The "State" as an
heuristic concept has not been widely employed in British constitutional or legal theory[1] and the present work does not make any

---

[1] For a lucid account of the reasons behind the absence of a "State tradition" in
Britain see K. Dyson, *The State Tradition in Western Europe* (1980). On the use
of the term "State" in British constitutional theory see G. Marshall, *Constitutional Theory* (1971), esp. Chap. 2. In Britain, argues Dyson, there is a "disin-
clination to explore ideas about the distinctive character of public authority.
Little or no attention is paid to state as a political concept which identifies the
nation in its corporate and collectivist capacity; as a legal institution with an
inherent responsibility for regulating matters of public concern; and as a socio-
cultural phenomenon which expresses a new unique form of associative bond,"
op. cit. p. 43. For an interesting judicial observation on the term state in British
constitutional law, see Lord Simon in *D.* v. *N.S.P.C.C.* [1977] 1 All E.R. 589 at
609–610. The term "State" occurs frequently in constitutional and administrative
usage in the U.K. We have Secretaries of State; Acts of State; State secrets; acts
which are prejudicial to the safety or interest of the State; State registered
nurses, etc. We also make do with an ambiguous variety of other epithets where
other systems would be inclined to use the term State. These include the
"Crown," "government," "public," "civil," "national," "British" etc.; see G.
Marshall, *op. cit.* Chap. 2. For a broad brush treatment of the role of the State in
Britain since 1945, see B. Jessop, "The Transformation of the State in Post-War
Britain" in R. Scase (Ed.), *The State in Western Europe* and more generally *The
Capitalist State* (1982).

direct contribution to a theoretical discussion of the concept of the State. It will become obvious, however, that in discussing what constitutes the official *loci* of power, the parameters of legitimate public activity, we are beset by definitional problems in delineating the public and private realms. They will be analysed in due course, but first some preliminary points require explanation.

It would not have been so long ago, perhaps, when the title *Grievances, Remedies and the State* would have been conceived by lawyers purely in "legal" terms—those remedies obtainable through the courts. For lawyers to concentrate almost exclusively upon the decisions of courts has been interpreted as an unjustifi-able restriction when studying the range of devices and institutions through which the state elects to implement policy, regulate activity, achieve accountability or remedy grievances.[2] Associating concern for the "legal" with the activities of courts of law alone would be difficult to defend. This is certainly not a novel point. Yet our constitutional consciousness has ensured a belief in the ultimate superiority of political forms of redress for grievances and accountability via Parliament, the intercession of elected representatives, the dignity of debate on the floor of the House, ministerial responsibility, question time and latterly the new Select Committee structure. But these are political forms, and only comparatively recently have they been studied seriously by lawyers as devices for remedying grievances and achieving accountability—functions which are implicit in the rule of law ideal.

The role of our courts of law in public law matters is limited by two important factors. From a practical point of view, the process of going to law is fraught with technical danger and uncertainty—judicial review of administrative action, for instance, is a notoriously opaque area of the law. The second factor is the theoretically more important one that our courts of law are inferior to Parliament, and the common law inferior as a form of law to parliamentary legislation to which the Crown has assented. This is not the place to develop the implications of this doctrine, but our constitutional history has witnessed a rigid division between law and politics. There are realms within which judges may not operate. As one commentator has said, the language of law itself is noticeably remote from politics. "On the one hand, the judiciary has a fierce independence; on the other, law is not regarded as the great interpreter of the pattern of politics."[3] Law may be successful, though not all would agree with the proposition, in presenting

---

[2] Ganz, "The Allocation of Decision-Making Functions" (1972) P.L. 25 and 299.
[3] Dyson, *The State Tradition in Western Europe* (1980).

itself as an autonomous institution, but its autonomy has been bought at a price. Its narrow, technical and arid nature, especially it might be argued in the field of government, has helped to ensure a "wholesome English contempt for legal technique."[4]

Scepticism in the belief that politicians and administrators could always be left to their own devices and the narrow role of legal institutions in public administration are to a great extent behind the emergence of various administrative devices for ensuring accountability and remedying complaints. The Comptroller and Auditor General (C. and A.G.) has a long and worthy tradition, beset as he is by financial constraints and a lack of sufficient staff for his tasks, and recent years have seen a renewed interest in his office, culminating in the National Audit Act 1983, described as "An Act to strengthen Parliamentary control and supervision of expenditure of public money by making new provision for the appointment and status of the C. and A.G. . . . " and the establishment of a Public Accounts Commission and National Audit Office. The provisions of the Act were weakened considerably from the initial Bill as the Government claimed that such an extension of Parliament's power would interfere with accountability by ministerial responsibility.[5] The Parliamentary Commissioner for Administration (P.C.A.) is a relative newcomer to these shores and unlike the C. and A.G. concentrates on individual grievances. Lawyers would be correct to demonstrate his inferior status to courts when protecting or assisting individuals who are seeking redress against state departments. According to one commentator his office is "a valuable adjunct to any system of administrative law."[6] The Commissioner has shown promise, as well as some diffidence, when tackling bureaucracy on behalf of individual complainants. The ombudsman theme we return to in a later chapter; though we should note here that the office has been extended into the field of local government and the health service.

Our courts are one of several available devices through which we may obtain remedies against the State and its agencies, and through which forms of accountability may be achieved. More to the point, their position in these tasks is in practice a secondary one. At the optimum level, courts may be viewed as a quality control mechanism over politicians, bureaucrats, etc. But their role in reality is a largely *ex post facto* one. They arrive invariably on the

---

[4] *Per* F.W. Maitland, cited in Dyson (*op. cit.* n.1, *supra*) and see Maitland, "The Crown as Corporation" (1901) 18 L.Q.R. 131.

[5] Cmnd. 8323 (1981) and also H.C. 236, Vol. 1, 1981–82.

[6] H.W.R. Wade, *Administrative Law* (5th ed.) p. 85.

scene after events have taken place. It would be idle to deny the importance of the presence of institutions such as courts to put right what appears to have gone wrong. That point is elementary. But courts have not in our constitution—and this is a submission— had a significant impact in influencing *a priori* the process of public decision-making with ideals such as fairness, impartiality or legitimacy. The battlefields of the seventeenth century ensured that decision making of constitutional significance and political importance is, in theory, the preserve of political institutions. "As the common law ceded pride of place to statute law . . . it was quite unable to provide a body of public-law principles in terms of which legislation could be framed. Hence the Rule of Law became a narrow, formal concept expressing a procedural philosophy and losing the substantive concerns that were apparent even in Dicey's later classic formulation."[7] It may well be, as a United States jurist commented on the position in England, that this inculcated a reluctance among lawyers to ask fundamental questions about governmental right as a consequence of such decisions being withdrawn from the courts.[8] The burden of the present work is not to suggest that there should be a shifting back to the courts of such a power. It is a more mundane, yet fundamental one, that a lack of such legal involvement or concern has not assisted in the creation of fair and open procedures in our governmental processes; has not assisted in the formulation of a critique against secrecy and arbitrary decision making. Lawyers in other words were not troubled by problems of government legitimation. It legitimated itself.

This statement is not, of course, *equally* applicable to local government, and the relationship of the "local state" to individuals or groups within their particular areas. The fact that the powers of local authorities are in essence exclusively statutory and can be interpreted by judges, as well as the judicial creation of a special fiduciary relationship between authorities and ratepayers, have both ensured the occasional judicial reprimand for unconstitutional behaviour by local authorities, most recently in *Bromley London Borough Council* v. *Greater London Council*.[9] The subject drawing forth judicial stricture is invariably expenditure. Though often, as in the GLC case, the judicial activity becomes a matter of great national controversy, it will be argued that the general thrust of the comments in the later stage of the above paragraph are also relevant to local authority administration.

---

[7] Dyson, *The State Tradition in Western Europe* (1980).
[8] R. Dworkin, "Philosophy and Politics" in B. Magee (Ed.), *Men of Ideas*.
[9] [1983] 1 A.C. 768.

Commentators of various schools of thought have noted the narrow impact on our public administration of lawyers, legal skills and techniques. Their services have been neither welcomed nor encouraged outside traditional legal *fora*. It may well be that the values and techniques which lawyers supposedly espouse are seen as belonging exclusively to those *fora*. What are the values, and what are the techniques of law? One author has very persuasively argued that our current political and legal forms are still deeply embedded in nineteenth century liberal-democratic constitutional theory.[10] Central to that theory was a firm belief, in varying forms, in the separation of the powers of government, the separation of the state from any sectional interest in society and the existence of all institutions, private and public, as well as individuals, under the autonomous rule of law. That the State—the *loci* of official power and authority—was enjoined to intervene in "private" relationships to counter the excesses of its own neutrality in, for instance, commercial and social welfare is a well-documented development. Just as important for our present purposes was the emergence of a kind of law which in its most developed form viewed people and institutions as possessors of abstract rights and duties to be freely exchanged in a market regulated by nothing save the Invisible Hand of optimum resource allocation. Law was emphasised as being an independent and autonomous method for dealing with disputes between abstract and equal individuals. It operated within institutions immediately recognisable as "legal," *i.e.* courts of law, and which possessed the same degree of independence and autonomy in their operation as did the method of law when employed for dispute settlement. Law was about rules which could be applied in a value-free manner and without any necessity to advert to the values inherent in the rules.

Our system of government and law came to make no formal distinction between its public and private law. As a consequence there emerged no developed legal concept of the "State," no form of law addressing itself—such as for instance the French *Droit Administratif*—to the peculiarities of the State's position and in particular its relationships and liabilities towards its citizens whether actual, or as often in immigration cases, putative. The result was a blurring of the distinction between the "public" and the "private" realms, a point made by Dicey himself.[11] Such a blurring facilitated the well-known feature of the government

---

[10] G. Poggi, *The Development of the Modern State* (1978). C. & M. J. C. Vile, *Constitutionalism and the Separation of Powers* (1967).
[11] Dicey, *Law and Public Opinion in England* (1914, 2nd ed.).

hiding behind a liability which in legal theory was common to all, but which in fact had come to bestow special immunities and privileges upon the state. The peculiarities of the state's position and the problems posed by the use of its powers—Friedmann, for instance, nicely describes the role of the state as regulator, entrepreneur, provider and adjudicator[12]—was not accompanied by the creation of any specific legal liability expressing as its concern the redress of problems posed by such myriad and even contradictory roles. In addition to the emergence of vast areas of law which seem to be a grey hybrid of public and private law concepts—here one thinks of labour law, social welfare law, and in particular family law—the blurring of the distinction between public and private had other consequences.

It would not be an overstatement to suggest that the common view of law in the United Kingdom is of an impartial and objective entity, which is basically concerned with the adjudication of disputes between individuals. This view, however, misses the more important point that law is the medium through which the State organises and regulates activities collectively, *i.e.* where primary reference is to the overall impact and utility of State policies as opposed to specific individual impact. Law, or legislation, has been the device through which a whole corpus of state activities has been created. A vast array of public bodies has been established covering all aspects of administration from executive decision-making, adjudicatory functions, resource allocation, "legislative" practices (by which is included statutory instruments and departmental rule-making; the rule-making by non-departmental bodies and local authorities and their representative associations, etc.,) and a host of activities too many to enumerate. Yet it is submitted that the pervasive influence of the former approach to law and also lawyering has had a narrowing effect on the contribution legal techniques have been able to make to government. This is the more surprising when one considers the broad range of techniques and skills involved in lawyering. Summers, for instance, has outlined five basic techniques of law that a society might use. These are the grievance remedial; the penal; the administrative-regulatory; the public benefit conferral and the private arranging techniques.[13] One may cavil at or approve this range, but it clearly embraces techniques which transcend the adjudication of collisions between individuals. To take the administrative-regulatory and public benefit conferral techniques, for instance, the point has been argued

---

[12] W. Friedmann, *The Rule of Law in a Mixed Economy* (1971).
[13] Summers (1971) 59 Cal.L.Rev. 733.

forcefully that the skills of lawyers are alien to the broad discretionary basis upon which public administration operates. Summers would disagree, though it must be remembered that he speaks from within a United States background with its emphasis upon legal processes in public administration. Lawyers, it has been argued, would introduce excessive formalism or legalism into, for example, the tribunals administering the supplementary benefit system.[14] On the other hand one cannot guarantee, and much of our public administration certainly does not support the belief that politicians and bureaucrats, left to themselves, will devise procedures or decision-making processes which will ensure fairness in interest representation, fairness in procedure, accessibility for interested members of the public or accountability where broad discretionary decision-making is involved. This theme will be developed in Chapters 2, 3, 4 and 5, but the point to be made at this stage is that inherent in the craft of "lawyering" is an awareness of the strength of procedural forms, indifferent though many lawyers may be to extending this awareness beyond the dignity of our "high courts of law."

A narrow approach to law and legal techniques would have been open to valid criticism had the state not developed from its nineteenth century image of being equal with its subjects under law while simultaneously possessing the authority of government and providing the framework under which free individuals allocated their resources. How much more so therefore when this image of state and law has not kept pace with changes in the social and economic system. According to Poggi, and others, these changes have wrought a progressive compenetration of state and society. Government of the "official" kind syphoned off many of its tasks and functions to intermediaries, both of a public and non-public nature. It engaged in activities hitherto the preserve of the private sector; institutions and corporations in the private sector emerged as powers almost, if not actually, equal with the state though obviously not accountable in the same political manner. In short, the form of government associated with the nineteenth century state has long disappeared as a real practice. Though whether as Middlemas, to take one example, has suggested this was because it could not accommodate the antagonisms of industrial society[15] is beyond the scope of this book.

The legacy of the nineteenth century is still very much with us however, not only in terms of its sketch of imagined constitutional

[14] Titmus, "Welfare 'Rights,' Law and Discretion" (1971) 42 P.Q. 113.
[15] *Politics in Industrial Society* (1979).

power, parliamentary supremacy for instance or appeals to Victorian values, but ironically in presenting us with the results of the "centralising tendency" of the nineteenth century State, a process which has not abated. If anything it has accelerated as witness the struggle between central and local government since 1979 which has seen more control going to central government. There has been ambivalence here, for while the state became more powerful and more centralised, Parliament and the courts exercised less real control. 1911 saw the process and its attendant bureaucracy buttressed more effectively by official secrecy laws[16] doing little to dispel the sociological truism that institutions develop interests of their own about which the public is best kept in ignorance.[17] Departmental secrecy was afforded judicial dispensation in *Local Government Board* v. *Arlidge*,[18] and wartime conditions along with ministerial and bureaucratic sensitivity encouraged a series of judicial decisions destructive of accountability and openness.

Given the brief sketch of historical developments outlined above one might ask "Why should it have been otherwise?" Law, some would argue, had become a process of legitimating state activity, not an ideal to inform the vast governmental enterprise with standards of fairness, openness and accountability.

The ideals under which our government supposedly operates are the ideals of the rule of law. The concept of the rule of law as traditionally understood is not a self-evident truth, but is informed by a particular moral/political outlook. However desirable some of the features of the concept are in the abstract, by for example insisting upon equality before the law or the supremacy of regular law over arbitrary action, the society within which the rule of law ideal was forged has been subjected to irreversible structural changes. To insist, for instance, upon strict equality before the law, may produce greater inequality in our society, as well as greater power to the powerful. Again to insist upon the supremacy of regular law and the realisation of that law through existing "legal" mechanisms, *i.e.* the courts, is to turn the blindest of eyes to the very limited role of courts in our public administration.[19] If, to put it at its bluntest, the ideals of legality are to be more appropriately addressed and given greater realisation, then we must start by

---

[16] Official Secrets Act 1911, ss.1 and 2.

[17] The first Official Secrets Act goes back to 1889. Prior to that there were various Treasury Minutes enjoining secrecy upon civil servants.

[18] [1915] A.C. 120.

[19] R. Unger, *Law in Modern Society* (1976); J. Winkler, "The Political Economy of Administrative Discretion" in Adler and Asquith (Eds.), *Discretion and Welfare* (1981).

understanding and expanding upon the mechanisms through which the ideals are to be realised. As will become apparent in the course of the book, this does not mean greater power to the courts.

It becomes obvious, for instance, that law—if restricted to the adjudication of disputes through the courts—has a limited role to play in achieving the ideals of legality, ironic as it may sound. The Crown Proceedings Act 1947, whereby the Crown was, for present purposes, to be subject to the same liability in contract and tort as any individual, could achieve little in ensuring the accountability of the modern State. In 1957 the Franks Committee in advocating openness, fairness and impartiality in the administrative process highlighted the dilemma of the "two unequal legal realms," the legal proper or the traditional areas which were the concern of law, and the administrative realm where the contained inequalities of the latter had not been concealed anywhere near as effectively as, some suggested, they had in the former.[20] The Tribunal and Enquiries Acts 1958 and 1971 were a commendable attempt to infiltrate the administrative process with principles of justice and legality, but critics have pointed out that they merely extended the model of law which "adjudicated in collisions between individuals" of which the State was one. They and other legal provisions in the form of judicial decision or statute, individualised disputes which may have arisen from collective interests and conflicts, in areas such as conditions of employment, redundancy, urban decay or rural development, forms of energy, homelessness, law and order.

More fundamentally, it was claimed that the legal provisions extended legal criteria forged by the structural constraints outlined above; their notion of fairness was a natural justice based firmly in the tradition of adversarial advocacy within a traditional legal forum. Their notion of relevance became that conducive to the relatively narrow ranging inquiry of a court of law. Their respect for administrative discretion in those areas where administrative discretion was to be respected was guaranteed by the oblique test of review established in *Associated Provincial Picture Houses Ltd.* v. *Wednesbury Corporation*[21] so that administrative laissez-faire was encouraged by the judiciary in all but the "most egregious" of abuses. Nobody could rightfully argue that the administrative process should be reduced to "a succession of justiciable controversies."[22] But such a stand-off attitude did not encourage a belief in

---

[20] Community Development Project, *Limits of the Law* (1977).
[21] [1948] 1 K.B. 223.
[22] de Smith, *Judicial Review of Administrative Action* (4th ed., 1980), p. 3.

fairness of procedures within the administrative system, which, beyond Franks, had not been forced to reconsider seriously its own standards of legality. The narrow basis upon which judicial intervention in administration in the United Kingdom may take place often evokes accusations of political bias where there is intervention; a Conservative judicial dislike of particular political programmes (*Secretary of State for Education and Science* v. *Tameside Metropolitan Borough Council*[23]; *Laker Airways* v. *Department of Trade*[24] and most recently *Bromley London Borough Council* v. *Greater London Council*[25]).

It could be argued that the judicial activism which blossomed in the 1960s, and though welcomed in various quarters,[26] operated out of several confusions. First, the narrow remit of affairs subject to "legal scrutiny" in our governmental and administrative apparatus meant that a sudden judicial activity would be viewed with distrust at the political level. Secondly, it operated out of a legal concern over issues about which commentators cannot agree as to their true constitutional moment. Judges showed deference to issues of taxation and rates as well as private enterprise, not to the protection of the poor and politically debilitated, aliens, immigrants and prisoners. Thirdly, while courts purport to maintain the rule of law, our constitutional order had dictated that certain areas are beyond colonisation by legal principles and legal ideals as interpreted by courts, either expressly or implicitly.

In recent years, not surprisingly perhaps, judges have failed to show themselves equal to the demands of fair and open administration. Opportunities to extend participation have been rejected.[27-28] There has been a reluctance to extend the notion of "fair procedure"[29] despite earlier precedents; to "ask realistic questions about the balance of political power," to encourage open government, freer availability of information or reasoned

[23] [1977] A.C. 1014.
[24] [1977] Q.B. 643.
[25] [1983] 1 A.C. 768.
[26] Sir Leslie Scarman, *English Law—The New Dimension* (1975); H.W.R. Wade, *Administrative Law* (5th ed., 1982), Chap. 1; Lord Diplock, "Administrative Law: Judicial Review Reviewed" (1974) 33 C.L.J. 233 and see his comments in *I.R.C.* v. *National Federation of Self Employed and Small Businesses* [1981] 2 W.L.R. 722.
[27-28] The *modus operandi* of distributing franchises by the Independent Broadcasting Authority was approved by Lord Denning in *Cinnamond* v. *British Airports Authority* and one should note the various jejune exercises at public participation encouraged by the Broadcasting Act 1981, s.19.
[29] *Bushell* v. *Secretary of State for the Environment* [1981] A.C. 75.

statements as a matter of political practice.[30] Nor have judges been prepared to encourage what one United States lawyer[31] has termed a "surrogate political process" with decisions such as *Gouriet* v. *Union of Post Office Workers*[32]; *I.R.C.* v. *National Federation of Self Employed and Small Businesses.*[33] It must be admitted that one would be suspicious if they were to give succour to such processes and one would also be concerned about the conditions under which surrogate political systems might be encouraged. The point of all this, however, is not to rue missed opportunities which courts and our legal process may have let slip. It is rather to notice the absence of adequate procedures for bringing a complaint against governmental bodies and the absence of effective ways of engaging the public in decision-making. Courts resolve some complaints. So too do Ombudsmen and politicians. But these methods are not foolproof, and nor are they the only ones in operation.

In 1979, the Select Committee structure of the House of Commons was reformed, in what many consider to be an attempt to wrest power from the executive and administrative branches of government and to receive reliable information about policy formulation. It is not without interest that the more successful of the Select Committees to date have adopted formal, almost legal-like procedures.[34] The extent to which the battle to secure open, accountable central government takes place in Westminster will be examined in Chapter 2. Commentators have ably described the secretion of the expenditure process from effective democratic scrutiny by the use of cash limits and the consequences of this for policy formulation.[35] The formality which political processes adopt to supervise executive functions at Westminster has been

---

[30] One notes *Burmah Oil* v. *Bank of England* [1980] A.C. 1090; but *cf. Air Canada* v. *Secretary of State (No. 2)* [1983] 2 A.C. 394; *Lonhro Ltd.* v. *Shell Petroleum Co. Ltd.* [1980] 1 W.L.R. 627, H.L.; *Home Office* v. *Harman* [1983] A.C. 280: *British Steel Corporation* v. *Granada Television* [1982] A.C. 1096; *R.* v. *Lancashire Police Committee, ex p. Hook* [1980] Q.B. 603; *R.* v. *Liverpool C.C., ex p. Liverpool Taxi Fleet Operators' Association* [1975] 1 W.L.R. 701; *Crake* v. *Supplementary Benefits Commission* [1982] 1 All E.R. 498; *Cannock Chase D.C.* v. *Kelly* [1978] 1 W.L.R. 1; *Elliott* v. *Southwark L.B.C.* [1976] 1 W.L.R. 499; *Secretary of State for Defence* v. *Guardian Newspapers Ltd.* [1984] 3 W.L.R. 986, H.L.; *R.* v. *Secretary of State for the Foreign and Commonwealth Office, ex p. the Council of Civil Service Unions* [1984] 3 W.L.R., 1174, H.L.
[31] Stewart, "Reformation of Administrative Law" (1975) 88 Harv.L.Rev. 1669.
[32] [1978] A.C. 435.
[33] [1981] 2 W.L.R. 722.
[34] A. Davies, *The Reformed Select Committees: The First Year.*
[35] M. Elliott (1977) 40 M.L.R. 569, and note T. Daintith "Law in the Field of Short-Term Economic Policy" (1976) 92 L.Q.R. 62.

noted with interest[36] and serves as a reminder that even though the *forms* of control of government may differ, a public lawyer's interest in the process of accountability and complaint resolution is not diminished simply because there is an absence of a judge or counsel, prerogative orders or writs. The pursuit of effective procedures for accountability and resolution of grievances is what counts.

This is not to suggest that public law is solely interested in procedural aspects of accountability. There are issues of substance—ideals of legality. Lewis states, in referring to work by David Trubek:

> "It has been argued elsewhere that the fundamental justification for a legal order in an open society related to its ability to contribute to equality, individuality and community, the latter implying sharing and participating in the larger enterprise.[37] We would not argue an ontological foundation for these values but at least we feel entitled to claim that the liberal notion of the rule of law (formal rationality, autonomy, equal treatment, rational discourse) together with the idea of participation by the ruled in the process of rule connects the expectation of the modern state with the 'moral heritage of the west.' "[38]

The task which the present work sets for itself is the examination of current practices and opportunities which exist for citizens to complain about and participate in the larger enterprise of governmental activity. Such a task must take this work beyond the traditional concerns of law and lawyers when seen in terms of adjudicating between individuals, though it will not be beyond the concerns of those lawyers who have sought to study the "regulatory activity of law" in its manifold forms in the modern State.[39] It will be argued that function is more important than form and many of the issues examined, albeit briefly, in this book should cut to the quick of legal concern.

To what extent do current practices in governmental bodies assist or negate the ideals of which Trubek[40] speaks? It would be fanciful and naive to anticipate that improved procedures for com-

---

[36] Elliott and Daintith, *supra.*

[37] See D. Trubek, "Complexity and Contradiction in the Legal Order" (1977) 11 *Law and Society* 529.

[38] Poggi, *op. cit.* n.10, *supra.*

[39] For a critique of this latter position, see F.A. Hayek, *Law, Legislation and Liberty*, Vol. 1.

[40] *Loc. cit.* n.37, *supra.*

plaining and participating will of themselves help to achieve the ideals. In many areas, such opportunities become the preserve of the most articulate, influential or wealthy sectors of the community.[41] Law and legal services have done little to counter this; some argue they can do little.[42]

The question may well be asked: to what extent would an improved system of complaints and participatory systems, or a more broadly based utilisation of existing methods create a "surrogate political system" supplementing and buttressing the elected model?[43] In the federal administrative law of the United States it has been noted how judges have actively encouraged such a process by virtue of litigation, especially where policy decisions of a complex and technical nature are concerned.[44] It is submitted that there are serious deficiencies in the manner in which our governmental institutions operate from the point of view of consumer service and satisfaction, and from the point of view of democratic involvement of the public they serve. It would be foolhardy to ignore such deficiencies or to rest complacent in the belief of the power of the electorate every few years rendering supererogatory further opportunities for complaint or involvement in decision-making. Nor should it come as too much of a surprise to discover that surrogate political processes already exist within the official political system.[45]

This latter feature is not simply related to the failure of the "official government" to resolve problems concerned with industrial change and conflict[46]; nor to the recent popular belief—though it is a belief which has to acknowledge the ideologies and changes in practice in the form of government of our present administration—in certain circles of "corporatism" as a system of government and control,[47] whereby individuals and less powerful

---

[41] Schwartz and Wade, *Legal Control of Government*, Chap. 2; McAuslan, *Land, Law and Planning*, Chap. 2.

[42] See *infra*, Chap. 6 and the Community Development Project's *Limits of the Law* and the stimulating study by Patrick McAuslan in *The Ideologies of Planning Law* (1980).

[43] Stewart, *loc. cit.* n.31, *supra.*

[44] Stewart *et al*, "Vermond Yankee and the Evolution of Administrative Procedure" (1977) 91 *Harv. L. Rev.* 1805.

[45] See Chaps. 2, 3, and 4.

[46] Middlemas, *op. cit.* n.15, *supra.*

[47] Winkler "Law, State and Economy: The Industry Act 1975 in Perspective" (1975) B.J.L.S. 103; Pahl and Winkler "The Coming Corporatism" (1974) *New Society*, October 10, p. 72; P.C. Schmitter and G. Lehmbruch (Eds.) *Trends Towards Corporatist Intermediation* (1979); *cf.* Middlemass "The Supremacy of Party" (1983) *New Statesman*, June 10 and 17; M.L. Harrison, *Welfare Corporatism* (1984).

groups are excluded from bargaining processes between government, the leaders of industry and finance, representative bodies of organised labour, local government, etc. More basically, our present State, as Stewart pointed out for the United States, simply cannot avoid delegating vast areas of executive, legislative and administrative activity to a multiplicity of permanent, ad hoc and varying institutions whatever the political ideology of the government. So much is a truism, but like all truisms it needs occasionally to be repeated. These institutions themselves in their relationships with individuals and communities generate expectations and are vehicles for debate of a kind not taking place elsewhere within the "official system." The public inquiry is a common illustration of this point. Such activities require more examination and research, for the procedures currently in operation in such debate or negotiation are of prime interest to the public lawyer. An attempt to understand the dialectic between ideals and procedures when set against current practices must surely be a foremost task for all students and teachers of public law.

In conclusion, this book is concerned with the resolution of grievances against State institutions, whether the grievances are real or subjectively perceived as such, whether justified or not. Not only is it concerned with their *a posteriori* resolution by the range of practices which I will discuss, but it also examines various opportunities which individuals or groups may possess to contribute towards public decision-making, providing potential at least for minimisation of their own grievances. This is a study within a democracy which orthodox wisdom generally labels "representative." This means that having elected our political representatives and reposed our trust in them, they make decisions on our behalf. Our attention will focus on practices which accompany the representative model of democracy and which gravitate that model towards a more participatory one. These practices occur at both an official and unofficial level, as we shall see, and their existence does not necessarily carry a more significant opportunity for *all* interests to participate more directly in public decision-making. Indeed the degree of informality often assists more articulate, more resourceful interests at the expense of those not so endowed, and that is an issue to which we must remain alive.

Chapter 2

CENTRAL GOVERNMENT

In this chapter, we begin to unravel a form of power that was never effectively colonised by the imperatives of legal order as interpreted by courts. The discussion highlights the *collective* nature of power and organisation arranged around central government, its departments and Ministers of State.

There will be an introductory discussion of government departments, their structure, organisation and administration. The discussion will then assess the methods adopted by departments to process complaints. I will concentrate upon statutory opportunities for appeal to tribunals, where departmental or parliamentary rules will be adjudicated upon "impartially;" resort to inquiries or other opportunities to be heard before a person appointed by a Minister; and the informal processing of complaints whether attending statutory or other procedures. The role of the Parliamentary Commissioner will be examined in Chapter 5.

Government Departments

First we have to be clear about what is meant by a government department as different sources would indicate differing institutions.[1] In June 1983, *The Times*[2] cited the Government as comprising the Cabinet, Departments of State and Ministers. There are some less than obvious inclusions in *The Times, e.g.* Management and Personnel Office. Notable exclusions include the Inland Revenue, Customs and Excise and the Cabinet Office. Other reference books[1] list as government departments bodies which are really governmental agencies such as the Commission for Racial Equality or the Equal Opportunities Commission. This chapter is concerned with those bodies which have a Secretary of State or Minister at their head who is responsible to Parliament for the

---

[1] *e.g.* sched. 2 to the Parliamentary Commissioner Act 1967; the *Civil Service Yearbook; The Municipal Digest; Central Government of Britain,* Central Office of Information (10th ed., 1979); Crown Proceedings Act 1947; and *The Times,* June 20, 1983, listing the new Government.
[2] June 20, 1983.

administration of the department. Governmental agencies are considered in Chapter 4. The Inland Revenue, Customs and Excise (for which the Chancellor of the Exchequer has responsibility) and the Export Credit Guarantee Department are included as are tribunals.

The last inclusion may seem strange as tribunals are sometimes lumped under the heading "Quango" but they have such a pronounced role to play in legitimating departmental administration that it seems convenient to deal with them at this juncture. Some of the discussion on this latter topic will be relevant to the theme of Chapter 4.

It is trite constitutional knowledge that the Crown or its Ministers govern though Cabinet decisions which are implemented through the departments of State usually following legislative approval. Our constitutional heritage has determined that "The Crown or its Ministers are restrained from ruling without a Parliament, since it is enacted that for the redress of all grievances and for the amending, strengthening and preserving of laws Parliaments ought to be held frequently."[3] Government departments owe their creation and organisation, along with their powers and duties in part to the royal prerogative and in part to Parliament. The seventeenth century ensured that most ministerial powers were eventually to be derived from Parliament in the form of statute, and apart from loans, Parliament alone provides ministers with the finance for their expenditure. But a department's " . . . internal arrangements . . . are hardly ever organised or directly interfered with by Parliament but have been a matter for the royal prerogative."[4] Since the nineteenth century, it has become usual to establish departments under statutory authority and to transfer functions between departments likewise.[5] Appointments of Secretaries of State or Ministers are effected under the royal prerogative and although most of the necessary powers are conferred upon them by statute, *qua* Secretary of State, they are not a statutory creation, but natural persons possessed of natural, prerogative and statutory powers. This phenomenon is of fundamental importance.[6] Some Secretaries of State are corporations sole and finally the prerogatives of the Crown are usually exercised by Her Majesty's Ministers.

[3] Bill of Rights 1689, cited in *Halsbury, infra.*
[4] *Halsbury's Laws of England,* (1974) Vol. 8, paras. 1156–1272.
[5] Ministers of the Crown Act 1975 being the general authority for the latter.
[6] Because for instance they can exercise their powers to contract under natural or prerogative power, not only statutory power, see Daintith, "Regulation by Contract: the New Prerogative" (1979) 32 C.L.P. 41.

Government departments, apart from the Scottish and Northern Ireland Offices, have their headquarters in London and some have a regional and even a local presence. At a regional level in England there are regional boards comprising senior officials from those departments with regional organisations and there is one committee for each standard statistical region. The boards, which are chaired by the Regional Director of the Department of the Environment (D.o.E.) in each region, meet quarterly to discuss the implementation of the Government's policies in their respective regions and the coordination of inter-departmental activities. The boards conduct close working relationships with local authorities,[7] and although their meetings are not open to the public, they occasionally meet with regional bodies of the C.B.I. or T.U.C. for discussion. Some departments have inspectorates who may investigate systemic shortcomings in local-departmental or local authority administration, *e.g.* education, prisons or the police.

Departments are split into sub-departments, divisions or sections dealing with specific areas of administration. The nature of departments differs enormously and includes the *functional*, *e.g.* the environment, education, employment; the *processual* concerned with finance and legal matters though obviously these are functions also; and the *territorial*, *e.g.* the Northern Ireland or Scottish Office, the "multi-dimensional" Departments.[8] To give an idea of the growth of departments, the Home Office in 1782 when it was established including the Ministers, consisted of 17 people and shared 26 other staff with the Foreign Office and it cost £15,639 12s. 9½d. At present, the Home Office has some 35,000 staff in 200 different units and buildings over the United Kingdom. "It is directly responsible for expenditure of about £2,000m. in 1982/83 and indirectly responsible for about £1,600m. more. Its major operational responsibility is prison administration, but it deals with nationality and immigration, law and order, Community Programmes and Equal Opportunities, broadcasting as well as technical and support services of various kinds for the police and emergency services and various inspectorates covering the police, the fire service, probation and after-care service, drugs and experiments on animals."[9]

Government departments are not simple, straightforward enti-

---

[7] Especially in the making of structure plans, see Chap. 3.
[8] Jones, "Central—Local Relations, Finance and the Law" (1979) 2 *Urban Law and Policy* 25.
[9] Mrs. S. Littler, speech to *UKIAS,* March 27, 1982. And see generally on departments Fulton, Cmnd. 3638 (1968).

ties but are extremely complex interrelated organisations of many dimensions. Some deal regularly and directly with the public—the D.H.S.S. and Department of Employment, the Inland Revenue, and Customs and Excise; some deal with citizens personally, but more often in their capacity as overlookers, appellate bodies or complaint recipients about local authority administration or as regulators of aspects of the economy or industry; some departments feature daily in the lives of citizens, yet will be reluctant to allow personal contact to be made with them other than in writing. The Home Office is a good example of this; prisoners' complaints can be dealt with by the board of visitors, which is appointed by the Home Secretary though they are not Home Office officials, governors or by petitioning the Home Secretary in writing; only rarely by personal contact with Departmental officials. Adjudication officers are appointed by the Home Secretary to hear appeals from the decisions of immigration officers, but they are not representatives of the Home Office. Complaints about the police are not made to the Home Office, but to the police themselves, though they can be supervised by the newly formed Police Complaints Authority (see Chapter 5).

Other departments remain aloof and removed from the man in the street. The Treasury fits into this category. It has certain appellate functions, *e.g.* the Chancellor of the Exchequer can receive appeals from those refused a licence or "recognition" to operate as a deposit-taking institution by the Bank of England, though the appeal is heard by a tribunal.[10] The Treasury, which is a central, if not *the* central agent of contemporary governmental policy is very far removed from public scrutiny, legal scrutiny and challenge—its decisions on finance are not justiciable at the suit of individuals before courts of law—and some would suggest effective parliamentary scrutiny, because of increasing resort to cash limits, as well as the absence of full and proper debate to discuss expenditure plans.[11]

The most important decisions in our constitution are not to be subject to individual complaint. A Government's economic record will speak for itself, and citizens can exercise their content or dis-

---

[10] Banking Act 1979, s.11.
[11] In spite of the provision of "green budgets" in the Autumn preceding the budget and more opportunity to debate estimates. It was interesting that the body of Ministers charged with reducing 1984–85 spending limits of departments by £2·5 billion in October 1983, was referred to as the "Star Chamber." See also H.C. 273 (1983–84), and *Structure and Form of Government Expenditure Reports*, Likierman, A. and Vass, P. (1984).

content through the ballot box.[12] The ballot box is the factor which legitimates the exercise of political power. The fact that the present Government secured 43·5 per cent. of the votes cast in the 1983 election and the support of 31·6 per cent. of the electorate, and yet achieved a majority of 144 in the Commons ought to provide a chastening reflection upon claims to the firmness of the legitimation basis for the exercise of governmental power, and helps to highlight the unfairness of an electoral system which makes no concessions to proportional representation. Ours is a political constitution, and ultimate responsibility for the exercise of power is by Ministers to political bodies, to Parliament. Along with legislative supremacy and omnicompetence, this is what parliamentary supremacy means. It was the former strand of the doctrine, that there is accountability by Ministers for the exercise of their power to Parliament which made M.P.s, according to Enoch Powell, "An assembly of kings." Such a sentiment has always been an overstatement, but now it constitutes simple exaggeration. Why is this so?

In popular terms, if individual ministerial responsibility means anything, it means resignation after events have gone wrong in a department for which the Minister is responsible whether caused by his own decisions or actions or those of the "servants to the Minister."[13] It may be true to say that ministerial responsibility would not have developed into such a central feature of our constitution had the movement toward the appointment of boards in the 1840s and 1850s and their autonomous development under the law not been hindered by the parliamentary élite who were jealous of their own position and were fretful of the power accompanying such regulation by boards in a burgeoning industrial economy.[14] The new powers, usually statutory, were concentrated increasingly in the hands of Ministers, and they were to be accountable to Parliament for their exercise. As a method of achieving accountability for policy, let alone the redress of individual grievances, the doctrine and practice were always symbolic rather than effective and have become increasingly so.

Nevil Johnson believes that the convention is not really about accountability and responsibility at all but "is fundamentally a doc-

---

[12] Englishmen are only free, according to Rousseau, at the moment they cast their ballots!

[13] Resignations seem to follow most readily after personal scandal in the last 20 years as opposed to administrative shortcomings. The resignation of Lord Carrington during the Falklands débâcle is an exception, although not all agreed that it was his responsibility.

[14] Nevil Johnson, *In Search of the Constitution* (1977).

trine about the manner in which public powers are to be established and located; it defines who is responsible for what rather than who is responsible for whom."[15] It is not a grievance remedial device of a collective or individual nature, but allows us to know rather in whom powers are reposed and who answers the questions. Johnson has gone so far as to say that if the "British have any notion of the State, then it is to be found in the doctrine of Ministerial Responsibility."[16] And George II was probably more astute and insightful than Enoch Powell when he allegedly opined "Ministers are Kings in this country" long before the nineteenth and twentieth centuries accumulated vast, additional power and patronage in their hands.

From a legal perspective, the most important feature of the success of ministerial responsibility as the putative method for achieving accountability was that it nipped in the bud the development of any wider ranging and specific public law accountability. Again and again, for instance, judges when faced by issues that were clearly justiciable and which concerned individual grievances against a department or governmental board would justify non-interference by declaring that the issue touched upon a matter of administration over which a department or board had authority or jurisdiction and for which a Minister was ultimately responsible to Parliament.[17] If, as has been argued, the doctrine is not an effective method for redressing grievances, then judicial resort to the doctrine merely helped to set back, and is still setting back, the development of a coherent system of administrative justice. This is a contentious point and it will be developed throughout much of this book, but it is interesting to note how frequently the government of the day has argued that efforts to ensure greater accountability of departments by increasing the powers of the Parliamentary Commissioner for Administration (P.C.A.) or Comptroller and Auditor General would interfere with ministerial responsibility.[18] And indeed, the Government has made its own inroad into the convention with its Personal Management Review for the civil service which insists that much more responsibility should be delegated to civil servants, especially line managers operating away from Whitehall. Further, "civil servants should be encouraged to show their personal commitment to the priorities of

---

[15] *Ibid.* p. 84.
[16] *Ibid.*
[17] *L.G.B.* v. *Arlidge* [1915] A.C. 120; *Bushell* v. *Secretary of State for the Environment* [1981] A.C. 75.
[18] *e.g.* Cmnd. 8323 (1981), see Chap. 5.

their political masters rather than to Parliament or the needs of the public."[19]

Behind our discussion so far lies one feature of overriding significance. That is, not only is ours a "hidden constitution," but that it is to a very great extent a "secret constitution" in as much as the business of central government from top to bottom is deemed prima facie to be deserving of protection by Official Secrets Acts and criminal law unless information under section 2 is disseminated by an "authorised" source—and what is an authorised source is not always totally clear.[20] *Justice* has at various stages recommended that Parliament should enact a Statement of Principles of Good Administration, which would include an exhortation to inform parties affected by administrative decisions of the fact that they were being taken. A "reasonable opportunity of making representations to the authority" and provision of necessary and accurate information expeditiously were also advocated. Failure to comply with the Statement should result in legal action.[21] By 1978, *Justice* was recommending a Code of Practice to apply to all bodies listed in Schedule 2 to the Parliamentary Commissioner Act 1967 which would urge disclosure upon request of information relating to administrative decisions "so far as is reasonable and practicable."[22] This non-statutory duty was subject to familiar exceptions, though in some, viz. that which was entrusted in confidence to government departments or the Cabinet, or Cabinet Committee documents, it would appear that the judiciary have made greater inroads than the *Justice* recommendations, as the former have insisted that even cabinet documents can be obtained on applications for discovery of documents.[23]

Governments have successfully fought off a Freedom of Information Act,[24] and have preferred the existing legislative provisions concerned with public records and vague codes of practice. An example of such a code was the Croham Directive of 1977,

---

[19] "Financial Management Initiatives for the Civil Service" *The Guardian*, May 24, 1983. Civil service unions have considered the introduction of a Code of Practice to give definition and clarification to their members' relationships to Parliament and M.P.s. See *The Times*, February 27, 1985, p. 1.

[20] See for instance the Departmental Committee on section 2 of the Official Secrets Act 1911, Vol. 1, Chap. 2, Cmnd. 5104, and the Ponting trial.

[21] *Justice, Administration under law* (1971).

[22] *Justice, Freedom of Information* (1978).

[23] *Burmah Oil Co.* v. *Bank of England* [1980] A.C. 1090; *Air Canada* v. *Secretary of State for Trade* (*No. 2*) [1983] 1 All E.R. 910 (H.L.).

[24] The Labour Government came very close to accepting one, but a Private Member's Bill fell with the Government in 1979; cf. Cmnd. 7592. For D. Steel's Freedom of Information Bill, see H.C. Deb., Vol. 55, col. 738, March 6, 1984.

named after the then head of the Home Civil Service, which impressed upon departments the desirability of releasing more background information behind policy decisions, though civil servants' advice and ministerial comments, as well as "other sensitive points" were to remain secret.[25] This can be seen as a desire to avoid duties in legislation, and to leave the provision of information totally within the discretion of the department. The Directive itself stated that adherence to its terms would avoid the need for legislation similar to "the formidably burdensome Freedom of Information Act in the U.S.A.," a point which the Government of the day endorsed.[26] "The essential and fundamental change in administrative perception, however" which Croham hoped his Directive might introduce, "never took place"[27] and in any event it has all but been overtaken by subsequent events. This has not prevented the First Division Association (the senior civil servants union) advocating a reactivation of the Directive within departments, and even supporting a Freedom of Information Act.

We have witnessed no reform of the much maligned Official Secrets Acts, especially s.2.[28] According to the present Government the "problem" of an over-secret state was, in line with the new Conservative philosophy, best resolved by reducing the size of the state; making what remained more efficient and effective; cutting the size of the civil service and erasing all non-departmental bodies; privatising wherever possible state assets. A minimal state has no need for vast secrets and bureaucratic fog, so the argument runs. The inexorable thrust of the market place is towards openness and rationality. The flaw is that the Government is excused from the full impact of most market disciplines. It has, and will maintain its preserve on official information. Among countless examples of its attitude,[29] one can cite the example of parliamentary Select Committees. These were reformulated in 1979 to supervise the activities and expenditure of departments. However, they have no right to demand a debate in the House

---

[25] Outer Circle Policy Unit (1980).

[26] Cmnd. 7285 (1978).

[27] Outer Circle Policy Unit (1980).

[28] The Conservative Government's Protection of Official Information Bill, which fell with the Anthony Blunt fiasco in 1979, would have been more restrictive than even the Official Secrets Act, s.2, which it was supposed to reform. Will the acquittal of Clive Ponting prompt a reconsideration?

[29] "Leaks" revealing what can at best be described as "double talk" by Government Ministers, are legion. See the "mole-hunt" in *Secretary of State* v. *Guardian Newspapers Ltd.* [1984] 3 W.L.R. 986, H.L.; and for the relationship between a Minister and a nationalised industry *British Steel Corporation* v. *Granada Television* [1982] A.C. 1096.

on the refusal of a Minister to give evidence or produce papers before a committee. In 1981, the Leader of the House pledged that he would "seek to provide time to enable the House to express its view."[30] Further, limitations on what can be produced by civil servants before Select Committees have been spelled out in a Memorandum of Guidance and includes advice given to Ministers, details of consultations between Ministers or inter departmental exchanges.[31] Select Committees have been advised that similar constraints operate upon the flow of advice and information from sources outside departments, *i.e.* from non civil servants. Not even M.P.s are to be allowed access to essential information as of right. One wonders how effective the remedy of a judgment of the House after debate would be, given a strong governmental hold on the House. It seems difficult to avoid the conclusion which the former chairman of the Treasury and Civil Service Committee came to that governments are still "obsessive over secrecy."[32]

Resolution of Grievances

It is surprising perhaps that in spite of many statutory appeal or complaints procedures, departments make widespread resort to informal methods for the resolution of grievances. What is more surprising is that there is little in the way of recorded research of such practices. The Prime Minister has impressed upon departments the need to resolve complaints from the public at as local and humble a level as possible, though the Whitehall Management and Personnel Office stated that there are no uniform instructions on grievance handling for departments; it is left to the departments and their officers to sort out for themselves. At a time when more people are becoming dependent upon the State for a variety of benefits or services, the number of those administering the schemes is diminishing. The Treasury Committee has said "in some cases, staff reductions may lead to a programme being administered less equitably than before."[33] Although there is a greater risk that "more mistakes will be made in Whitehall,"[34] the Whitehall Management and Personnel Office has stated that officials must ask themselves "Is too much attention given to the wishes of individuals and to equity, and not enough attention to the needs of

---

[30] H.C. Deb., January 11, 1981.
[31] H.C. 92, 1982–83. *Quaere* whether refusals would constitute a contempt of Parliament?
[32] H.C. 584, 1979–80 and Outer Circle Policy Unit, (1980); and see generally D. Wass, *Government and the Governed* (1984).
[33] H.C. 236, Vol. I, para. 4, 1981–82.
[34] Lady Young, Lord Privy Seal, Civil Service College (1982).

the department."[35] It is against these sentiments that we can study the resolution of grievances and the options available in a *representative* democratic state.

The Courts

In chapter 6 I will examine those areas where courts offer redress against the State and comments relevant to departments of state will be amplified at that point. It will be seen how the common law in its historical development has achieved much in the protection of individual freedom. But the common law has always perceived its range of interests narrowly—a pragmatic, proprietary basis of protection of individual right and entitlement the *modus operandi* of which has usually found it difficult to adapt to sudden and profound upheavals in social and economic structure. Even Dicey accepted that the Revolution Settlement in England was not a victory for immanent rights of man, but a defence of proprietary interests interpreted by inherently conservative common lawyers.[36] Judicial deference to the executive and the reality of the legislative supremacy of Parliament will be returned to.

Political Redress

A second alternative was to offer political redress of grievances. Parliament after all was to be a vehicle for the redress of all grievances[37] as well as being the vehicle for legislative amendment and reform. Ministerial responsibility, operating through procedures such as Question Time in the House and Adjournment Debates,[38] has been referred to. Many regard M.P.s first and foremost as trouble-shooters on behalf of constituents and virtually all departments invariably identified their intervention as the first method of complaint resolution. In 1981, the Department of Employment received in the region of 8,000 letters from M.P.s dealing with constituents' complaints. The D.H.S.S. stated their average to be 22,000–25,000 *per annum* and the Home Office 22,500 letters from M.P.s in 1981, though some of these were

---

[35] *The Guardian*, August 26, 1982.

[36] Dicey, *Law and Public Opinion* (2nd ed., 1914), p. 82. For Dicey, this was its strength. "A revolution, not made, but prevented" opined Burke on the events of 1688–89.

[37] Under the Bill of Rights, *supra*.

[38] For those matters on which successive administrations have refused to answer questions, see G. Wilson, *Cases and Materials on Constitutional and Administrative Law* (1976), pp. 146–150.

requests for information and concerned bodies other than central departments. In the debates on the Parliamentary Commissioner Bill, an estimated figure of 300,000 was given as the number of complaints which M.P.s received *per annum* from constituents[39] and more recent figures suggest that M.P.s collectively write anything from 3,000–16,000 letters per week on their constituents' behalf to departments.[40] A study in 1977 stated that the M.P. under observation received and wrote 5,011 letters in one year on behalf of constituents.[41]

Morrell's study put into question the efficacy of an M.P. as a trouble-shooter when s/he operated without appropriate back-up staff. There is a close connection between the effectiveness of an M.P. and his/her personal status, knowledge of the system and connections. The Department of Employment for instance described a convention whereby M.P.s who were Privy Councillors would always receive a personal letter from the Minister. Personal factors are important in order to break through the practice of routinised replies; and most departments "are likely to have a standard procedure dealing with M.P.s correspondence on behalf of constituents."[42] A further factor to bear in mind is the relative obscurity of many M.P.s in the eyes of constituents. The Opinion Research Centre, for instance, in a 1978 survey claimed that only 46 per cent. of those questioned could name their M.P.s. Among younger voters, the figure was 30 per cent.[43] The creation of the Parliamentary Ombudsman was an implicit acknowledgment of the adventitious nature of M.P. intervention.

Further intervention by M.P.s on behalf of complainants can take place at proceedings concerned with collective or policy issues. Officials acknowledged that individual grievances are raised under the cover of a policy relating to departmental administration. This has happened at Select Committees—and a Committee has been used to help settle an industrial dispute. A further opportunity may well arise in the legislative process—especially at Standing Committee stage when M.P.s will advance the interests of their sponsors. An authoritative study has shown the general impact of M.P.s at this level not to be substantial.[44] The power or influence of collective or institutional interests outside Parliament, and the pressure or persuasion which they can bring to bear on a

---

[39] H.C. Deb., Vol. 734, col. 89.
[40] Norton (1982).
[41] Morrell, (1977).
[42] Sir Cecil Clothier, letter to the author.
[43] *The Times*, April 5, 1978.
[44] Griffith, *Parliamentary Scrutiny of Government Bills* (1974).

Government, is *the* important feature and is never more fully demonstrated than when such an interest prevents an issue emerging in legislation or shapes the legislation. Such might be achieved to maintain self regulation, statutory or otherwise, as opposed to governmental control (the Stock Exchange, the Press, etc.,) or to facilitate as cosy a relationship as possible in what could be irksome regulation, such as health and safety at work.[45] Consultation with "interested parties" before making regulations or general decisions provides the possibility of influence.[46] More overt are the private and local bill procedures which offer an opportunity for legal representation of grievances from affected interests at committee stage. It has become obvious that we have moved from *ex post facto* redress of grievances by political processes or *persona* to *a priori* moulding of decisions to suit particular interests and reduce possible grievances felt by those interests. "Because the process of bargaining and compromise has gone on largely within departments and has been sheltered by confidentiality, we know relatively little about how alternatives are weighed and how consequences are mapped out."[47]

The political processes we have described whereby a government or department can be persuaded to change its mind after complaint are of course important. More difficult is to establish *how* they are important. Indifferent performance by M.P.s on constituents' behalf could well effect election results and a government's future. But if one asks how effective in changing decisions are these efforts, the answer must be, hardly at all. Their importance invariably is at the symbolic level. If it were otherwise, we would have a very different style of government and very different governments. Too frequent a back-bench revolt, for instance, by the government party would produce government by Parliament, not government through Parliament.

Tribunals

As mentioned earlier, tribunals are invariably bodies which are overtly independent of departments and it might appear a little

---

[45] For such an issue in the North Sea Oil Fields, see Carson, *The Other Price of Britain's Oil* (1981).

[46] For a classic statement on what constitutes appropriate consultation, see Morris J. in *Rollo* v. *Minister of Town and Country Planning* [1947] 2 All E.R. 488 at 496 and a qualification by Lord Morris in *Port Louis Corp.* v. *Att.-Gen. of Mauritius* [1965] A.C. 111. Also, *Agricultural, etc., Board* v. *Aylesbury Mushrooms* [1972] 1 All E.R. 280.

[47] Ashford, *Policy and Politics in Britain* (1981).

strange to deal with them in this chapter. They are such a central feature of dispute resolution by adjudication in cases involving departments and individuals that it seems most appropriate to deal with them now. What are the motives behind the establishment of tribunals?

First of all, to provide an apparently autonomous form of dispute settlement by adjudicatory devices in governmental or governmentally approved programmes, originally in the field of industrial expansion and then social welfare.[48] Their primary aim is dispute resolution, but at a more subliminal level there is also the legitimation of power by the governors over the governed. The popular image presented is of an individual locked in conflict with a department, or other embodiment of the State. The Franks Report[49] on tribunals and inquiries states that "Our terms of reference involve the consideration of an important part of the relationship between the individual and authority" and the seeking of a balance between "private right and public advantage, between fair play for the individual and efficiency of administration."[50] Further, "We consider that tribunals should properly be regarded as machinery provided by Parliament for adjudication rather than as part of the machinery for administration." The emphasis was upon individual manifestation of conflict which could be subjected to a justiciable process less formal than a court of law. Tribunals would apply, impartially and even-handedly, rules which have been made by departments and approved by Parliament.

It has been argued that the classification adopted by Franks does not embrace all tribunals. A substantial majority may fall under its spread, but a significant minority are not "court substitutes" but "policy oriented tribunals."[51] Franks's recommendations were of direct relevance to the former type of institution, *i.e.* that decision-making before such tribunals should be conducted in accordance with "openness, fairness and impartiality." A judicial body of any sort which lacked these *desiderata* would lack credibility. With many of the tribunals falling under the court substitute heading, the department can tolerate impartiality in determination of disputes between it and an individual claimant. The jurisdiction of the tribunal and the subject-matter it adjudicates upon are

---

[48] Though as Wraith and Hutchesson show, the "administrative tribunal as a judicial phenomenon" has its origins deep in antiquity, *Administrative Tribunals* (1973).

[49] Cmnd. 218.

[50] *Ibid.* para. 5.

[51] Abel-Smith and Stevens, (1968), Farmer (1974).

restricted so that decisions are unlikely to upset the policy of the minister or government. There will be strict controls over the appointment of tribunal chairmen and members who are usually appointed by the Lord Chancellor, or by the minister presiding over the department which is involved. For the individuals in dispute with the department, their claim or grievance is for them often a matter of supreme importance; in the wider context of constitutional decision-making, such tribunals adjudicate on relatively small claims and comparatively trifling issues. Impartiality in such decisions is permissible, though the D.H.S.S. has had frequent recourse to legislation, regulations and rather questionable administrative practices to reverse the decisions of Social Security Commissioners.

Plausible arguments have also been advanced that by judicialising the administrative process to this extent, a depoliticisation of such decision-making is achieved.[52] A concentration upon technicalities concerned with the amount of individual entitlement to social security, supplementary benefit, unemployment benefit or whether a dismissal was fair or unfair or caused by redundancy directs attention away from political choices lying behind such decisions. The extent, for instance, of state assistance to the impoverished, the infirm, the unemployed or the exercise of managerial prerogative or movement of capital is effectively ignored.

For policy oriented bodies, the impact of Franks's recommendations ring less persuasively. Tribunals which licence or which regulate economic activity, monopolies and mergers, trading practices and trade relationships, and transport activities to name a few, can, if not subjected to ministerial control, quite easily wield power and make decisions upsetting the policy of a government. Ministers invariably have power to issue directions and supervise by direct intervention or by reserving appellate powers from such tribunals.[53] The problems these bodies pose for government are: how can they appear autonomous and expert and yet be controlled without appearing to be controlled? How can they be controlled without a minister having to account to Parliament on their behalf? How can they assist in the formulation of policy without upsetting the overall aim and strategy of departments? Even if policy oriented bodies

---

[52] Prosser, "Poverty, Ideology, and Legality . . . " (1977) 4 B.J.L.S. 539. Duncanson, "Balloonists, Bills of Rights and Dinosaurs." (1977) P.L. 391.

[53] On the Civil Aviation Authority, see Chap. 4. For an interesting recent example of the Secretary of State overriding a majority recommendation of the Monopolies and Mergers Commission, see *R.* v. *Secretary of State for Trade, ex p. Anderson Strathclyde* [1983] 2 All E.R. 233.

operate within policy parameters established in Whitehall, or court substitute bodies for that matter, there is no guarantee that the judiciary will abstain from intervention in such bodies' decision-making processes at the suit of complainants. *Anisminic* v. *Foreign Compensation Commission*[54] extended considerably the power of the High Court to review the decisions of quasi-judicial tribunals when the House of Lords decided that virtually all errors of law made by inferior tribunals took them outside their jurisdictional powers.[55] There is no doubt that the ideals of openness, fairness and impartiality in decision-making in themselves are desirable. But many tribunals which are listed in the Schedule to the Tribunal and Inquiries Act and subject to the supervision of the Council on Tribunals are susceptible to a degree of ministerial control or influence which will bring into question their impartiality. Their high policy content often necessitates a relationship with ministers and departments which is the antithesis of public candour and openness.

A second reason for the increasing utilisation of tribunals by government was the requirement of expertise and/or technical knowledge to be applied in a judicial manner in the resolution of grievances or disputes. One does not have to be a lawyer in order to act judicially, but the inclusion of a lawyer whether as chairman or member has been common. In the field of social welfare, increasing resort has been made to the use of lawyers as chairmen of social security and medical tribunals. The Health and Social Services and Social Security Adjudications Act 1983 has combined the former national insurance and supplementary benefit tribunals into Social Security Appeal Tribunals. Part of these "rationalising tendencies" includes directions for chairmen of Social Security Appeal Tribunals, including full-time chairmen, to be lawyers. Objections to these plans from the T.U.C. did not prevail with the Government, although the latter agreed that a separate panel of "work peoples representatives" would be constituted from which one of the wing persons would automatically be selected. This concession was necessary to save the bill falling before the June 1983 election.[55a]

A third reason for resort to tribunals was their relative speed and

---

[54] [1969] 2 A.C. 147.

[55] And see *Re Racal Communications Ltd.* [1980] A.C. 374. The more one moves away from an adjudicatory process, the less appropriate is the test in *Anisminic*, of course. For regulatory, recommendatory, etc., bodies, challenge on grounds of *vires* and discretion is the usual method, along with unfair procedure.

[55a] *Cf.* Health and Social Security Act 1984, s.16, which ends this "concession."

informality of procedure. It need only be said that speed and procedure vary enormously as is to be expected for bodies created on an "ad hoc and pragmatic" basis owing their *raison d'être* to the exigencies of political legitimation and administrative convenience as the industrial revolution gradually metamorphosed into the welfare state.

The legacy of Franks was the Tribunals and Inquiries Act 1958[56] described at the time by Lord Denning as "a first chapter in a new Bill of Rights."[57] The legislation provided in essence that for tribunals listed in the Schedule to the Act, procedural rules[58] were not to be effective until after departments had consulted with the Council on Tribunals, a body created by the legislation. As well as acting in an advisory and consultative capacity with government and its departments, the Council also supervises tribunals listed in Schedule 1 to the Act and inquiries. It enjoys no executive powers.[59] Listed tribunals had to provide a statement of reasons for decisions, either written or oral, when requested save in exceptional circumstances such as national security or unless specifically exempted. Reasons so given were to be considered part of the record of proceedings thereby extending the possibility of judicial review for error of law within, or post *Anisminic,* without jurisdiction. Rights of appeal on a point of law to the High Court were to be available generally and there were limitations on the efficacy of statutory clauses restricting or otherwise ousting the jurisdiction of the High Court to review tribunal decisions.[60] The presumption was that tribunals exercising judicial functions would sit in public unless exempted.[61] Legal aid is available only before the Lands Tribunal, the Commons Commissioners, the Employment Appeal Tribunal, and since 1982, the Mental Health Review Tribunal which reviews cases of patients in mental hospitals to decide whether they should be released.[62] The Council on Tribunals recommended in evidence to the Royal Commission on Legal Services that legal aid should be extended to all tribunals over which it had supervision. The Government has not agreed to this.[63]

The Council in fact writes informative annual reports, but there is much evidence to suggest that its proposals on more contentious

---

[56] See now Tribunals and Inquiries Act 1971.
[57] H.L. Deb., Vol. 208, col. 605.
[58] Made under statutory instrument.
[59] See Harlow and Rawlings, *Law and Administration* (1984) Chap. 6.
[60] With reference to tribunals created under statute prior to August 1, 1958.
[61] For a recent and important exemption, see the Mental Health Act 1983, s.78.
[62] See *X* v. *U.K.* 4 E.H.R.R. 181. S.I. 1982 No. 1582.
[63] Cmnd. 9077. See (1984–85; H.C. 151).

issues are not taken seriously by government which is under no duty to take a "hard look" at the Council's suggestions after the latter has been consulted.[64] For the first nine years of its existence, the Council spent much of its time responding to individual complaints. It was denied the statutory powers which Franks had recommended and its chairman stated in 1970: "The Council's principal difficulty is that they have no effective means of securing attention for the tribunal system as a whole."

Considering the doubtless good intention and many beneficent effects of Franks, it might appear churlish to stand back and make a critique of its overall impact more than a quarter of a century after he reported. As the Report has long been a focal point of administrative justice in the United Kingdom, certain points require development.

First, the Report and the subsequent legislation only covered statutory tribunals. There are many bodies which are non-statutory, but which conform to judicial techniques, of a kind. The Criminal Injuries Compensation Board is one example. Created to award *ex gratia* payments to victims suffering physical injury as a result of violent crime, etc., it follows no statutory guidelines and coupled with some unexpected judicial review it has made some haphazard and rather inconsistent awards never contemplated in the origins of the scheme. Discretion and uncertainty have merely been compounded.

Secondly, there are many statutory bodies which are essentially tribunals but which are excluded from the schedule to the Act. As well as the more usual examples,[65] one might add boards of visitors in H.M. prisons whose dual tasks of adjudicating over the more serious disciplinary charges against prisoners and acting as complaints' mechanisms for prisoners have been the subject of much concern. The power of punishment of boards is, in any language, enormous, yet they often operate with a minimum of procedural protection for prisoners.[66] It is not always clear why some bodies are included and some are excluded from the provisions of the legislation, though it doubtless relates to unarticulated assumptions concerning national security, public policy and the appropriate extent to which the ideals of legality should operate in public administration.

---

[64] See, *e.g.* its Report for 1981/82 (1982–83; H.C. 64).

[65] Foreign Compensation Commission, Gaming Board, Legal Aid Committees, Parole Board, etc.

[66] See the author's "The Closed Society etc." (1981) 32 *N.I.L.O.* 117, and "Legal Order and Prison Administration" (1983) 34 *N.I.L.O.* 269. It has recently been decided that boards may allow a prisoner legal representation, see Chap. 6.

A third weakness of the Franks Report was its failure to examine the "ad hoc" methods of raising objections about departmental decisions. This was the stranger as a widely regarded reason for setting up the Committee in the first place was to investigate the ad hoc responses to the Crichel Down fiasco. I return to this topic later, but apart from some fairly brief treatment in the Whyatt Report of 1961, it has received little attention.

A fourth point is that Franks's brief did not cover those instances where a department, instead of handing an appeal to a tribunal, or inquiry (*infra*), deals with the matter itself. On many occasions, decisions on appeal or arising from a statutory opportunity to register a complaint or simply as an ad hoc response to informal appeals are dealt with by departmental officials themselves. Examples are complaints under sections 68 and 99 of the Education Act 1944 or the whole array of licensing and approval functions under investment and insurance legislation which has spawned a body of "law" known only to departmental officials.[67] More examples will follow. Why are some decision-making processes handed over to "independent" bodies and others not, when the political or security aspects would not seem to necessitate any distinction? Sometimes it might be possible to discern rational distinction in the choice of forum or method for decision-making.[68] At other times, one is left with the distinct impression that it is simply the result of "muddling through" which gives to much of our public administration the appearance of an "unsystematic hotch-potch." The thought might be prompted that a malevolent *primum mobile* lies behind such a division of labour, thereby seeking to impede deliberately rational exposition of decision-making and accountability. We can take some comfort in the fact that governors are rarely efficient enough to effect such a conspiracy. Nevertheless, departments have made serious errors of judgment when instead of handing over a grievance to an established independent statutory procedure, they have attempted to resolve the matter informally. In *Sachsenhausen*, an early and important investigation of the Parliamentary Commissioner, the Foreign Office was distributing compensation from the West German Government to victims of Nazi atrocities. There was an expert body at hand to deal with such matters, the Foreign Compensation Commission, but the Foreign Office chose to deal with the cases informally itself, and engaged in rather heavy-handed administra-

[67] Gower, *Review of Investor Protection* (1982).
[68] And see Ganz, "The Allocation of Decision-Making Functions" (1972) P.L. 215, 299.

tion after drawing up pettifogging distinctions between classes of victims.

The last weakness of the impact of the Franks Report in achieving "openness, fairness and impartiality" in the administrative process was glanced at when we looked at policy oriented tribunals, though it concerns all those bodies which are part of, or concerned with, the organisation and development of governmental policy. These are connected with the overtly collective dimensions to public or governmental decision-making. It may be claimed on behalf of the State that its role is to be a minimal one, but such claims are in large part political rhetoric. The economic structure of advanced capitalism requires State support through the provision of a system of law and legal institutions and other bodies instructed to achieve a fair market system, a spirit of competition as well as establishing basic economic direction through Government decisions on fiscal and expenditure policy. This is apart from the activities performed by local government, health authorities and the public sector at large. Neither Franks, nor anybody else for that matter, explored what was required in the interests of administrative justice in decision-making of a collective dimension. A proliferation of multi-purpose, protean advisory agencies will remain a fixture of governmental apparatus for the foreseeable future. Though the decisions of policy oriented bodies may impinge directly upon individuals as with Monopolies and Mergers Commission investigations, their primary reference is to aspects of the collective weal: competitiveness, a fair market, consumer choice. Through the achievement of collective aims governments hope to create a climate in which individual grievances will be minimised. The pursuit of sound economic policy through economic expansion and growth has been the policy of every British government since the Second World War hard though this may be to reconcile with the evidence. In pursuit of this aim there has been and will be persistent resort to policy oriented bodies operating informally to assist departmental officials and their political overlords in the preparation of appropriate strategies. Sometimes such bodies operate by making rules which define the policy of regulation, *e.g.* the Transport Tribunal; sometimes they do not. There is often negotiation with the regulated, *e.g.* by the Director General of Fair Trading under the Fair Trading Act 1973 and the 1980 Competition Act. Often they proceed by informal processes, such as the Monopolies and Mergers Commission, and their recommendations are sometimes—though not with the Monopolies and Mergers Commission—made in confidence to the Minister. Details behind these processes will invariably be a mystery and opportunities to participate and be informed remain oblique.

Informal control over such bodies has been achieved in the past, and doubtless for the future, by a Minister's power of appointment. Moving beyond the bodies which are our present concern, this feature of control is pervasive throughout the public sector: *e.g.* in regional and district health authorities; city institutions such as the Policy-Holders' Protection Board; Insurance Brokers' Registration Council; or through patronage exercised by the Bank of England; or ministerial permission to the Stock Exchange to operate as "the only recognised Stock Exchange." Governmental control by regulation of private activities is witnessed by the degree to which building societies have become increasingly regulated by statute and administrative practice.[69] Less direct, but nonetheless significant informal control over domestic or private bodies is achieved when a Government accepts ultimate responsibility by legislating, *e.g.* the General Medical Council and the Medical Act 1858, but leaves the details of the regulation to the body itself. This scenario was recently advocated by Professor Gower for statutory self-regulation of the investor market in securities.

What is common throughout the modes of organisation outlined in the preceding two paragraphs, is that the inescapable necessity for social and economic survival has impelled successive Governments to organise collectively and often by informal means the processes necessary for the continuation and reproduction of social life. On these issues, Franks has little relevance. The individualistic outlook of the Report owes much to the *gesellschaft* notion of justice and law perfected by the law and legal profession in the nineteenth and early twentieth centuries—atomic individual versus atomic individual one of whom happens to be the State. Such an outlook overlooks the fact that the problems which tribunals were to address were not simple emanations of unfair practices in the individualisation of disputes, but were inherently caused by increasing collective processes of production, consumption, centralisation of authority and a secretive state, many relevant decision-making processes of which it did not fully understand or which were excluded from the Report's terms of reference. The concentration upon the individual manifestation of dispute and the narrow focus of its terms of reference helped to

---

[69] McAuslan, "Administrative Law, Collective Consumption and Judicial Policy" (1983) Vol. 46 M.L.R.1.

maintain the myth that law, and law-like processes represent consensus, and politics—the preserve of politicians—represents conflict.

In many areas of collective control and organisation, opportunities for individual or group challenge, complaint or redress are not present. In economic policy, expenditure and taxation decisions of the Government—apart from challenge of personal assessment in the latter—are inevitably beyond legal or effective administrative challenge, and, many would still maintain, also beyond effective political challenge, in spite of recent reform.[70] Informal economic pressure has often been used to influence the money supply, the level of wages and prices and where formal mechanism exists for investigation or examination of abuses of market domination, informal "deals" made "off the record" are far from rare, making informed outside comment or complaint unlikely. Of course, provision by Government of open and impartial grievance procedures through which to complain about such collective processes would present the opportunity to upset Government policy. This could not be tolerated. When Government has provided a collective grievance mechanism such as the Advisory Conciliation and Arbitration Service in the field of labour relations it achieved more to "encourage the extension of collective bargaining" by use of informal means rather than by its formal powers, the latter of which were repealed in 1980.[71] Regional assistance to industry is yet another feature of economic policy which is particularly resistant to individual grievance—by legal or administrative devices.[72]

What we have then, even under a Government espousing the philosophy of individualism, is a series of devices the collective governmental nature of which render individual challenge largely nugatory.

---

[70] See *op. cit.* n. 11, *supra.* The Public Accounts Committee can make scathing *ex post facto* reports of wasted expenditure, as in De Lorean, H.C. 127 (1983–84), and the Accounting Officer in each department, *i.e.* a permanent secretary can put on record his disagreement with a Minister on a decision of the latter which he regards as imprudent, especially if it relates to public funds.

[71] 2,000 unions were recognised for bargaining purposes under the former, and 1,400 under the latter. The decision of the House of Lords in *Grunwick Processing Laboratories* v. *ACAS* [1978] A.C. 665 did much to reduce the formal recommendatory powers of recognition of unions which ACAS possessed until 1980. Under s.3 of the Employment Act 1980, the Secretary of State has power to issue Codes of Practice on industrial relations, effectively superceding those of ACAS.

[72] *infra.*

Public inquiries

The second term of reference of Franks concerned public inquiries about which Wraith and Lamb have said that it would be "pointless to try to apply any coherent system to the use of the term inquiry, public inquiry, local inquiry, public local inquiry and 'opportunity to be heard; it is safe to say that none exists."[73] The procedure suitable as an appeal mechanism to the Secretary of State against a local authority decision affecting an individual's proprietary rights may not be appropriate for discussion of proposals affecting a wide range of local, regional or national interests such as: the siting of a nuclear reprocessing plant; whether a pressurised water nuclear reactor plant should be established or where should a major international airport be positioned? The statutory details for the procedure in all the above instances are virtually identical[74]; administrative concession has brought considerable difference in practice. In planning appeals for instance, the matter can be disposed by a written procedure supplemented by site visits or by an informal hearing.[75] For inquiries into projects of major significance, departments concerned have invariably relied upon the usual statutory procedure supplemented by pre-inquiry hearings and appointing as an inspector an eminent person, often a lawyer, assisted if necessary by a panel of experts.[76] The Department of Energy utilised its powers under section 34 of the Electricity Act 1957 to hold an inquiry into the proposed siting of a pressurised water nuclear reactor at Sizewell when an application was made for the Minister's consent under section 2 of the Electric Lighting Act 1909 for the placing of high voltage lines. The frequent choice of a lawyer chairman is not without significance, McAuslan believes. A panel with a broad range of talents is more likely to upset official or officially sponsored plans. Discussion of highly technical and inherently controversial issues is more likely

---

[73] Wraith and Lamb, *Public Inquiries as an Instrument of Government* (1971).

[74] Public inquiries fall under three main heads: statutory inquiries which are mandatory and for which the Lord Chancellor has power to make regulations detailing procedure. They are under the supervision of the Council on Tribunals, and the Tribunal and Inquiries Act 1971 applies to them; statutory inquiries which are discretionary, though if "designated" they are subject to similar controls as the inquiries above; and non-statutory inquiries operating without supervision, apart from the common law. *N.B.* Planning Inquiries (Attendance of Public) Act 1982. Inspectors' Reports are usually published.

[75] *Infra.*

[76] Planning Inquiry Commissions, which provided a statutory procedure under the Town and Country Planning Act 1971, ss.47–49 for investigation into major proposals, have never been employed.

to be kept within a narrow rein by a figure who is, by virtue of his legal training and public position, sympathetically disposed towards the official line,[77] though this may not always be the case.

There appears to be a problem concerning the appropriateness of a procedure whereby the Secretary of State acts as an appellate authority in an issue between, say a local authority and an individual where he can act on the hearing inspector's recommendations impartially, and those inquiries which touch on issues of wide public concern and in the outcome of which the department has a very close interest. Here the inquiry is not aimed at settling an individual grievance or complaint. These latter inquiries are primarily concerned with the provision of information and recommendations to the Minister better to inform his decision, and raising objections is subordinate to this function. The information obtained from these inquiries and the recommendations of the inspector form but one part, possibly a substantial part, of the total information which the Minister will consider when s/he determines what conclusions are in the public interest as s/he interprets that. This point is set in relief when one considers that *officially* the range of discussion at inquiries is supposed to be restricted to matters which do not touch upon the merits or the policy dimension underlying a proposal in question, though as a matter of *practice,* discussion of policy or merits invariably finds its way into the proceedings. It is also restricted by placing third parties, *i.e.* those with no direct legal (proprietary) interests at a disadvantage to those with such interests. At major inquiries, third parties are invariably the major protestors. They have no individual legal rights to insist on being present and to be heard at the inquiry or to challenge the ultimate decision of the Minister.[78] General administrative practice has been to allow them a greater opportunity to participate and present their own case, though as recent events at Sizewell illustrate, their participation and how effectively they participate is at the total discretion of the inspector. Sir Frank Layfield Q.C. informed Friends of the Earth that safety issues involved in the proposed construction of Britain's first nuclear pressurised-water reactor could not be adjourned, even though the review on safety by the Nuclear Installation Inspectorate (N.I.I.) had been delayed and was not available. One of the reasons given by the Secretary of State for Energy for not publicly funding the

---

[77] McAuslan, *The Ideologies of Planning Law* (1980).
[78] Though *cf. Turner* v. *Secretary of State* (1973) 28 P. & C.R. 123; *Wilson* v. *Secretary of State* [1974] 1 All E.R. 428; and in particular *R.* v. *Hammersmith L.B.C. ex p. "People Before Profit"* (1982) 80 L.G.R. 322.

objectors' case was that safety aspects were to be investigated by the N.I.I.[79] Awarding of costs by one party to another at an inquiry is extremely rare. The cost of presenting the Central Electricity Generating Board's (C.E.G.B.) case at Sizewell was estimated in December 1983 to be about £10 million! Contrariwise, the longer a topic is deferred, the costlier it will be for objectors to cross examine it.

"Policy" includes the merits of a proposal and even the need for a proposal. The inspector would be correct to stop examination of these matters by objectors, unless, as at Sizewell, need and economics are written into the terms of reference or the inspector believes they are questioning the specific application of policy, and not the policy itself. Government is accountable to Parliament for policy, not to objectors. The importance of what constitutes "policy," and the judicial interpretation of the term require further elaboration. The basic procedure for planning and development, highway and compulsory purchase schemes, is publication of the proposal, receipt of objections thereto, and where bargains cannot be struck to assuage objectors, the holding of an inquiry before an inspector. At the conclusion of the inquiry, the inspector sends his report and recommendations to the Secretary of State, who can accept or reject the recommendations, though if he disagrees on a point of fact or considers new evidence, he has to provide the opportunity for a reopening of the inquiry. The House of Lords has held that where the Minister takes into consideration new evidence which constitutes part of the *factual* basis of the policy behind the proposal, there is no breach of natural justice where he refuses to re-open the inquiry. The Secretary of State is also entitled to receive new evidence and advice from *within* his own department after the inquiry (and which may result in a change in the proposal) without being under an obligation to put this new evidence before the objectors.[80] The Minister and his officials are constitutionally one and the same, and he was not therefore taking new evidence into account but talking to himself, as it were.[81] The feeling of unfair treatment among the objectors

---

[79] The inspector became very critical of the delay by the C.E.G.B. and N.I.I. (*The Guardian*, January 18, 1984).

[80] *Bushell* v. *Secretary of State for the Environment* [1981] A.C. 75. No inquiries procedure rules were in operation which specifically covered the inquiry in *Bushell*.

[81] *Cf.* the comments of Tudor Evans J. on whether the Minister could have imputed to him statements by senior civil servants on the punitive nature of the control unit in Wakefield Prison; *Williams* v. *Home Office* (*No. 2*) [1981] 1 All E.R. 1211. *Cf. Carltona* v. *Commissioners of Works* [1943] 2 All E.R. 560.

was evoked largely by the refusal of the inspector to allow cross-examination of the factual basis supporting the policy which involved the prediction of future traffic flows along particular routes and which was employed as a justification for building a motorway. This refusal, the majority held, did not constitute a breach of natural justice, as the factual basis was an inherent part of the policy. This Lord Edmund Davies found too much to accept, and indeed cited Franks in support of his dissent. Subsequently, the factual basis was altered without any opportunity of challenge.

Certain key points call for comment. Lord Diplock insisted that an inquiry is not a proceeding in a civil court of law, and it should not be attended by overlong procedural niceties. Too many challenges to public decision-making would seize up the administrative and civil processes of government. This is certainly a valid point. The judgment affirms a belief in the division of labour in government—policy is for the executive and legislature, not the judiciary nor the public at large. Again this basically is a widely accepted implication of government under our representative democracy. However, ought not a valid, constructive and possibly valuable improvement on policy be welcome after a public hearing, especially where a policy is to have a constraining influence on our future development, resources and style of life? Do the arguments of the majority in the *Bushell* case carry full conviction with the realisation that it is the facts and their correctness which we are talking about, not an overt evaluation of the policy itself. It seems that officialdom wishes to maintain its preserve on *all* features of decision-making, and the feeling is widespread that participatory exercises are ineffective, irrelevant and tokenism.

Criticism of "The Big Public Inquiry" by the Outer Circle Policy Unit (O.C.P.U.)[82] seems particularly apt after *Bushell*. The inquiry emerges *after* the real decision has effectively been made; a department usually has a very close interest or commitment in the outcome; the procedural rules do not ensure that enough time is afforded to study such information as is provided; traditional inquiries impose a "yes/no" solution to a highly complex proposal which is not susceptible to such a straightforward response. It is modelled on legal/adversarial lines, and a looser more flexible procedure might allow better examination of the wider dimensions involved.[83]

The O.C.P.U.'s suggested balance in procedure to accommo-

---

[82] (1979).
[83] *Ibid.*

date the legitimate requirements of the administration and fair treatment for the interested parties beyond mere tokenism, is a Project Inquiry. This would operate as the inquiry into major proposals and would investigate impartially, thoroughly and in public the *need* for a project, its cost, risks and benefit, "in short all the foreseeable economic, social and environmental implications and repercussions of the project" . . . all the material facts would be brought out and tested. The Project Inquiry—which would be non-statutory and preferably not chaired by a lawyer[84]—would precede a Standing Commission or Select Committee of Parliament. These latter would scrutinise general policy before traditional local inquiries examined specific planning applications. The Project Inquiry would proceed in two stages; a stage of investigation followed by a stage of argument taking a maximum of 30 months. Commissioners to sit on the Project Inquiry would be chosen by reference to two broad criteria: "a sufficient degree of expertise and the maximum degree of impartiality" though the Secretary of State would appoint them after "very wide consultation." These recommendations have not been accepted as necessary by the Government[85] and nor have the recommendations for a pool of public funding for objectors.

The majority of their Lordships in *Bushell* work from a paradigm of governmental decision-making which is symptomatic of representative democracy in the nineteenth century. There was a signal failure to acknowledge a point emphasised by the O.C.P.U.: the democratic implications of the fact that policy formulation is a cumulative process, developed at various stages and by various bodies of a governmental, quasi governmental and private character meshing in often confidential debate or dialogue long before any parliamentary appraisal let alone public participation programme is countenanced. In the United States this realisation was partly responsible for federal judges insisting that policy, when developed by the big regulatory agencies, should take the form of rule-making, *i.e.* delegated legislation. Under the Administrative Procedure Act a formal procedure with interested parties participating in rule-making will sometimes be followed. At the other end of the spectrum was a "notice and comment" procedure,

[84] *per* O.C.P.U.
[85] See the proposals of the Government in 1978 for major inquiries, (1978) J.P.L. 732. The Council on Tribunals is working on a code of practice for major public inquiries. See also the views of the Royal Town Planning Institute (1982), paras. 6.8–6.31, and *A Fairer and Faster Route to Major Road Construction*, N.E.D.O. (December 1984).

whereby interested parties would be informed of proposed rule-making and asked for their comments. This latter process was supplemented by decisions of federal courts which insisted on a "hybrid" procedure—not quite a full judicial hearing but a substantial fleshing out of the "notice and comment" procedure. The hybrid procedure, though still in existence, has been subject to attack by the Supreme Court,[86] and rule-making as a whole has met with executive opposition in the drive towards "deregulation."[87] Nevertheless, opportunity to participate in policy formulation by regulatory bodies in the United States far surpasses any British analogue apart that is from the planning process in land use and inquiries. But with big inquiries there is much room for development:

> "It is now becoming urgent that the institutions and procedures which make and carry out national policies for the planning of our industries, and decisions about their associated "works" should [adapt themselves to maintain government by consent]. . . . There are to-day also mounting calls for more open government. These include proposals for new procedures for submitting central policy-making in general to more profound, critical and expert scrutiny than is provided by existing arrangements.[88]

Formal and informal internal resolution of grievances

The last category of practices for processing complaints concerns the methods adopted *within* departments themselves to resolve grievances. These can follow a statutory opportunity to appeal or make complaint to the Secretary of State or may attend other statutory procedures. Local authorities are, for example, under a range of duties to make arrangements for one or more classes of services for disabled persons.[89] The Secretary of State, if of opinion that an authority has failed to discharge relevant func-

---

[86] *Vermont Yankee Nuclear Power Corp.* v. *NRDC Inc.* 519 U.S. 435 (1978) Stewart, R.B. *et al.* (1977–78) 91 Harv.L.Rev. 1805.
[87] Lewis, N. and Harden, I. (1983) 34 N.I.L.Q. 207; Verkuil, P.R. (1980) 80 Col.L.R. 943; and judicial opposition in *Sierra Club* v. *Castle* 657 F.2d 298 (1981). Though *cf. Motor Vehicle Manufacturers' Assoc.* v. *State Farm Mutual Automobile Insurance Co.* 51 U.S.L.W. 4953 (1983) where the Supreme Court held that de-regulation may well be subject to rule-making procedures requiring a "thorough, probing and in-depth" review.
[88] O.C.P.U. (1979).
[89] Chronically Sick and Disabled Persons Act 1970, s.2, and National Assistance Act 1948, s.29.

tions, has certain declaratory powers and power to perform the functions himself after an inquiry.[90] This is carried out within the department itself by staff of at least Principal level and can involve deliberations with the Secretary of State. Unlike the power of the Secretary of State to hear complaints about the behaviour of an educational authority,[91] this provision does not appear to have given the impetus to local authorities to devise adequate complaints procedures for members of the public,[92] although complaints to the Secretary of State from individuals and representative bodies are far from rare. In 1981, for example, The Royal Association for Disability and Rehabilitation reported 12 authorities to the Secretary of State for allegedly not complying with statutory duties.

The Department of Trade and Industry issues and revokes "Exemption Dealers" Orders which means that dealers in securities are exempted from the licensing requirements of the Prevention of Fraud (Investments) Act 1958. Revocation of these Orders is only permissible after the Department specify particulars of the grounds of revocation and invite representations, which can be given orally if required. Unlike licensing decisions under the 1958 Act, there is no reference to a tribunal. Likewise, the Department of Trade and Industry may declare a unit trust to be authorised for securities dealing if satisfied of various things, a provision which has precipitated a vast amount of internal law within the Department unknown to outsiders.[93] Those insurance companies which are not self-regulating, unlike Lloyd's which is self-regulating, are regulated and controlled under the Insurance Companies Acts by the Department of Trade and Industry. Insurance companies have to be "authorised" and there is no appeal from the Secretary of State's decision. On the initial interpretation of what constitutes "securities" to establish whether a licence is necessary, the discretion of the statute is in fact confined by Departmental rules. These set a "rigid precedent" on what constitutes securities and upon which transactions are, or are not, forbidden. "This leads to a voluminous rule-book known only to the Department and followed slavishly"[94] similar to the erstwhile secret "A" code in

---

[90] National Assistance Act 1948, s.36.

[91] *Infra.*

[92] In spite of an earlier precedent, there is a possibility of judicial relief by way of a declaration, where the local authority's action is clearly *ultra vires, Roberts* v. *Dorset C.C.* (1977) 75 L.G.R. 462, though *Wyatt* v. *Hillingdon L.B.C.* (1978) 76 L.G.R. 727 holds that s.76 offers the exclusive remedy.

[93] Gower, *op.cit.* n. 67, *supra.*

[94] *Ibid.*

social security regulation. We will shortly examine more informal processes attending statutory appeal procedures, etc., but it should be noted that when a department maintains ultimate control in this manner, it creates a procedural framework in which policy on a given matter will prevail without hindrance from "independent" bodies. A simple alteration in procedure has potential for fundamental change. Free competition in transport policies, for instance, could flourish by the simple incorporation of a right of appeal as in section 35 of the Transport Act 1980.[95] This allowed an application for permission by a private concern to compete with public transport in the metropolis and provided for an appeal from the decision of the London Transport Executive to the Secretary of State.[96]

The last option available to departments is to deal with a grievance by their own procedure where no statutory guidelines are established. Very few complainants make their complaints by personal appearance at headquarters—though many departments said the practice was far from unknown. Appearances at departmental local or regional offices is more common, and the more local the office, the more likely that a complaint will be made personally. It is far more common for a complaint to be made in writing and for the complaint to be handed down to as local a level as is appropriate.

The reply from most departments to the question how they resolved such complaints was by "ad hoc methods" with "few formal internal procedures." The departments most likely to receive a significant number of such informal complaints are those whose administration brings them into regular contact with the public—the D.H.S.S., the Inland Revenue, the Department of Employment, the Home Office and the Department of the Environment are leading contenders. The P.C.A. has identified the following types of complaint as recurring frequently:

    (a) against the conduct of a particular member of staff
    (b) about a department's general handling of a specific case
    (c) those made by M.P.s on the constituents' behalf
    (d) about government or department policy.

In spite of frequent departmental claims to ad hoc methods for resolving complaints, regular practices have been noted by the P.C.A. and this was reinforced by my own examination. In category (a) there were regular, internal and rather formal pro-

---

[95] Amending the Transport (London) Act 1969.
[96] See Chap. 4.

cedures involving trade union representations. In Category (b) complaints were invariably in writing and where there is a local network, letters received by the centre are handed to the local level. It was the P.C.A.'s impression that interviews would seldom be refused if requested "or if the department felt it was a sensible way of progressing," and the presence of the complainant can often have a direct effect on a positive outcome in his favour. Of all the departments, only the Home Office stated categorically that interviews with complainants would never be given, though it should be remembered that there is a wide range of institutions which act as grievance remedial devices *inter alia* in areas over which the Home Office assumes ultimate responsibility. These include the newly formed Police Complaints Authority; the Commission for Racial Equality; the Broadcasting Complaints Commission and boards of visitors in H.M. Prisons and will be examined elsewhere. In spite of a statutory appeal process, the Home Office receives about 13,000 letters a year from M.P.s on immigration matters,[97] and the discretionary decisions on naturalisation and citizenship under the British Nationality Act 1981, are dealt with by *written* application.[98] P.C.A. reports refer frequently to other departments conducting interviews if requested and it is not uncommon for complainants to be accompanied by friends, representatives from claimants' unions or relatives. His reports have also cited departments possessing internal standing procedures for complaint handling.

All of this leaves the distinct impression that fairness of treatment can often be dependent upon variables such as luck and good fortune as to whom it is who happens to receive a complaint. Government officials supported the view that the cantankerous and/or knowledgeable invariably manipulate opportunities in a fashion not repeated by others. Sometimes it might happen that departments, divisions or offices are complaint-conscious—an internal instruction sent out to civil servants on one job creation scheme urged them not to "lose their temper, argue, interrupt, lecture or be sarcastic to complainants." Sometimes they are not.

---

[97] In 1982, 14,261 immigration appeals were referred to adjudicators, though they disposed of 16,875 appeals. For M.P. representation and informal exercise of ministerial discretion in individual immigrants' favour, see Harlow C. and Rawlings R. *op.cit.* n. 59 *supra.*

[98] With over 80,000 registrations in 1982, it is understandable that a written procedure is followed. The fee for application has caused frequent complaint of unconscionable profit-making by the Home Office, though this fee has been reduced. More difficult cases will be dealt with by interview: Standing Committee F. British Nationality Bill, Official Report, cols. 691–696.

Looking more specifically at departments, one regional office of the D.o.E. stated that complaints of a group or collective nature on for example inner city funding, housing or planning were made at regional offices by representative groups. The Department itself had no central procedural point for complaints made to head-quarters as these were dealt with on a divisional basis. This was the same for most other departments. One regional office of the D.o.E. had set up a specific section to deal with one subject gener-ating numerous complaints against local authorities. This involved the sale of council houses where authorities were proving to be too dilatory or imposed unduly restrictive covenants in the sale of houses to the public.[99] Complaints about local authorities and other public bodies were frequently made to the D.o.E., as well as complaints about functions which were the responsibility of other departments in which case the D.o.E. acts as a "sieve and co-ordi-nator." Interviews with complainants did not take place as a mat-ter of course, though there was a readiness to see organisations with a grievance.

The D.o.E. had produced an informal hearing for a trial period to hear planning appeals where the public inquiry or appeal by written procedure was unsuitable. Objections to planning decisions can vary from those about proposals with national sig-nificance, to those of little importance. The Department utilises a variety of devices to hear objections or appeals; inquiries where the Secretary of State makes the final decision and inquiries where the inspector does. An oral inquiry may be dispensed with, and a written procedure may be employed, again with either the Sec-retary of State or the inspector making the final decision. The informal procedure is the latest addition to the efforts to marry departmental efficiency and procedural fairness from the Depart-ment's point of view.

The informal hearing concentrates upon speed and informality and legal representation is not anticipated. It will not be used when issues are controversial or complex, and choice of the pro-cedure rests with the Department. Although the Inquiries Pro-cedure Rules can apply with some modifications, the emphasis is upon informal negotiation around a table. Although "interested persons" may attend if they wish, notice of the hearing is not generally advertised. No party can claim costs and the procedure is expected to be used in about 250 cases a year.

---

[99] Housing Act 1980, Pt.I, Chap. I. For the process of haggling between central and local government on specific applications to buy, see Lord Denning's judgment in *Norwich C.C.* v. *Secretary of State* [1982] 1 All E.R. 737.

In the Department of Transport the regional offices will deal with complaints about road schemes and "surprisingly on road schemes we find that the actual volume of complaints as distinct from negotiations with those affected during the progress of road schemes is quite small." This is important because if after negotiations between public authorities and the Department, the authorities subsequently withdraw objection to the road scheme, any duty to hold an inquiry under the appropriate legislation evaporates.[1] It has been claimed that these general procedures represent a regress from public debate to enable "a reduction in procedural delays in the construction and improvement of highways."[2] A decision by the Secretary of State not to hold a public inquiry is extremely difficult to review in a court of law.[3] Any "deals" negotiated privately by public or private parties are unlikely in the vast majority of cases to be set aside.

With the D.H.S.S., a ready awareness of complaints made by the public was displayed; in spite of well-publicised statutory appeal procedures to local tribunals and the Social Security Commissioners established under the Social Security Act 1980. In the year ending in 1982, there was a total of 129,909 appeals against decisions on supplementary benefit claims. Of these, 73,825 did not go before a tribunal and 43,790 of those were superceded by an Appeals Officer in informal proceedings where he reviews the original decision. This review is often supplemented by visits and interviews and it is interesting to note that so called "Secretary of State decisions" from which there is no appeal, and decisions by the Secretary under section 95 of the Social Security Act 1975 from which again there are no rights of appeal are supplemented by considerable informal safeguards if need be by way of internal review. Some internal procedures are highly secret, *e.g.* the activities of the social security fraud squad. For claimants who had allegedly made a fraudulent claim for social security where less than £50 is involved, there is no prosecution, though they will be dissuaded from making a claim where the investigators *believe* fraud to be present. In 1981/82 there were 87,833 "fraudulent" claims which did not lead to prosecution.[4] The figure for 1982/83 was 125,333.

For general social security complaints, there was little that could

<hr />

[1] Highways Act 1980, Sched. 1, paras. 7(2) and 14(2).

[2] McAuslan, *op.cit.* n.77, *supra.*

[3] *Shorman* v. *Secretary of State for the Environment* (1977) J.P.L. 98; though *cf. R.* v. *Secretary of State for the Environment ex p. Binney, The Times,* October 8, 1983.

[4] H.C. Deb. Vol. 29, col. 445 (October 27, 1982). The D.H.S.S. have refused to publish the *Fraud Investigators' Guide.*

be described as a formal complaints procedure, the D.H.S.S. said, though two individual senior officers described a very similar and clearly defined internal and non-publicised process for dealing with complaints made orally or in writing at local or regional offices. Claimants are advised by claimants' unions to complain before appealing about assessment, in fact. On the supplementary benefit side there was an internal procedure specifying the grade of officer who should handle a complaint, whether it should be designated "urgent" or requiring a reply from a Minister, as well as the degree of liaison needed between headquarters and a local office. Successful complaints often emanated from the intervention of pressure groups such as C.P.A.G. or MENCAP and it was acknowledged that the best recourse was for a pressure group to take the issue up with a Minister which counters the official exhortation to deal with grievances at as low a level as possible. Although managers in local D.H.S.S. offices will interview complainants, this is not publicised. Also kept for internal consumption is the D.H.S.S.'s Office Administration Code which carries instructions on how to reply to complaints. In Scotland, some local offices have gone so far as to display the name of the person to whom members of the public can complain—a "customer consciousness officer." Apart from the Code, advice on how to deal with complainants was a matter of local practice and custom.

We will look at complaints upon health aspects of the Department's responsibility in Chapter 5.

Without wishing to reiterate familiar themes, the Department of Employment echoed the points made by the D.H.S.S. à propos of individual complaints at local level—good practices existed and were of local discretion and practice, a feature that was also true of Jobcentres under the Manpower Services Commission. Where decisions are open to compromise, as is often the case with taxation, more formalised supplements to statutory procedures are often resorted to and this was certainly true of the Inland Revenue where H.M. Inspectors of Taxes are afforded "full discretion to negotiate and agree with tax-payers and their professional advisers the amount of tax which is due and are expected to find solutions to their problems." Well-defined internal procedures for complaints exist at central, regional and local levels. Unlike the Inland Revenue, Customs and Excise do process complaints centrally as a general practice. The Board openly acknowledged what one suspects is common practice: that the manner in which a complaint is handled varies "according to both the gravity of the complaint and the *standing* of the complainant." The Board possessed "a very developed process for complaints from M.P.s" and there was a "clearly identified" hierarchy for replies, dependent upon the importance of the complainant: complaints forwarded by constituency M.P.s and letters directed from the chairman or chief executive of a large organisation will get a reply from the chairman, a director of a company from a commissioner and an individual from an Assistant Secretary or Principal.

Most departments could cite instances of individual complaints on administrative and more routine matters changing the outcome of a decision. Although some departments mentioned that policy reviews had taken place as a consequence of an individual or group complaint, only the Department of Employment offered a specific example of this. This Department, as would be expected given its relationship with the forces of capital and labour, is the frequent recipient of complaints from employers' associations, trade unions or public corporations about policy concerns. Implementation of the Vredeling Directive into English law has been the subject of one such complaint. Briefly, this would make worker participation in company decision-making legally binding and complaints of large companies, with which there was official sympathy, argued that change should be by way of custom and agreement, not legislation. The point was not missed that for reform in trade unions' affairs, however, legislation was seen as the prime instrument of change.[5]

The Department of Energy received only in the region of 15 complaints directly each year, and it was willing to interview general complainants, who could be represented where desirable. This happened most frequently with large companies affected by the Department's regulatory activities to advise them of statutory obligations under, *e.g.* the Health and Safety at Work, etc., Act 1974. A recent study[6] has identified how the influence of the regulated can have a decisive influence not only upon the attitudes of the regulators towards their statutory duties, but on the very framework of regulation that is adopted, and concerned regulation of health and safety in the North Sea Oil Fields. Such a theme has many analogues in public administration, in areas as diverse as the regulation of the Stock Exchange and insurance market; financial markets and the City and their relationship to the Bank of England and the Treasury; professional associations and their ability to per-

---

[5] With legislation in 1980, 1982 and 1984. S.1 of the Employment Act 1982 has some faint encouragement for "Employee *involvement* in [employer] company's affairs." The word "participation" was expressly excluded, and the provision only refers to companies employing over 250 people.

[6] Carson (1981), *op. cit.*

suade Governments to allow them to regulate, or continue to regulate, themselves. Planning agreements are a familiar example of negotiated outcomes between private corporations and Government departments whereby the former would trade their technical knowledge and expertise in return for permission to exploit resources and "sympathetic" regulation by Government or its agencies.

Two departments have maintained a strictly internal and confidential approach to complaint resolution. The first concerns the Department of Trade and Industry and its responsibility for the disbursement of funds for regional assistance to industry, a policy which has been in operation, with one short interval, since the 1960s as a method of encouraging industrial expansion in depressed areas. The details of the scheme under the 1982 Act are complex, and they also tie in with other programmes to encourage regional development. The Department has maintained total control over the disbursement of funds or grants under the legislation,[7] and this has been supported by judicial deference leaving the exercise of discretion almost totally within the Department[8] and offers limited scope for the P.C.A. to find maladministration.[9] There is no appeal from refusal or revocation of an award, though the Department encourages early discussion between applicants and the Regional Development Grant Office, and details of grants over £25,000 are published in *British Business* (those under Pt. II of the Act). Selective Financial Assistance to industry is made under sections 7 and 8—while the former is concerned with Assisted Areas, the latter is not restricted. Powers to award are couched in extremely broad discretionary terms, and applications are considered by various regional advisory boards before a final decision is made by the Secretary of State. The Department offered the following account of its practices *vis à vis* all complaints, including those under the 1982 Act:

"A complaint will be dealt with fully and carefully by the responsible division to ensure the complainant receives equitable treatment and a fully considered reply. There are, however, no formal procedures for dealing with complaints and any arrangement, correspondence, meetings, legal representation etc. which will provide satisfaction will be used. Essen-

---

[7] Industrial Development Act 1982. Changes in the priorities and bases of regional aid have recently been announced *Regional Industrial Development*, 1983 (Cmnd. 9111). Aid is to be reduced by £300 m. for 1985/86.

[8] *British Oxygen Co.* v. *Board of Trade* [1971] A.C. 610.

[9] See Chap. 5.

tially they will be dealt with *"ad hoc"* in the light of the particular circumstances. Very few complaints end up with the P.C.A., tribunals or courts . . . an indication of the success of the practices and procedural arrangements for handling complaints."

Views from trade competitors on grants are not sought and most information is treated as highly confidential because it falls under the broad rubric of "trade secret." What is clear is that the Department wishes to keep such decisions expressing a central component of economic policy, firmly within the grasp of the Department.

The Department of Education and Science (D.E.S.) is particularly secretive about its treatment of complaints on school education. It receives "many thousands of complaints each year about all aspects of the educational system." In relation to school education, parents and consumers have, since 1944, possessed certain legal rights, difficult though these are to realise in the courts.[10] The proper recourse is to complain to the Secretary of State under section 68 or 99 of the Education Act 1944. Judicial decision has interpreted section 68 as offering extremely limited scope for intervention by the Secretary of State in a local authority's affairs.[11] The Secretary of State does not have to give reasons for refusing a complaint under the sections, and although the D.E.S. does not keep a central record of complaints received, complaints on school allocation are maintained: 1978—1,012; 1979—1,083; 1980—795; 1981—824; 1982—313 (*sic*). These complaints resulted in *one* direction by the Secretary of State, although the Department said that authorities often changed their decisions after an investigation with the emergence of new facts. The Department has, however, been reluctant to reveal the manner in which it processes complaints, though an informed guess has speculated that as well as interviewing officers in the relevant education authority, the D.E.S. will study the advice of the Schools' Inspectors and examine the written statement of the complainant who will, however, rarely be interviewed.[11a]

---

[10] *e.g. Watt* v. *Kesteven C.C.* [1955] 1 Q.B. 408: *Cummings* v. *Birkenhead Corp.* [1972] Ch. 12; *cf. Meade* v. *Haringey L.B.C.* [1979] 1 W.L.R. 637; *R.* v. *Hereford and Worcester L.E.A., ex p. Jones* [1981] 1 W.L.R. 768.

[11] *Secretary of State for Education and Science* v. *Tameside M.B.C.* [1977] A.C. 1014.

[11a] Education Committee, *Second Report* (1981–82; H.C. 116, Vol. 1). Leaders of pressure groups objecting to school closures may occasionally be granted interviews at the D.E.S., Meredith (1984) J.S.W.L. 208.

The secrecy of the process and the claims by the Department of limited powers of intervention offer ample cover for highly contentious decisions of a political nature affecting education. Government cuts on education expenditure have led many authorities to publicise falling standards. Complaints to the Secretary of State are unlikely to be met with sympathy. The cuts have been the result of D.E.S. policy and anyway, the matter is within the jurisdiction of the local education authority the centre will argue. Complaints about school syllabi may not result in direct intervention, but Departmental publication of Inspectors' Reports highlighting criticism can provide much ammunition for attack by parents on the grounds of political ideology to which the Department may be sympathetic. Certainly, political ideology was felt to be a central feature when the D.E.S. and Inspectorate advertised events after receipt of a complaint from a polytechnic lecturer in 1983 which alleged that her former sociology department was infiltrated by Marxist indoctrination. Selective use of information, and selective encouragement of complaints on ideological grounds is a dangerous game. Less sensationally, seemingly perplexing decisions by the Secretary of State on closure of schools have been made with an apparent total absence of consistency. In short, in spite of rhetoric about parent participation in education at a local level[12] the most important decisions affecting the standards and nature of education lie beyond challenge—short of successful back-bench revolt—when political overlords at the centre are committed to particular programmes. The results are often chaotic and one feels that more judicious treatment of complaints and treatment that is seen to be so, would be highly desirable.

Conclusion

The wide variety of options open to departments and citizens confronted by, or wishing to articulate grievances offer a confused and confusing picture. The enormity of the contemporary enterprise of government has forced upon departments a multiplicity of procedures, techniques and *fora* through which sometimes the powerful and baneful effects of government may be given antidote. The following seem particularly pressing: the enactment of a statutory code of good administrative practice and open government; the giving of reasoned decisions as a matter of course; the publication of *internal* grievance procedures and processes which affect inter-

---

[12] See Chap. 3.

Chapter 3

LOCAL GOVERNMENT

Local Government Organisation and Administration

Local Government has been witness to enormous changes in its structure in recent years. The widely criticised reorganisation of local government by the Local Government Act 1972 was a response to the growth of activity and bureaucratic development of local government. The changes have not solved the problem of rational organisation—on what basis are authorities to be organised to carry out their functions efficiently?—nor concomitant problems for citizens caused by authorities becoming repositories of vast amounts of information, expertise and resources.

The 1972 legislation introduced a system of metropolitan counties and non-metropolitan counties, sub-divided into metropolitan districts and non-metropolitan districts respectively.[1] Non-metropolitan districts are further sub-divided into parish councils. Various recommendations to establish local "neighbourhood councils" for urban areas on a statutory basis have not been pursued as far as the statute book.[2] London has its own local government structure.[3]

A cursory glance at Part IX of the 1972 legislation indicates the enormous variety of functions performed by local authorities in England and Wales and which are divided between the various tiers of authorities.[4] Local authority administration is further char-

---

[1] England and Wales are divided into six metropolitan counties, 47 non-metropolitan counties, 36 metropolitan districts and 333 non-metropolitan districts. Scotland is divided into a two tier system of regional and district authorities, with three Island authorities and various community councils. Northern Ireland has 26 district councils, though local government lost many of its more important functions in the province in 1973. What follows details the result of work carried out on local government in England and Wales. See the work cited at note 54 *infra*; more recently, the author has been in receipt of a research grant from the Local Government Legal Society and the Town Clerks' Education Trust to study open government and administrative practices in local government.

[2] There are about 10,000 parish councils, mainly in rural areas.

[3] London comprises the Greater London Council which is further divided into the City and 32 london boroughs (12 inner and 20 outer boroughs).

[4] And a further complicating factor has been the change-over of name from one description to another for departments, *e.g.*—public health, environmental, etc.

53

acterised by the presence and combination of elected councillors (members) and paid officials.[5]

The Government has taken steps to bring about the abolition of the six metropolitan counties and the GLC, and to replace them for administrative purposes by joint nominated boards and non elected public bodies. Together with powers for "rate-capping," *i.e.* controlling the amount of rates raised by authorities, this development represents the culmination of bitter relationships between central and local government as the former has sought to control the expenditure and effective independence of the latter.[6] More effective control by the centre does not augur well for local accountability and democracy, but it is sad to say that the record of local government has often left much to be desired. This general record has persisted in spite of the strenuous efforts made by many authorities to improve their image and practices in relation to local communities.

The reorganisation under the 1972 Act cannot be fully appreciated without reference to the report, *The New Local Authorities, Management and Structure*.[7] This report represented "an attempt to secure unity of purpose in the affairs of a local authority through adjusting activities to changing needs and problems. This involves making assumptions explicit, methodically reviewing policy, and attempting to measure outputs."[8] The report was claimed to have had an "astonishing impact" in introducing what Bains referred to as a "corporate approach" to local authority management and planning.[9] A departmental approach to administration, lacking appropriate co-ordination, was no longer adequate for the brave new world facing local authority administration. McAuslan, amongst others has supported the point that the corporate management approach pays too little regard to the democratic basis of local government. The role of the public and councillors is decreased as emphasis is placed upon a Policy and Resources

---

[5] The latter displaying expertise, it is claimed, matching if not surpassing that of their central Government counterparts (Jones, "Central-Local Relations, Finance and the Law" (1979) 2 *Urban Law and Policy* 25. See Stewart, J. *Local Government: The Conditions of Local Choice* (1983) for a recent appraisal of these relationships and resulting tensions. For central-local relations and the law see: Loughlin, *Local Government, the Law and the Constitution* (1983).

[6] See Local Government (Interim Provisions) Act 1984 and the Rates Act 1984.

[7] Bains Report, *The New Local Authorities, Management and Structure* (1972).

[8] Lewis and Harden, "Law and the Local State" (1982) 5 *Urban Law and Policy* 65.

[9] Hambleton, *Policy, Planning and Local Government* (1978).

Committee (with only a few "heavy weight" councillors present) shaping major decisions. This committee's meetings are commonly preceded by the Chief Executive's Principal Chief Officers' Management Team Committee "filtering out that which it is, for one reason or another, impolitic to put before the councillors."[10] Criticisms have been made suggesting that the corporate approach has reduced the effective role of many councillors, is mechanistic, developed further the hiatus between the council and local people and local organisations and that it depoliticised policy-making. This last aspect has various causes, chief among them being a stress on the managerial and technical aspects of policy-making and an overdue reverence for professionalisation in political decision-making. Recently, it has been stated that a disenchantment with the diminution of overt political discussion in policy formulation and the common concentration upon professional/ bureaucratic values has become discernible in local authority administration:

> "Again and again we detect the earnest raising of questions as to how political values and priorities get fed into the corporate processes which have traditionally been seen to be officer-managed activities. These developments have more recently been accompanied by attempts to secure outside or consumer input, not least in an attempt to politicise the local population into defending their services against attack from the 'centre' (central government)."[11]

The problem of "alienated local government" and the barriers this presents against the airing and effective resolution of grievances, as well as participation in decision-making, is particularly acute in the urban and especially inner urban areas. These latter areas often display a concentration of poverty, lack of opportunity, poor housing and racial tension. The problems caused by "alienated local government" are not, however, confined to those areas. Various attempts have been made to deal with the causes and consequences of inner urban decay ranging from the Community Development Project—a government sponsored attempt to involve the community in local affairs which ultimately proved to be unpopular with the government—to the employment of management consultants and planning consultants by the Department of Environment (D.o.E.). The latter undertook various urban studies which hoped, *inter alia*, to "formulate

---

[10] McAuslan, *The Ideologies of Planning Law* (1980), Chap. 9.
[11] Lewis and Harden, *loc. cit.* n. 8, *supra*.

guidelines to help local authorities in developing a "total approach" to the urban environment and to propose advice which the D.o.E. could commend to local authorities." One study of Rotherham outlined the "total approach" being concerned with "problem identification," "co-ordination," "the need to avoid or resolve conflicts," *etc.* Poverty in urban areas was also to be a feature of study. More recent attempts to rejuvenate inner urban areas will be detailed later in the chapter.

In 1977, a White Paper, *Policy for the Inner Cities*[12] was published and 1978 saw the Inner Urban Areas Act. The White Paper voiced the desirability of involving local people in urban regeneration, but the 1978 Act, as well as the Local Government Grants (Social Need) Act 1969, under which grants are made by the D.o.E. to areas of special need, are both silent as regards consultation and participation from affected communities. Again Lewis and Harden[13] have said:

> "Indeed the government vigorously resisted attempts to amend the Inner Urban Areas Bill to require consultation with voluntary groups, and local authority practice appears generally to have reflected the lack of any adequate consultation dimension in the legislation and circulars."

After the White Paper, we saw the introduction of Inner City Partnerships between central government and a number of major cities[14]—"the latest in a series of attempts to secure a better co-ordinated and directed approach"[15] to inner city problems. D.o.E. pressure, however, prevented meetings of partnership committees being open to the public. Lord Scarman in his report on the Brixton riots in 1981 made the following observations à propos of the partnerships:

> "In the result, there emerges a lack of co-ordinated policy for the control of services which must be central to any strategy designed to tackle the related, but not identical problems of inner city decline and minority disadvantage."[15]

On greater community involvement in urban programmes, he said:

---

[12] Cmnd. 6845.

[13] *loc. cit.* n. 8, *supra.*

[14] Some cities are designated as "programme authorities." Here "urban aid bids are made through locally prepared programmes," Lewis and Harden *loc. cit.* n. 8, *supra.*

[15] Scarman, *The Brixton Disorders*, April 10–12, 1981, Cmnd. 8427, (1981), para. 6.6.

"(L)ocal communities should be more fully involved in the decisions which affect them. A 'top down' approach to regeneration does not seem to have worked. Local communities must be fully and effectively involved in the management and financing of specific projects. I should like to see, for example, greater consultation than exists at present between local authorities and community groups about the allocation of resources to projects under the Urban Programme."[15]

Reading this statement it is difficult to overlook the fact that the last official attempt at involving the community in such decision making, a "bottom-up" approach as opposed to a "top-down" one, met with scepticism and eventual disapproval from the government. The Community Development Project, which was the scheme in question, had become too successful in getting local communities *involved* in decision-making rather than merely being *informed* about decision-making.[16]

A selection from the statutory duties, circular guidelines and current practices for participation in local decision-making will be examined later in the chapter. Our attention now turns to current practices, some statutory, some not, for the reception, resolution and airing of complaints by the public about local government activities.

Complaints—The Background

A chief executive of one authority replied to a question about the availability of grievance procedures for members of the public in his authority "that the seventeenth century had established his accountability in legal terms to the courts, and his political accountability to Parliament."[17] Less grandly, the feeling is very largely present among authorities that existing devices for remedying complaints via the elected representative or by the process of the complaint through the local authority committee structure justified a certain complacency. This should not be confused with indifference on their part, as there was always, and many executives pointed this out, the Commission for Local Administration (C.L.A.) in the background.[18] It is a sobering thought, however, that with the C.L.A., apart from London and the South East,

---

[16] The community development project was disbanded in 1977. See their *Limits of the Law* (1977) and McAuslan *op. cit.* n. 10, *supra*, Chap. 9.
[17] This was not representative of any wide feeling, it must be said. See n. 54, *infra*.
[18] See Chap. 5 for the local ombudsman.

planning complaints have until very recently been numerically
dominant—in spite of a statutory procedure for appeals to the Secretary of State, planning inquiries, and resort to the courts,[19]
although the D.o.E. has asked authorities to settle planning complaints informally and locally.[20] Some of the statutory prohibitions
on what the C.L.A. can investigate contain their own mysteries.
They are not allowed for instance to investigate complaints about
commercial activities which have included the allocation of market
stalls and alleged mishandling of concessionary bus passes, though
they can investigate complaints about council house allocation.[21]

In one respect of course, what the chief executive asserted is
correct. For over 100 years, various statutory rights of appeal, and
more recently of statutory review have existed to a range of courts
against local authority decisions and actions. The law of contract
and tort applies to them. In addition there is opportunity for
judicial review under Rules of the Supreme Court, Ord. 53.[22]
Several points call for comment, however. Resort to the courts can
be time-consuming, expensive and fraught with uncertainty. The
law of judicial review can be complex to the point of being almost
unpredictable.[23] More pertinent perhaps is the claim that judges
tend to respond in litigation to the interests of those owning private property, or to the claims of "public interest" as identified by
public officials. They do not show themselves being particularly
sympathetic to larger community claims or to group interests relating to "public participation" and which cannot be easily attached
to legal right or political influence.[24] Judicial interference in local
authority administration has frequently been accused of being
motivated by a conservative dislike of forward planning exercises
involving broad social purposes. Whether or not this is so, the
influence of judicial decision-making upon the internal procedures
and processes of local government administration has been, until
recently, minimal. Some areas of administration from the point of
view of the consumer may be more procedurally aware than

---

[19] The increase in the number of housing complaints is partly due to the "right to
buy" provision of the Housing Act 1980, Pt. 1, Chap. 1.

[20] D.o.E. Circular No. 38/81, *Planning and Enforcement Appeals*.

[21] Justice, *The Local Ombudsman—The First Five Years* (1980), para. 36.

[22] See Chap. 6, *infra*.

[23] S.A. de Smith's, *Judicial Review of Administrative Action* (4th ed., 1980) is a
brave effort to make sense of the quagmire. See, however, the views of Lord
Diplock in *I.R.C.* v. *National Federation of Self Employed and Small Businesses*
[1981] 2 W.L.R. 722 and his paeans of praise for the judicial development of
administrative law, Chap. 6 *infra*.

[24] McAuslan, *op. cit.* n. 10, *supra*.

others; matters relating to licensing might fall under this category. This could owe something to the impact of judicial decisions,[25] but as a general proposition the statement on judicial influence appears to be correct. This is so whether the particular aspect is fairness of procedure, openness of proceedings or provision of information and the availability of reasoned decisions. Courts are only a long-stop. At a fundamental level, complaints should be dealt with effectively by the authorities themselves. If they lack appropriate complaints procedures for the public, authorities should be prompted to put their own house in order.

As to the chief executive's statement that political responsibility is owed to Parliament, this is not functionally correct. His political overlords are the Secretary of State in the D.o.E., Department of Education and Science, etc., and the leader of the council. This is not the place to discuss these extremely complex relationships.[26] Suffice it to say, the relationship between central government and local government centres around finance, and more pronounced centripetal tendencies in this relationship have confused the issue of accountability of local government.[27] Is accountability owed to the local electorate, the ratepayers, central government or the national taxpayer? The rhetoric would have us believe that it is owed to all. The reality is not so clear-cut.[28] From the point of view of a complainant on the street all of this might appear a little confusing and it would be of little comfort to answer his problem: "Vote differently at the next local or central election or frame your complaint into a legal issue for the courts."

Ratepayers, Electors and Objections to the Accounts

Much importance has recently been placed by central government, and indeed judicial decisions, upon the duties owed by local authorities to their ratepayers. The emphasis is upon "value for

---

[25] See, *e.g. R.* v. *Liverpool Corporation ex p. Liverpool Taxi Fleet Operators' Association.* [1972] 2 Q.B. 299 in relation to taxi-cab licensing. See *Hillingdon L.B.C.* v. *Paulssen* [1977] J.P.L. 518 on s.159 of the Local Government Act 1972.

[26] See Griffith, *Central Departments and Local Authorities* (1966); Layfield, *Local Government Finance*, Cmnd. 6813, (1976). Jones, "Central-Local Relationships, Finance and the Law" (1979) 2 *Urban Law and Policy* 25.

[27] Layfield (1976) is a particularly powerful statement. For the tendencies see Local Government, Planning and Land Act 1980, Pts. 6 and 8; the Local Government (Finance) Act 1982; the Rates Act 1984, the Transport Act 1983, and the Local Government (Interim Provisions) Act 1984.

[28] Layfield, *supra*, n. 26.

money" for rate-payers in local government administration. In law
the position which local authorities occupy, *vis à vis* the ratepayer, has been compared with that of a trustee (though not
actually a trustee)[29] owing fiduciary duties, duties of special good
faith, to rate-payers within their respective areas. This legal relationship, which is the creature of judicial decision, has been
recently reaffirmed in the widely debated, and hotly disputed judgment of the House of Lords in *Bromley London Borough Council*
v. *Greater London Council.*[30] The House of Lords held that the
GLC's statutory power to award grants to the London Transport
Executive supplementing revenue from the fare-paying public was
restricted by various factors. The most important for present purposes was the fiduciary duty to rate-payers and the council's obligation to balance that duty against its duty to transport users when
making a grant. The decision by the GLC to reduce fares by 25.per
cent. transferred the cost of doing so (about £69 million) from
transport users to rate-payers. This was held to be unfair. It also
incurred loss of £50 million from the rate support grant (from central government) to the GLC which the rate-payers would have to
make good "without any compensating improvement in transport
services." Because the last aspect was a "thriftless use of rate-
payers' money" it amounted to a breach of the fiduciary relationship. This has important consequences where authorities in future
spend above the target set by the D.o.E. They could incur penalties by way of reduction of rate support grant, thereby bringing
into possible effect this last feature of the Law Lords' ruling.[31]

While we have recently seen a spate of litigation on rating issues
it is interesting to observe that in relation to the public inspection
of local authority accounts, etc., at each audit, the opportunity for
inspection is open to "any person interested." It is, however, a
"local government elector" for the area, or his representative who
has "an opportunity to question the auditor about the accounts" or
"attend before the auditor and make objections" on various
related matters. The auditor must receive written notice of the
proposed objection and the grounds on which it is to be made, and
the notice must be sent to the authority. The right is not restricted
to a ratepayer.[32]

---

[29] *Per* Jenkins L.J. *Prescott* v. *Birmingham Corporation* [1955] Ch. 210.

[30] [1983] 1 A.C. 768.

[31] See the Transport Act 1983 and the controls on the maximum amount of revenue
grants which authorities can make in any year.

[32] Local Government (Finance) Act 1982, s.17 and note s.24 on the right to inspect
statements of accounts and auditor's reports. See *Code of Local Government
Audit Practice for England and Wales* (1983).

While obligations owed to ratepayers or those owed in connection with financial issues are of course important, this chapter will argue that the present range of obligations which the authorities owe to the putative recipients of their administrative services and activities, and to their electors is seriously underdeveloped.[33] Concentration will be placed upon complaints procedures for the *general* public and the provision of opportunities to participate in decision-making.

Complaining to Local Government

(a) The Commission For Local Administration (C.L.A.) Code of Practice

The Redcliffe-Maud Committee (1974), strongly recommended that authorities should develop clear arrangements for receiving and investigating complaints from members of the public. In 1978, the C.L.A., its representative body and the Local Authority Associations produced A Code of Practice for Handling Complaints by Local Authorities and Water Authorities.[34] This gives the appearance of being essentially a checklist for action and provides an outline model procedure for handling complaints. The Code tended to be "defensive" in tone, to ensure greater management efficiency, the monitoring of overall performance and corporate responsibility. Its eyes seemed more firmly set on internal processes rather than external devices to deal with complaints or receive the views of the public and as such seemed influenced by the thrust of the Bains Report which had encouraged a greater "internal corporate sense."[35] This would create greater efficiency as judged by internal standards of performance. The Code was not noticeable for its discussion of consumer needs, although the 1982 supplement shows more awareness of that dimension. What evidence there is would suggest that the influence of the Code has been negligible. The *Justice* Report[36] noted that local authority responses were generally critical of the Code and less than 20 per

---

[33] Ratepayers have been afforded special and general access as a class to challenge the *ultra vires* activity of local authorities before the High Court, see Chap. 6 *infra*. In *I.R.C.* v. *National Federation of Self-Employed and Small Businesses* [1981] 2 W.L.R. 722, Lord Diplock thought the special position of ratepayers, *via à vis* electors, anomalous, "But now that local government franchise is not limited to ratepayers, this distinction between the two applicants strikes me as carrying technicality to the limits of absurdity . . . "

[34] See also the supplement (1982).

[35] Bains Report, *loc. cit.* n. 7, *supra*.

[36] *Justice, The Local Ombudsman, The First Five Years* (1980).

cent. of the authorities interviewed "had taken, or appeared likely to take significant steps to improve their arrangements for dealing with complaints in response to the Code." In spite of a revamping or reshaping of complaints' procedures by some authorities, *Justice* felt that good procedures were "thin on the ground."

Criticism can be levelled against the complaints' model itself as emphasis was clearly directed towards management efficiency— ensuring that a local authority is not "caught-out" by making elementary mistakes. The *Justice* Report for instance had noted "that the majority of authorities have developed procedures for dealing with complaints referred to the C.L.A." but not *before* they are referred. Publicity for the procedures recommended in the Code and "consumerism" are mentioned occasionally, but provision for these and participation are on the tepid side. For example:

> "There should be a willingness to see enquirers and complainants . . . particularly where the issues are complicated or the facts need to be clarified."[37]

It is interesting to compare this minimum standard with the practice of some authorities which allow a complainant to be present at a committee accompanied by a legal representative. This has been noted especially in the field of planning and hackney-cab licences. This apparent forbearance on the part of authorities could be a recognition of the obvious complexity which traditionally attends these subject-matters. But such committees would rarely deal with manifest issues of law rather than fact and/or interpretation of terms such as "reasonableness."

In spite of the attempt in the Code and the supplement to alert authorities to the need for publicity, there is a possible danger that the rather exiguous suggestions which it contained may be construed as the optimum rather than a *de minimis* provision. In spite of improvements in the supplement there is no emphasis upon actually informing the complainant at the time s/he makes a complaint of available procedures, let alone actual details of such procedures, a point which the *Justice* Report supported. It found publicity of such procedures as existed to be sparse.

Part 3 of the Code, dealing with complaints referred to a Local Commissioner, may have been expected to relate less to members of the public than to officers and elected councillors. However, it does seem that even here there was and remains scope, notwithstanding the 1982 supplement, for clearer information being avail-

---

[37] C.L.A. Code para. 2.3.

able to members of the public at various stages. For example, the suggestion in paragraph 3.3 that the complainant be informed of progress on his complaint and "if appropriate" be afforded a copy of the Authority's report on his complaint, while welcome does appear to be distinctly weak.

A complaint is defined in terms going beyond "maladministration."[38] The Code of Practice also draws attention to the desirability of providing information, recording complaints and actually interviewing complainants. The absence of these practices in local administration has elicited criticism in the past.[39]

Nonetheless, the point is repeated that the thrust of the Code is in the direction of internal efficiency, rather than catering fully for the consumers' needs, a point emphasised to some extent by the fact that the Code is merely a recommendation and authorities have shown themselves to be unwilling to comply with non-statutory standards from outside agencies. This point was supported in the findings of the *Justice* Report.[40] Although some authorities complained that the Code, if implemented, would produce too much centralisation of complaints' handling, and that this is a matter better left to departments themselves, one must question whether such procedures ought not to be based in statute, with opportunities for them to be tailored to an individual authority's particular needs.

What is interesting to note is that the *raison d'être* for the Complaints Procedure was the unsatisfactory nature of local authority voluntary procedures. Many chief executives said in response to research questions that the persistent and obstreperous tend to achieve more in the way of redress than the meek and mild. As one American commentator noted "The squeaky wheels get the grease."[41] More specifically, a chief executive of a large district council declared:

> "In my experience the manner in which people take up and pursue their complaints varies enormously and depends often on their knowledge of the local government system, the complexity and seriousness of the issue and indeed on their personality."

This was a view shared implicitly by the C.L.A. both in reports of

[38] Chap. 5, *infra*.
[39] See discussion of the C.L.A. investigations in Chap. 5., *infra*.
[40] *Justice*, (1980).
[41] Friedmann *Comparative Aspects of Complaint and Attitudes Towards Complaining in Canada and the U.K.* (1974).

investigations, and in the findings of a survey in its Third Annual Report, and to some extent by the *Justice* Report.[42]

(b) Ad hoc inquiries in local government

In passing one should note the report *Ad Hoc Inquiries in Local Government* (1978) by the Society of Local Authority Chief Executives (SOLACE). This deals with the more serious inquiry into local authority misadventures. The document cited the range of opportunities open to local authorities to conduct such inquiries and noted:

> "they do not operate within any framework of procedural rules and there have been occasional shortcomings."[43]

This point was supported by the Local Authority Associations (L.A.A.) in their reply in 1980[44] and they also believed that local inquiries under the *aegis* of the authority were to be preferred to ministerial inquiries. The use of inquiries in government has been studied in the previous chapter but they are often resorted to by local authorities either under statute or on a non-statutory and ad hoc basis. In this latter class, the Council on Tribunals will have no supervisory powers, nor will there be an inspector appointed by central government. The response of the L.A.A. is interesting as it preferred the inquiries discussed by SOLACE to be non-statutory. In fact, their response shows quite clearly that they prefer discretion and vagueness both for the setting up of such inquiries and the procedures which they should adopt; in other words greater local authority control. Although it was difficult to lay down ground rules as to when a local inquiry was justified it placed greater emphasis upon "serious internal investigations" feeling that "political sensitivity to local feelings of the authority concerned can be relied upon to ensure that the right approach is adopted."[45] For "minor complaints" the L.A.A. felt that the Code of the C.L.A., etc., "was likely to be most helpful"—a feeling which the *Justice* Report has not supported.[46]

The Code of Practice drafted by the L.A.A. for "Formal Local Inquiries" is not of course binding and it would be at the authority's discretion whether or not the Code was adopted for "the more serious internal investigations." The Code recommends a

---

[42] *Justice* (1980).
[43] *Ad Hoc Inquiries in Local Government* (1978), para. 1.2.
[44] L.A.A. (1980).
[45] *Ibid.*, para. 9.
[46] *Justice*, (1980).

lawyer chairman and an independent panel with a "lay member." Interestingly, complainants and those complained against shall have a right to call their own witnesses, subject to the panel's agreement and that it is in the panel's discretion to allow bodies representing "the public interest" to address it, either directly or through a legal representative.

In spite of these various codes of practice which we have examined, many chief executives in reply to queries felt that the committee system and the role of the elected representative render superfluous further procedural devices for complainants. It is to these topics that our attention now turns.

(c) *Committee, sub-committee, members and complaints*

Authorities are given wide powers to "arrange for the discharge of their functions" by allocating them to committees, sub-committees and officers, as well as joint committees. Some form of "appeal" to a committee or sub-committee from an officer's decision is common among English local authorities. As to the former, the public have since 1972 a general right to be admitted,[47] as they do to council meetings by virtue of section 1 of the Public Bodies (Admission to Meetings) Act 1960, though some chief executives spoke of "allowing" members of the public to be present at committees. For sub-committees legislation is silent with probably no legal right for the public to be present,[48] and sub-committees will, more often than committees, be the bodies dealing with such appeals.

Where sub-committees are used as informal appeal mechanisms, there is a general division between those which allow the complainant to state his case in writing and those which allow a personal appearance,[49] the former being much more common practice and written appeals are a regular feature for instance in the field of housing. There are examples of such authorities resorting to different forms of procedure, other than the committee, for allocation of council tenancies. Allocations were made by an officer "conference" involving the transfer officer, clearance officer, lettings officer, and senior allocation officer.[50]

---

[47] Local Government Act 1972, s.100.

[48] *Tenby Corporation* v. *Mason* [1908] 1 Ch. 457, *per* Cozens-Hardy M.R. at p. 466. *N.B.* note 37, *infra.*

[49] Lewis and Birkinshaw, "Taking Complaints Seriously" in *Welfare Law and Policy* (Partington and Jowell eds. 1979).

[50] Lewis and Livock, "Council House Allocation Procedures" (1979) 2 *Urban Law and Policy* 133.

C.L.A. reports have highlighted egregious abuses in committee and sub-committee procedure.[51] The C.L.A. has also commended a council's practice of permitting citizens to attend a committee and state their case.[52] A *locus classicus* for public lawyers must be an investigation and further report at Slough,[53] where there were substantial abuses of procedural regularity when hearsay evidence of a particularly damning kind was admitted by a councillor against a homeless applicant for housing, and in the absence of the applicant. There was no opportunity for this evidence to be challenged. In previous field research a lack of basic safeguards was found to be common.[54] Indeed Slough on further investigation replied:

> "It is permissible and indeed common for local authority committees of this nature to receive and act upon uncorroborated statements which appear to them to come from a reliable source."

It is possible to distil from the C.L.A.'s reports recommendations for a Code of Good Practice in local authority administration though discussion of this will be reserved until Chapter 5.

The law relating to attendance at committees and especially sub-committees by the public and press is in need of amendment. The law is contained in the Public Bodies (Admission to Meetings) Act 1960[55] which applied originally to council meetings, but which now extends to committees, joint committees and advisory committees of local authorities by virtue of the Local Government Act 1972.[56] Section 1(1) of the 1960 Act states: "Subject to subsection (2), any meeting of a local authority or other body exercising public functions, being an authority or other body to which this Act applies, shall be open to the public." The Act does not apply to sub-committees and admission to these, as of writing, depends upon the total discretion of the authority. Subsection (2) allows the public to be excluded from council or committee meetings where "publicity would be prejudicial to the public interest by reason of the confidential nature of the business to be transacted or for other special reason stated in the resolution arising from the nature of that busi-

---

[51] See *infra.* and Inv.2774C (S. Lakeland D.C.) and Inv.C/77 (Wirral D.C.).

[52] Inv.1372/C/77 and Inv.496/H/78, 508/H/78, 460/C/78.

[53] See Chap.5, *infra*, Inv.387/H/77.

[54] Lewis and Birkinshaw, "Local Authorities and the Resolution of Grievances— Some Second Thoughts" (1979) *Local Government Studies* 7. See generally the same "Taking Complaints Seriously" in Partington and Jowell (Eds.), *Welfare Law and Policy* (1979).

[55] c. 67. See n. 37, *infra*.

[56] c. 70.

ness or of the proceedings." Lord Widgery's decision in *R. v. Liverpool City Council, ex p. Liverpool Taxi Fleet Operators' Association*[57] held that section 1(2) of the 1960 Act—which states that resolutions excluding the public from the meeting are to be minuted along with the reasons for exclusion—is directory only. A study of the minutes of several councils has shown how authorities seem to pass resolutions as a matter of course with as much ceremony as a vote of thanks.[58]

In the *Liverpool City Council* litigation, the relevant committee of the council which was discussing the allocation of taxi-cab licences invited those who wished to make representations to attend the meeting. The meeting was held in a council room which contained 55 seats—14 of which were available for the public and the Press. As 40 members of the public wished to be present, the chairwoman decided to exclude all members of the public, though the Press could attend, on the grounds of lack of space and the undesirability of allowing individual applicants for licences to be heard by rival applicants. These were the reasons which were accepted as adequate, but they had not been properly stated in the resolution and minutes as required by section 1(2). As the requirement was only directory however, it was not an error which would vitiate the proceedings in law and the meeting would not be set aside by the court.

In spite of exhortations in Circulars[59] and support from the Dobry Report for more openness in committee and sub-committee meetings[60] one is left with a strong sense that improvements have not been forthcoming.

In a generally pessimistic account of openness in local government, it must be said that officers are sometimes hopelessly confused by the oblique dealings of their putative political overlords—the councillors. In the Slough investigation (above), the commissioner stated:

> "(I)t was clear that there was a divergence between the attitudes of councillors and officers towards homelessness, and that it was common for the officers' recommendations not to be accepted. The officers confirmed this and said that they found it difficult to understand the Sub-committee's decisions

---

[57] [1975] 1 W.L.R. 701; and see: *R. v. Brent Health Authority ex p. Francis* [1985] 1 All E.R. 74.

[58] Lewis and Birkinshaw, "Local Authorities and the Resolution of Grievances—Some Second Thoughts" (1979) *Local Government Studies* 7.

[59] D.o.E. Circular 45/75: *Publicity for the Work of Local Authorities*.

[60] Dobry (1975).

when no reasons were given for them or because of their inconsistency."[61]

The role of the member in representing citizens has revealed serious shortcomings. According to the Maud Report[62] a councillor required the capacity to "understand sympathetically the problems . . . of constituents and to (be able) to convey them to the authority. . . . " It will be recalled that many authorities suggested that problems were best resolved through the intercession of the member. Reference has already been made to the belief, held in various quarters[63] that the role of the councillor has been diminishing in local government. Doubtless, this may not be a universal reflection of developments in local government, but the frequency with which it has allegedly come to pass is sufficient to raise questions about the utility of the member as the "people's champion." Can they get to the right people? Can they make their presence felt at influential places? Can they obtain the necessary information?—for it is a trite observation that without this their utility for a complainant will be severely limited.

Recently a majority of the Court of Appeal[64] has maintained that a councillor does not have a roving commission to go through council documents and that he is only entitled to such documents as are reasonably necessary for him to perform his duties. An "improper or indirect" motive has been held to disbar his entitlement to documents. Such a motive has been held to exist where a member wanted documents to assist an elector in litigation against an authority, *i.e.* where from the elector's point of view the member might require the information most urgently.[65] What if the member was assisting a complainant and not a litigant? Such an approach has equated a local authority with an individual litigant or commercial corporation with secrets to be kept and protected by law, even against those whom they purport to serve. Yet preventing a member from looking at the books destroys his utility where it could be required most. The implications for practice are enormous. A more recent decision of the House of Lords has emphasised that the decision on whether to disclose documents to

---

[61] Inv.387/H/77.

[62] *Committee on Management of Local Government* (1967) Vol. 2, p, 143.

[63] Cockburn *op. cit.* n. 35, *infra*, McAuslan *op. cit.* n. 10, *supra*.

[64] *R.* v. *Lancashire C.C. Police Committee, ex. p. Hook* [1980] Q.B. 603.

[65] *R.* v. *Hampstead B.C. ex p. Woodward* (1917) 116 L.T. 213 and *R.* v. *Barnes B.C. ex p. Conlan* [1938] 3 All E.R. 226; In *R* v. *Southwold Corp. ex p. Wrightson* (1907) 97 L.T. 431, it was suggested that the fact that a member was critical of a council's policy was not adequate to prevent his sight of documents.

a councillor is essentially for the Council itself, or for the relevant committee where there has been a delegation of authority.[66] If a request by a councillor is interpreted as being hostile to the council and refused, the chances of the councillor successfully challenging such a decision upon judicial review are in reality minimal if he is not a member of the committee whose documents he wishes to see.[67]

In *Hook's* case there were suspicions of party political feuding. Such feuding has, not surprisingly, been reported by the C.L.A. investigation reports. In Inv.4862/C opposition members of the city council were not allowed to appear at the housing sub-committee at which allocations and disputes were dealt with. It was noted that the authority complained against had replied to a questionnaire that the usual method by which a complaint was taken up was via the ward member. Indeed, Lord Denning dissenting in *Hook* said that lack of information for members, if taken too far, could lead to rule by caucus. The implications for an individual complainant are obvious. The recent *Justice* Report on the C.L.A.[68] noted serious misgivings about the role of the councillor assisting complainants. A comment such as "too interested in policy-making and not in individual grievances" was fairly typical. One executive stated that complaining through a councillor was useful "as long as the authority had a clear practice about what it did to put the matter right at local level."

> "Even where such procedures existed, they did not always seem to work satisfactorily, either because councillors thought they could make political capital out of a reference to the C.L.A. or because they were alarmed at the prospect of becoming involved in a complaint against the authority or

---

[66] *R.* v. *Birmingham City D.C.*, *ex p. O.* [1983] A.C. 578, where the Council allowed access.

[67] An allegation that the council or committee was motivated by improper or irrelevant considerations in the exercise of a discretion would have to be proved by the councillor. It is fairly clear that a concern about self interest, loss of face or prevention of public criticism against the council would be irrelevant or improper motivation for the purposes of the *Associated Provincial Picture Houses Ltd.* v. *Wednesbury Corporation* [1948] 1 K.B. 223 (C.A.) test and *cf. Padfield and Others* v. *Minister of Agriculture, Fisheries and Food* [1968] A.C. 997. Unless the council *stated* that these were the reasons for non-disclosure, a councillor would be unlikely to prove that they were. Where a councillor is a member of a specific committee, his entitlement to see documents of that committee, or its sub-committees, is very strong: *R.* v. *Hackney L.B.C. ex p. Gamper, The Times*, November 15, 1984.

[68] *Justice*, (1980).

because they had simply forgotten what the correct procedures were."[69]

The report found that complainants in its survey were largely negative about the role of councillors.[70] The report further stated that the lower socio-economic groups were more likely to contact the councillor than any other groups. Not surprisingly the report noted: "What is clear from the surveys is that the ability of complainants to obtain a positive response from the responsible authority is in part related to factors such as social class and length of education," those higher up the social scale invariably being more successful in finding redress.

Statutory Requirements

Quite apart from a range of appeals procedures from the decisions of local authorities to courts or the Secretary of State who possesses various default powers, there are numerous statutory duties on authorities to provide individuals with an opportunity of presenting a case against them in less formal surroundings than courts of law or central government offices. There are also statutory obligations upon authorities to produce information and/or reasons in writing for their decisions. Reference has already been made to the right to inspect accounts at audit, make representations thereon and challenge related items. The legislation which unified rent and rate rebate schemes and rent allowance schemes making them the responsibility of local authorities, and not the D.H.S.S. has been widely criticised for its over-hasty implementation causing administrative chaos and individual hardship. It is ironical to note that Regulations have introduced a detailed procedure for claimants to make representations in writing; to apply for further review before a review board appointed by the authority at which s/he can be legally represented; call witnesses; cross examine, etc. Claimants receive a statement of reasons for a decision in writing and the board's findings on material questions of fact.[71] There has been criticism of these boards as their members are not independent of the appointing authority.[72]

---

[69] Para. 254.

[70] Though it must of course be remembered that the sample deals with those who by complaining to the Commission had *a fortiori* not been satisfied with local treatment.

[71] S.I. 1982 No. 1124, Pt. 8 and D.H.S.S. H.B. (82) 2.

[72] M. Partington and H. Bolderton, *Housing Benefits Review Procedures: A Preliminary Analysis* (1984).

(a) *General provisions*

It has been observed that some statutory obligations have a tendency to produce additional administrative practices which result in increased procedural protection, or at least increased opportunity to present one's case to a decision-maker, a practice noted recently by the Court of Appeal and encouraged by the High Court.[73] For example, an appeal lies to the Secretary of State against a local authority which refuses or revokes a disposal licence for controlled waste,[74] yet authorities often display a willingness to conduct informal meetings with applicants or licensees as a matter of course. Research has found supplementation of even quite detailed statutory procedures by informal negotiation to be common. Such informal practices are not made public knowledge and can quite easily gravitate towards the interests of the obstreperous, the knowledgeable, the powerful. Although licensing is an area notoriously lacking in procedural coherence, there are many statutory provisions extending procedural protection to individuals,[75] *e.g.* control and licensing of sex establishments and refreshment premises.[76] The Rent (Agriculture) Act 1976 and the activities of the Agricultural Dwelling-House Advisory Committee (ADHAC) caused particular interest.[77] Briefly, the Act places upon local authorities a duty to "do their utmost" to rehouse farmworkers where a farmer can establish "agricultural need" for the premises in question. Any of the parties concerned can call upon the advice of an ADHAC which is tendered in writing to all participants. In fact, hearings before these bodies, and representations of farmer or tenant have been numerous.

Looked at as a whole these provisions seem to do much to advance the argument that whether or not a procedural protection exists is largely fortuitous and that a statutory provision once produced tends to bring in its wake supplementary safeguards and devices. Whether this is always the case is open to empirical examination. MENCAP for instance, have suggested that the default

---

[73] *R.* v. *Secretary of State for the Environment ex p. Powis* [1981] 1 W.L.R. 584; *Steeples* v. *Derbyshire C.C.* [1984] 3 All E.R. 468 at 495.

[74] Control of Pollution Act 1974, s.10.

[75] *e.g.* Residential Homes Act 1980, s.3, especially subs. 4; Public Health Act 1936, (c. 49), s.238(3).

[76] Local Government (Miscellaneous Provisions) Act 1982, s.2 and Sched. 3 and s.5 respectively. With reference to public entertainment licensing under s.1 and Sched. 1 of the 1982 legislation, and a strong judicial statement of procedural fairness extending well beyond the statutory language, see *R.* v. *Huntingdon D.C., ex p. Cowan* [1984] 1 All E.R. 58.

[77] s.29.

powers of the Secretary of State under the Chronically Sick and Disabled Persons Act have proved "largely ineffective" in prompting such procedural protection. They have argued for a statutory regional appeals procedure against an authority's assessment of the needs of an individual who is chronically sick or disabled.

(b) Education

For a statutory complaints or appeals procedure, that provided by the Education Act 1980 is of outstanding interest. Before spelling out the more interesting procedural features of the statute it should be noted that it was normal for education authorities to provide some form of appeals structure in education matters before the 1980 Act. As opposed to the examples in the next section, the regularity of these structures was striking. It would, perhaps, be explained to a certain extent by the requirements of the Education Act 1944. Sections 37 and 76 provide for a degree of parental choice in the matter of secondary schooling. These particular provisions have not been heavily utilised,[78] but section 68 has been frequently invoked.[79] The extra-statutory safeguards adopted by education authorities had been formed, it is suggested with a view to minimising instructions issuing from the Department of Education and Science. The types of procedures available offered a variety of appeals procedures, appeals panels, etc., (sometimes they even cover discretionary education awards) with examples of some authorities actually admitting parental evidence directly. There was a specific example of one county authority's appeal panel upholding 79 out of 353 such appeals.

Turning to the Education Act 1980, section 6 provides that arrangements shall be made by every local education authority to enable the parents of a child in the area of the authority to express a preference of school(s) for his or her child and to give reasons for this preference. This duty is hedged in with exceptions in section 6(3). Of present interest is section 7 which states that all education authorities shall make arrangements to enable the parent of a child

---

[78] *Watt* v. *Kesteven C.C.* [1955] 1 Q.B. 408; *Cummings* v. *Birkenhead Corporation* [1972] Ch. 12; *Winward* v. *Cheshire C.C.* (1978) 122 S.J. 582.

[79] See Chapter 22 and notice in relation to s.99, *Meade* v. *Haringey L.B.C.* [1979] I.C.R. 494: and see Chap. 6, *infra.* Successful petition to the Secretary of State under s.68 is rare. For interesting references to complaints to the Secretary of State from public sector tenants who were being frustrated in their efforts to buy their freeholds and for the Secretary of State's reaction by his use of s.23 of the Housing Act 1980, see Lord Denning's judgment in *Norwich C.C.* v. *Secretary of State for the Environment* [1982] 1 All E.R. 737, 740–741.

to appeal against decisions of local education authorities or governors of voluntary schools. Local education authorities shall establish appeal committees. The decisions of committees are binding on local authorities or governors. They are subject to the supervision of the Council on Tribunals, and the jurisdiction of the C.L.A. Schedule 2 to the Act sets out the constitution of the Committees in a manner which seeks to avoid suspicion of bias or partiality, though the members are appointed by the authority or governors from persons nominated by the authority or governors. Part II details the procedure. The appellant, who must set out grounds of appeal in writing has the right to be afforded the opportunity of appearing and making oral representations and to be accompanied by a friend or to be represented. The decision, by simple majority if necessary, shall be communicated to the appellant in writing. The appeals are heard in private. The Education Act 1981, contains considerable detail on procedures to be followed by an authority in assessing "special educational needs" of a child which utilise the same appeal procedure as under the 1980 Act.[80] Decisions of the committees are not binding in the 1981 legislation.

Although these provisions may appear akin to taking a sledgehammer to crack a nut, it is not surprising that a relatively copious procedure should be provided for such an area as education. School allocations frequently affect vociferous and articulate members of the community, and their heavy utilisation of non-statutory procedures ultimately led to government support for a statutory procedural form. It is interesting to make comparison with public housing and a class of consumer which invariably lacks articulate groups.

(c) Housing

The Housing Act 1980[81] as well as introducing a right for tenants to buy their council houses, has produced important changes in the

---

[80] The details are contained in ss.5, 7 and 8 and provide for information about the procedure for making an assessment; who is making it; the right to make representations and submit written evidence; right of appeal in writing to the Secretary of State; the provision of a "meeting" to discuss an authority's assessment and the relevant advice they received with the "appropriate person"; right of appeal against an authority's statement of need (1980 procedure) and a final appeal to the Secretary of State, who can *inter alia* direct the authority to cease to maintain the statement.

[81] Described by Michael Heseltine as follows: "No single piece of legislation has enabled the transfer of so much capital wealth from the state to the people."

legal position between landlords and tenants in the public sector, providing security of tenure for what the Act defines as "secure tenants."[82] More important for our present purposes, are the provisions relating to housing management, especially consultation with secure tenants under section 43. Successful housing management enterprises *involving* the residents were applauded by the Scarman Report.[83] Prior to the changes introduced by the Housing Act, constant criticism had been made about the frequent arbitrary, almost feudal presumptions operating behind allocation and transfer of council tenancies.

Allocation and transfer of public sector tenancies had witnessed a baffling variety of practices as regards notification, information and points schemes for allocation and transfer of houses. There were examples of good practices by housing authorities, often responding ad hoc to consumer pressure or problems. Some authorities were developing tenancy agreements making provision for the production of information to tenants on council policies and procedures concerning tenancy matters. What does the Act require?

If the "landlord authority" is one within section 42(1)—essentially all public landlords—and relates to "housing management" as defined in section 42(2)—then the landlord authority shall within 12 months of commencement of that part of the Act make, and thereafter maintain, such arrangements as it considers appropriate to enable those of its secure tenants who are likely to be substantially affected by a matter of housing management . . . to be informed of the proposals and to make their views known. The landlord authority is under the familiar duty to consider any representations made to it in accordance with arrangements made by the authority under this section. The landlord authority must publish details of the arrangements to be made available at the authority's principal office for inspection and to be furnished on payment of a reasonable fee, to any member of the public who requests them. Similar provisions apply to housing associations. It should be made plain that these provisions are not directly comparable with the appeal provisions contained in the Education Act 1980. Those latter provisions provide, on paper at least, firmer procedural opportunities to complain and appeal.

It is to be noted that the provisions are expressed in vague and subjective terms, and in general will not be easy to upset, *e.g.* "appropriate arrangements," "likely to be substantially affected."

[82] ss.28–34.
[83] Scarman, 1981, para. 6.14.

Also "housing management" does not include matters relating to rent payable under the secure tenancy and any charge for services and facilities provided by the landlord authority.[84] So often in the past the feeling has been present that exercises aimed at involving tenants in management schemes have amounted to no more than mere "tokenism" on the authority's part. Such gestures from authorities lead to disillusion and cynicism though there is no doubting that effective and participatory schemes involving tenants may have much to offer. That said, it should be noted that there are qualifications to be made about the Housing Act. Although the authority must consider representations from the tenants, nowhere is there any machinery to ensure that authorities take the representations seriously. The statute sets out a bare framework, the rest will be left to the good will, no doubt, of authorities. It will also be interesting to note what forms possible legal challenge may take if, or when, there is an alleged failure to comply with these provisions as their vagueness appears to offer little that could be encashed in terms of hard legal rights in the courts.

Section 44 deals with provision of information about housing allocation: every landlord authority shall publish a summary of its rules as regards priority between applicants and transfer of tenancies; a set of these rules together with procedural rules must be made available for inspection—separate provisions for publicity apply for housing associations. A summary of the rules is available without charge, and a set of rules furnished on payment of a reasonable fee. Of further interest in this section is the duty upon the authority to make available, to an applicant for housing, details of particulars which he has given to the authority about himself and his family and which the authority has recorded as being relevant to his application—it does not include details which he has not given but have been obtained from other sources. Information, however obtained, and if not disclosed, can place the consumer of public services at a great disadvantage.

This section, though incomplete, is welcome as it has been noted in the past that a statutory duty to provide information and give reasons may supply the ammunition to launch an attack on unjustified or questionable public decision-making.[85] Absence of any duty to provide reasons for an adverse decision has proved fatal on more than one occasion. In *Cannock Chase District Council* v.

---

[84] Housing Act 1980, s.42(3).
[85] For a recent statement on the legal effect of not supplying adequate reasons where there is a duty to supply reasons, see *Crake* v. *S.B.C.* [1982] 1 All E.R. 498.

Kelly[86] a mother and five children were evicted from a council house, though it was accepted by the authority that there were no blemishes or arrears of rent on her part. The Court of Appeal held that it was up to her to prove abuse of power or unreasonable behaviour and in the absence of a duty to supply reasons for the eviction, this would be virtually impossible for her to establish, as indeed it proved in the particular case. Be that as it may, the statutory framework offers what at first glance is an improvement on the previous fragmented and haphazard practices of housing authorities. But it has not been without its critics. Lewis and Harden believe that the requirements are "not only jejune and little more than common practice of the majority of housing departments these days, but detailed empirical evidence exists to show that the form in which the information is required to be presented will probably even obscure the real allocation exercise."[87] As the usual method for processing complaints about allocation and transfer of tenancies is via the Housing, etc., committee, or rather sub-committee, readers are reminded of the discussion on committees above.

(d) Homeless cases

We have seen in this section a series of statutory procedures whereby complainants or individuals with a grievance may make contact with agencies or persons independent of the authority complained against, and how such possibilities can assist in the more obvious presence of informal practices among authorities dealing with complaints to reduce the risk of outside intervention. We have noted specific statutory procedures aimed at local resolution of grievances, before the C.L.A. is involved. It might be convenient at this juncture to describe the development of one Act, the controversial Housing (Homeless Persons) Act 1977, which imposed various duties upon housing authorities in 1978 towards the homeless. Those receiving the full benefit of the Act have to be "non-intentionally" homeless and in "priority need," *e.g.* with children.[88]

The interest in the legislation lies in the fact that it does not establish a particular procedure for applications, or complaints/appeals, nor does the statute allow for appeal, either to the Sec-

[86] [1978] 1 W.L.R. 1. See now *Wandsworth L.B.C.* v. *Winder* [1984] 3 W.L.R. 1254, H.L.
[87] Lewis and Harden, *loc. cit.* n. 8, *supra*.
[88] In 1980, 62,420 households were accepted as homeless in England (D.o.E. figures). In 1981, 70,000.

retary of State or to the courts. The statute does say that applications, where the authority believes homelessness or the threat of homelessness to exist, will be subject to "appropriate inquiries."[89] By section 3(2), the authority conducts such inquiries to satisfy itself on: first, whether the homelessness was intentional and secondly, whether there is a "priority need." Given the importance of these inquiries, for if the findings are adverse to the applicants the authority will not be under a duty "to secure that accommodation becomes available," how fair are these inquiries when set against the legal paradigm of due process? If the decision is adverse in any wise to the applicant, reasons must be made available for collection for a reasonable time at the council offices.[90] The decisions are reviewable in the courts, indeed the Act has spawned an enormous progeny of litigation,[91] and local authority associations mooted for a time establishing their own domestic appeal forum to deal with applicants' complaints.[92]

The Code of Guidance issued with the Act speaks of all issues under section 3 being conducted *in the course of a single interview.* What about the possibility of having a friend or representative present? What about being informed of impressions or conclusions and being able to disabuse the interviewer or examiner of such impressions? The possibility of hearsay evidence being taken into consideration in the absence of the applicant when deciding homeless cases has been witnessed again and again.[93] What safeguards exist to prevent this taking place if the decision-maker is under no positive structural constraint to comply with basic principles of natural justice or the less wooden test of fair procedure.[94] Is there an opportunity for an appeal against a decision of an authority to a higher domestic appeal body?

In a study of 20 authorities and their responses to the Act, the author found procedural safeguards to be thin.[95] It was common for the initial interviewer not to be the person making the final

---

[89] Housing (Homeless Persons) Act 1977, s.3(1).

[90] *Ibid.* s.8(9).

[91] See Chap. 6.

[92] Housing Homeless Persons Bill—Report of Association of L.B. Housing Officers (1977).

[93] See C.L.A. Inv.387/H/77; and: *R.* v. *Southampton City Council ex p. Ward, The Times,* February 24, 1984.

[94] *Re H.K.* [1967] 2 Q.B. 617; *R.* v. *Liverpool Corporation, ex p. Liverpool Taxi Fleet Operators' Association* [1972] 2 Q.B. 299; *McInnes* v. *Onslow-Fane* [1978] 1 W.L.R. 1520; *Att.-Gen. of Hong Kong* v. *Ng Yuen Shiu* [1983] 2 A.C. 629, P.C.

[95] "Homelessness and the Law—The Effects and Response to Legislation" (1982) 5 *Urban Law and Policy* 255.

decision. Only six authorities made decisions via the appropriate sub-committee and therefore offering at least the basic appearance of formal constraint in decision-making. In most other cases, the decision was taken by a more senior officer in the housing authority. Eight of the authorities allowed the applicant and a friend or representative to be present after interview, but none of these authorities invited or encouraged their presence. Twelve authorities did not allow their presence after interview either alone or with a friend. Only one authority provided a set procedure for an internal appeal against its own decision, and this appeal was a written appeal. The procedural side, in other words, appeared undeveloped from the point of view of obvious safeguards for fairness in action. The study also indicated that the duty to give reasons under section 8(9) was carried out in a rather desultory fashion. In the absence of an insistence by the courts that full and proper reasons be given, exiguous reasons afford sparse opportunity to challenge an authority's decision.

Non-Statutory Procedures

All authorities in England were asked about details of any complaints' procedures over and above statutory requirements which were used to handle complaints whether formal or informal, structured or loose.

The replies suggested, excluding planning matters, that formal procedures other than the committee system existed and included an executive Ombudsman (*infra*) or a centralised and institutionalised method of dealing with disputes—14 authorities; use of committee and sub-committee especially for housing—78 authorities; informal procedures where the processing of complaints tended to follow a set pattern, generally internal in nature inasmuch as the complainant was not invited to be present at any stage, *e.g.* complaint sent to the chief executive who would refer the issue to the head of the department concerned—43 authorities. One hundred and forty five replied that they either possessed no procedures, which obviously cannot be taken at face value, or they resorted to ad hoc methods which revealed little consistency, *e.g.* complaint to the chief executive's office, ward councillor, M.P., etc. Twenty two replies said that there was provision for a complainant to be interviewed or for public participation, *i.e.* members of the public are actively invited to attend committee meetings, public information meetings or, for example, before the 1980 Housing Act, area tenants sub-committees were encouraged. At the more structured end it included invitations to attend the various bodies hearing the complaints, or complainants were given "a formal interview." Fifteen authorities said that they provided public information, *e.g.* information points, mini-cityhalls, pre-franked postcards. Apart from the use of the committee and sub-committee for complaint resolution, some authorities stated that the full council might hear an aggrieved party concerning such diverse matters as house improvement, rent assessment, Sunday trading, the introduction of taxi-meters, etc. No doubt such deliberations might prove extremely satisfactory but their unsystematic nature is unlikely to excite the general public to unsolicited action.

Under the first "formal type" several authorities were noted which kept central registers of complaints for the inspection of councillors. One of these authorities provided even more copious information, *e.g.* the nature of the complaints, their findings and response, all for public consumption. Personal social service departments tend to feature prominently in the practice of some authorities in keeping departmental registers, whether or not centrally collated. It would appear this is a response to widely publicised tragedies of child deaths.

We encountered examples of grievance procedures of a regular but informal nature which ran something like:

(1) complaint to departmental head
(2) to chief executive
(3) to elected representative
(4) to committee/sub-committee via ward members
(5) to full council
(6) to C.L.A.[96]

One county authority had detailed procedures for personal social services and education which were internal documents but were made available to the complainant at the stage of dissatisfaction with the Chief Executive's response. Another city authority possessed a detailed grievance procedure of such interest that it was followed up with fieldwork. It provided, at its ultimate stage, a panel of enquiry with independent membership. Though clearly documented in the council minutes, the more the procedure was pursued, the further it receded. Most people contacted in the city had not heard of the procedure, though various pressure groups and officers of the authority thought that such a system represented a useful advance in authority/community relations.

The procedure in question had in fact lain fallow since its accept-

[96] Lewis and Birkinshaw, "Taking Complaints Seriously" in Partington and Jowell (Eds.) *Welfare Law and Policy* (1979), and n. 1, *supra.*

ance and the minuted instruction to publicise the procedure
appeared to have been overlooked. What is perhaps of even
greater interest is that in scope it appeared very similar to internal
procedures which were frequently noted in other authorities, but
which in fact were simply defensive mechanisms operating against
the background of a possible investigation by the C.L.A. In fact, it
is of interest to note that this same city authority took almost *every*
item relating to a controversial development plan within one area
for 18 months after passing the "exclusion of the public" resolution under section 1(2) of the Public Bodies (Admission to Meetings) Act 1960. Local residents' groups felt that the authority was
not enlightened in its administration towards local residents, but
invariably displayed a "high-handed" approach.

Some authorities possessed an "executive ombudsman," an
inhouse ombudsman appointed by the authority.[97] There was one
notable example in an Inner London Borough. Though the device
is not without potential problems the strong impression was con-
veyed that his presence considerably reduced resort to outside
agencies such as courts, C.L.A. or elsewhere. This fitted in with a
theme which must be constantly stressed; local authorities themselves are the bodies who could and should deal effectively and
efficiently with disputes and complaints at a local level. This is not,
however, to deny the residuary role which external agencies must
naturally be expected to perform on the occasions when domestic
decision-making proves partial or unfair.

Local Authority Decision-Making and Public Participation

Some of the procedures discussed so far, *e.g.* the committee and
sub-committee, may well be utilised by individuals or groups who
wish to participate in the process of decision-making itself—to
influence a policy or decision with a group interest *a priori* rather
than complain about administrative practices as individuals *a posteriori*. The tenants' management schemes under the Housing Act
1980 constitute legislative encouragement for participation. It will
be recalled that misgivings were voiced about that procedure and
the genuineness behind the intention of actually *involving* tenants.
In local authority practice, we do not have to look too far to discern planning or policy-making exercises for future activity where
involvement of the community may be not only desirable from the
perspective of legitimation, but beneficial inasmuch as their contri-

---

[97] A.S. Wyner (Ed.), *Executive Ombudsmen in the U.S.A.* (1973).

bution may assist in better policy-making. This subject has, however, generated a tremendous amount of conflict from bureaucracy, both central and local, as the programmes we are about to discuss involve a close working relationship between the centre and localities.

At county level, we have the structure plan exercises—a "broad brush treatment of future policies on land use and the allocation of public resources in respect of public development. . . . "[98] Local plans filling in details of the structure plans are made by district and sometimes county authorities.

The subject of urban renewal, rejuvenation, *etc.*, has generated a vast array of statutory schemes aimed at urban and inner urban areas. Mention was made in the introduction of the urban partnerships and other urban programmes. Other schemes, having as their central concern the conservation and restoration of areas within particular authorities, are general improvement areas under the Housing Act 1969 (as amended by the Housing Acts of 1974 and 1980) and housing action areas under the 1974 Housing Act. Where areas were declared general improvement areas or housing action areas by authorities, they engaged in renewal, *etc.*, of dwellings rather than slum clearance. In an attempt to develop commercial expansion, private enterprise and urban renewal, we have seen the creation of Urban Development Corporations and Enterprise Zones.[99]

In a discussion of participation in local government, one commentator has drawn attention to the existence at a local level of three identifiable types of government ranging from "old style" government, based upon rigid party political control and hierarchical structure, to "representative mechanistic" models, to a type placing emphasis upon "new style" participation.[1] The study claimed that even this third type often in reality lacked the procedural and institutional structures which encouraged participation or enabled the public to elicit information from the authority about its plans and the "facts and figures" upon which those plans were based. And yet officials in such authorities were often surprised at "tepid" responses from those invited to participate. What opportunities have existed for the public to participate in the schemes outlined above? Have opportunities which exist been laid

---

[98] McAuslan, *The Ideologies of Planning Law* (1980). They constitute an authoritative general guide in determining applications for planning permission.

[99] Local Government, Planning and Land Act 1980, ss.135–172 and Scheds. 26–31; and s.179 and Sched. 32 respectively.

[1] Chamberlayne, "The Politics of Participation" (1978) 4 *The London Journal* 47.

down in statute, circular or are they left to the unstructured discretion of authorities?

(a) *Structure and local plans*

Looking at structure and local plans first, before they are submitted to the Secretary of State, the local planning authority is required to "take such steps *as will in their opinion secure*" adequate publicity for their survey in connection with the plan, their proposals, and that the public is informed of opportunities to make representations and that there are suitable opportunities for such. These have to be considered by the authority. The grave procedural deficiencies in these steps from the point of view of effective participation have been detailed by McAuslan.[2] The "Examination in Public" which takes place in relation to structure plans after they have been submitted to the Secretary of State has also attracted much criticism. Local plans can be dealt with at a local inquiry before an inspector appointed on behalf of the authority though inquiries are not obligatory if there are no objections.[3] McAuslan has claimed that a vague and relatively unstructured procedure such as the Examination in Public would not allow the opportunity to challenge the details of a structure plan in a way that the Greater London Development Plan for instance was criticised at a special inquiry held to examine that plan.[4] Procedures at inquiries tend to be more formalised as noted in the previous chapter. The subject-matter and procedure at an Examination is left, ultimately, up to the virtually unfettered discretion of the Secretary of State, who appoints a person or persons to conduct an examination in public "of such matters affecting his consideration of the plan *as he considers* ought to be so examined." Nobody has a right to be present.[5] Research on Examinations has described the overbearing influence of officials, both central and local, and powerful industrial or commercial interests.[6]

---

[2] McAuslan, *op. cit.* n. 98, *supra.*

[3] For caustic judicial comment on the adverse reaction of an authority to the recommendations of an inspector after such an inquiry, see *R.* v. *Hammersmith and Fulham B.C. ex p. People Before Profit* (1983) 80 *L.G.R.* 322, and Chap. 6, *infra.* And see: *Great Portland Estates p.l.c.* v. *Westminster City Council* [1984] 3 All E.R. 744 (H.L.).

[4] Structure plans replaced old style development plans; for details, see McAuslan, *Land, Law and Planning* (1975).

[5] The details of the procedures are contained in the Town and Country Planning Act 1971 (c. 78), Pt. 2, as amended, and regulations.

[6] McAuslan, *op. cit.* n. 98, *supra*; Reade "Town and Country Planning" in Harrison, M. L. *Corporatism and the Welfare State* (1984).

Meagre as these provisions are, they should be seen in the context of D.o.E. Circular 23/81 and the Town and Country Planning (Structure and Local Plans) Regulations 1982,[7] explaining the changes in structure and local plan exercises contained in the Local Government, Planning and Land Act 1980.[8] Essentially, an expedited form of procedure for local plans has come into operation and enables local plans to be adopted or altered in advance of the approval or alteration of the structure plans. In the event of a conflict between local and structure plans, local plans are now to prevail.[9] It is important to note therefore that local plans can be adopted without any inquiry or before an Examination in Public for the respective structure plan. The circular stated boldly that the statutory public participation exercises were considered adequate, "and planning authorities should not normally need to do more."[10] "Only one stage of publicity and public participation will normally be necessary for a plan or alteration and a period of six weeks for the making of representations on the draft plan should be adequate, though authorities may consider representations received outside this period."[11]

The Secretary of State has power to dispense with the Examination in Public on an alteration or replacement of a structure plan "where no further information is required and it is possible to reach a decision on a submitted plan on the basis of the objections and other representations received about it."[12] Successful legal challenge to such a decision is unlikely.[13] Local authorities likewise now have power to dispense with inquiries into a local plan. Amongst other changes, the duty to give adequate publicity to a report of the survey in connection with a structure plan and reports of results of review relevant to proposals for the alteration of a structure plan are removed. These are not issues which seize the popular imagination as cutting to the quick of democratic ideals; their intricacy would prevent that. But the whole process reveals a considerable diminution of the possibility for public involvement, considerable bureaucratic sensitivity (central government's) to outside (citizen) interference and complete reversal of the tenor of

---

[7] S.I. 1982 No. 555; and see D.o.E. Circular 22/84.
[8] ss.88–89 and Sched. 14.
[9] para. 10(*d*), Sched. 14.
[10] D.o.E. Circular 23/81 para. 15.
[11] *Ibid.* para. 16.
[12] *Ibid.* para. 17.
[13] *E.H. Bradley & Sons* v. *Secretary of State for the Environment* (1983) J.P.L. 43. An application to quash a structure plan under s.244 Town and Country Planning Act 1971.

the now far distant Skeffington report advocating greater participation in the planning process by the public.[14] The circular stated, ironically or cynically depending on your point of view:

> "The contribution of the individual citizen and of interest groups to the preparation of structure and local plans remains one of the central features of the development plan system."[15]

(b) *General improvement areas and housing action areas*

The general improvement areas and housing action areas which affect whole areas contain no details for public participation in the statutes. Instead, details on participation were covered in circulars which are not binding in law. *Public Participation and Information*[16] urged that "authorities should not only develop new channels of communication between themselves and the residents of housing action areas (which were more run-down areas than general improvement areas) but should also use local organisations and groups by whom information already passes within communities,"[17] though authorities are reminded that the "Act leaves the *manner and amount of publicity to the discretion* of the local authority."[18] *Renewal Strategies* states: "In considering areas suitable for declaration, authorities have the opportunity to see how, in the areas they select, they can, in a practical way, involve neighbourhood councils, associations of residents and tenants, voluntary bodies and the community generally. . . . "[19] Details of these two schemes and differences between them have been noted elsewhere.[20] While of course the details of particular exercises in participation depend upon the attitudes of individual authorities, the record being somewhat mixed,[21] the failure to provide hard statutory machinery to achieve participation has allowed bureaucracy to ride high on the rhetorical wagon of good intent, but to produce little in the way of effective goods where real motivation is absent.

[14] Skeffington Report *People and Planning* (1968) and see the Royal Town Planning Institute, *The Public and Planning: Means to Better Participation* (1982).

[15] D.o.E. Circular 23/81, para. 15.

[16] D.o.E. Circular 14/75.

[17] *Ibid.* para. 32.

[18] *Ibid.* para. 31.

[19] Circular 13/75, para. 28.

[20] McAuslan *op. cit.* n. 98, *supra.*

[21] Lambert, Blackaby and Paris, *Housing Policy and the State* (1978); Paris and Blackaby "Not much Improvement" in Kantor (Ed.) *The Governable City* (1979).

The circulars do no more than encourage what the more aware authorities would have done in any event.

(c) *Urban partnerships and urban programmes*

Lack of formal statutory opportunity for consultation and participation by voluntary and local groups in the urban partnerships and other urban programmes has been referred to earlier, though the D.o.E. has emphasised the importance of consultation with private business in inner city programmes.[22] In their study Lewis and Harden detail the efforts of one English city in its attempts to involve the community in its urban programme and planning in relation to housing investment programmes, education programmes,[23] etc. While the study shows what can be achieved if the spirit of democratic involvement is present in town halls, it brings home yet again the anaemic and indifferent quality of our present devices for involving the public in our local state. The public are often represented or constituted by local/national voluntary bodies which engage in participatory exercises. Many voluntary bodies rely, of course, on grants from central government and its agencies, and these are subject to withdrawal or reduction.

(*d*) *Urban development corporations and enterprise zones*

This section is concluded by outlining the urban development corporation and enterprise zones. The schemes are one political

---

[22] Lewis and Harden, "Law and the Local State" (1982) 5 *Urban Law and Policy* 65; D.o.E. Circulars 19/81, para. 4; 38/81; 16/82, para. 3; 17/83, para. 5 and see incidentally D.o.E. Circular 23/81, para. 3.

[23] After the Taylor Report (Taylor, 1977) some authorities encouraged community participation by appointing parents to school governing bodies—this is now mandatory under the Education Act 1980, s.2. The Government has announced plans to allow parents to form the majority of governors in the case of county, maintained special schools, and voluntary controlled schools. "On many aspects of the character and running of each school the local education authority should continue to have the final say," Cmnd. 9242 (1984). It will be interesting to study what public participation, if any, will follow the rather sparse notification, etc., provisions in the Education Act 1980 ss.12–16 and which are concerned with "establishment; discontinuance and alterations of schools" by local education authorities. On previous legislative provisions concerning school reorganisation, etc., see *Bradbury* v. *Enfield L.B.C.* [1967] 1 W.L.R. 1311; *Lee* v. *Department of Education and Science* (1967) 66 L.G.R. 211; *Coney* v. *Choyce*; *Ludden* v. *Choyce* [1975] 1 W.L.R. 422, all dealing with the Education Act 1944, s.13. Meredith argues that the provisions under ss.12–16 have afforded the opportunity for the Department of Education and Science to achieve a "deeper direct involvement" in the restructuring of schools, against L.E.A. wishes, and have allowed little real opportunity for parents, etc., participation in reorganisation, see (1984) J.S.W.L. 208.

response and interpretation as to the best way of resurrecting moribund urban areas. Briefly, the urban development corporation is a public corporation given a large array of statutory powers in relation to housing, planning, etc. They will assume many local authority functions and are the creatures of central government. They present us with some of the classic issues of accountability of "quangos" (see Chapter 4). Enterprise zones are specific zones within authorities where fiscal and administrative controls are relaxed to encourage commercial development.

Urban development corporations are under a duty to prepare a code of practice for consultation with local authorities, with no enforcement provision to ensure urban development corporations comply with their own code. The creation of an enterprise zone scheme can be challenged in the High Court and proposals for such schemes have to be published. Yet nowhere do the statutes refer to consultation let alone participation with a broader community of interests within the respective areas. In a way it is naïve to expect such provisions as these schemes are seen by their progenitors as exercises in economic and managerial efficiency in which the ideal of public participation is ill placed, if not counter-productive.[24]

The two schemes make explicit what has been implicit in the development of local administration for more than a decade and a half. The movement towards more centralised management reflected in the corporate tendencies within local administration along with greater control over local government by the centre, would be hampered by increased participation, or duties to consult local communities in a meaningful manner. Government plans to replace Metropolitan Counties and the GLC with non-elected boards are a continuation of such tendencies.

Publicity and Information

Information about the existence of complaints procedures is vital. Information for voluntary bodies in participatory exercises is essential—discussion is useless without it. Many of the developments looked at in our local administration have had the effect not of extending discussion and information, but it is claimed, of limiting it. Local authority information, it should be added, is not protected by the Official Secrets Acts.

[24] For recent details, see *Inner Cities Policy: England* (D.o.E., April 1983). The London Dockland Development Corporation has been severely criticised for its autocratic decision-making and failure to consult the GLC, local councils and residents, *The Guardian*, September 17 and October 27, 1983.

Without publicly available information, complaints will clearly be harder to pursue. Some good practices do exist among local authorities: pre-franked, pre-addressed postcards for the registration of grievances, information on complaints centres, an information and public relations officer responsible to a Public Information Committee which encouraged public participation exercises; detailed public documents were also found which advertise the functions and procedures of the authority.

More generally, the position and roles of local government have become complex and multifarious—part judicial, part provider, part entrepreneur. Its developing role has obviously enough increased bureaucratisation and the attendant inevitable information gathering. Little of this, however, is made available to the individual with a grievance who finds neither statutory assistance nor beneficial administrative practice. Refusal to disclose information causes antagonism:

> "Perhaps part of the reason for the quickening growth of law centres, community groups etc. is a reaction to the changing role of local government from protector and protagonist to opponent and antagonist."[25]

The problem is particularly acute when a committee relies heavily upon an officer presenting "expert" evidence or opinion as frequently happens in, for example, planning matters. Documentation containing such opinions should be readily available for inspection by those affected prior to its presentation before a body enjoying executive power.[26]

The subject of planning produces, along with housing, the greatest number of complaints referred to the C.L.A. Often they are from "third parties" complaining about planning permission to a developer. Many commentators and official reports have referred to the practice of "planning agreements" between authorities and developers whereby the authorities hope to achieve a planning "gain" in return for grant of development permission upon certain conditions.[27] Short of the agreement being *ultra vires* or illegal in some other respect, there is little that a third party can do, or little

---

[25] P.H.A.S. Interim Report (1976), p. 26.

[26] See C.L.A.Inv.83/C/77, para. 38. *N.B.* see n. 37, *infra.*

[27] See Jowell, J. (1977) 30 C.L.P. 63; Property Advisory Group. *Planning Gains* (1981); D.o.E. Circ. 22/83 and *Richmond upon Thames L.B.C.* v. *Secretary of State for the Environment, The Times,* May 16, 1983. The agreements are made by undertaking, contractual or otherwise, or under s.52 of the Town and Country Planning Act 1971.

that he is likely to know about if the authority and developer find the agreement mutually beneficial.

These problems undoubtedly flow from the complexity of local authority administration and services and the general impression is often evoked of a series of activities being conducted according to a highly professionalised and bureaucratised interpretation of the public interest. With this version of political life, it is of little surprise that local and central government have not seriously encouraged open administration and freedom of information. Section 228 of the Local Government Act 1972, allows for the inspection of minutes of Council meetings and the chance to make copies thereof by electors in the local authority area as well as other documents in the authority's possession. One major authority examined did not allow electors to peruse minutes and insisted they identify which specific item they wished to see.[28] Inspecting the minutes of committees exercising delegated as opposed to referred powers does not appear to be covered[29] though this issue may be ripe for litigation given that the public may attend *all* committee meetings.[30]

The Local Government Planning and Land Act 1980 has provision for the Secretary of State to issue to local authorities "a code of recommended practice" on the publication of information by such authorities concerning the discharge of their functions and other matters which he considers to be related. The code may specify that information be made available for inspection by members of the public at an authority's offices or elsewhere.[31] The code may additionally specify the steps which authorities are to take to inform the public of the availability of the information.[32] By section 3, the Secretary of State may make regulations to ensure the publication of information contained in the code. One must, however, immediately draw attention to the extensive resort to subjective and discretionary phrases in which the Secretary of State's powers under Part II of the statute are couched. The expressions are vague, subjective and virtually impossible to challenge. There is widespread evidence to show that public interest in authorities' annual reports has been minimal if not non-existent, largely because, authorities felt, the information which they had to provide was if not useless, then not very useful.

---

[28] Housing Emergency Office, Inform Action Series No. 1, *Access to Local Government Meetings and Information* (1981).
[29] *Wilson* v. *Evans* [1962] 2 Q.B. 383.
[30] Local Government Act 1972, s.100.
[31] S.2(7)(c) Local Government, Planning and Land Act 1980.
[32] *Ibid.* s.2(8).

Under Part II, codes of information have been published concerning sundry topics such as "Explaining the Local Authority Rate Bill," "Local Authority Annual Reports" and codes on the provision of information on manpower and employment of disabled people and planning applications. From the point of view of openness and political responsibility to the general electorate, the codes so far have been somewhat tepid, displaying by and large a concern for corporate efficiency, financial constraint and value for money for ratepayers. Important as these points may be, openness and accountability ought to be informed by greater vision than this.

The Education Act 1980, s.8 details the giving of information about schools and admissions programmes for county and voluntary controlled schools, opportunity to express parental choice and any information required by the Secretary of State.

Interesting as these statutory developments are, there are many who are convinced that they are partial in the kinds of information which they seek to make public and very limited in what they actually aim to achieve. Without doubt there is some justification in this allegation, especially that the range of beneficiaries is limited. However, there are many examples of legislation passed with narrow intentions but employed for very broad purposes—the Freedom of Information legislation in the United States being an example.[33] Certainly action groups have been urged to lobby the Secretary of State to issue further codes covering a wider range of interests under the Local Government, Planning and Land Act 1980, though so far such lobbying has not been effective.

Conclusions

Provision of information is at the heart of successful challenge against the state, local or otherwise. Many of the interests and groups affected by the lack of visible structures are not likely to resort to the courts; perhaps a significant number will be unlikely to approach the C.L.A.[34] Moreover there are those who argue that the development of the "local state" is such that it is incapable of responding to the needs of any but bureaucratic or dominant economic interests.[35] The point may be overstated, but it has been forcefully argued.

There are also voices suggesting that the present system, by and

---

[33] See S.Dresner, *Open Government: Lessons from America* (O.C.P.U.).
[34] See *infra*. Chap. 5.
[35] Cockburn, *The Local State* (1977).

large, works in a satisfactory manner. To create new devices would undermine representative democracy and professional efficiency. Besides assuming to make knowledge claims of when political democracy has reached full fruition, there are simply too many complacent assertions about the working of the present system which I hope this chapter has helped to assess and which appear to be over-sanguine.

I leave this chapter by posing several questions. Should there be statutory grievance procedures for members of the public provided by local authorities? What form(s) should they take? Should we create on a statutory basis local "neighbourhood councils" which would have to be consulted and allowed to participate in a constructive manner in the authority's policy-making? Recommendations for the establishment of "local neighbourhood councils" have met with a tepid response from central government and a hostile response from local government.[36] Should we possess a Freedom of Information Act for local government? A Private Member's Bill on this topic has been introduced.[37]

Where it seems that the authority may not be able to dispose fairly and adequately of a complaint by, for instance, a departmental complaints procedure, which should attract the attention of senior and experienced officers in the department, then it may be found that a final "tribunal" of administrative review should be established. Appointments from outside the authority, and local government generally, may be deemed appropriate. If the procedure were internal, such as for instance setting up the Performance Review Committee as a reviewing body for complainants then representation of opposition members on the committee would be desirable. Complainants should be allowed to be present and be assisted or represented if required.

---

[36] See *Neighbourhood Councils in England*, Consultation Paper LG4/743/4 D.o.E. (1975).

[37] November 1984. The Bill would open up sub-committees to the public; only allow exclusion of the public from *all* committees under the 1960 Act for specified reasons; and increase the public's and members' rights to inspect, obtain reports, documents etc. See my *Open Government, Freedom of Information and Local Government* (1985) and (1981) P.L. 545.

Chapter 4

NON-DEPARTMENTAL BODIES, PUBLIC
CORPORATIONS AND QUASI-GOVERNMENT

As government intervened more pervasively into the affairs of civil
society, it found it increasingly convenient to effect its intervention
indirectly; that is, not by establishing a government department
with a Minister at its head who was responsible to Parliament, but
by creating or using non-departmental bodies operating locally, as
well as local government, to assist in government and regulation.
The nineteenth and twentieth centuries saw a centralisation of
power in central government and also witnessed a proliferation of
non-departmental bodies, the latter constituting one of the chief
causes and effects of what has been termed the "compenetration
of state and civil society." This describes that stage of social organisation in advanced capitalist societies where the division between
the realm of the public and the official, and the private spheres
becomes impossible to discern.[1] "Quasi-government" refers to the
process whereby a government resorts to non-departmental and
non-elected bodies to implement its policies, regulate activities on
its behalf, or manage its commercial interests, which include
nationalised industries.

After making various introductory comments, I will look specifically at the institutions which the Government has provided to act
as watchdogs for the consumer interest and as complaints mechanisms for the consumer against nationalised industries. The argument will be advanced that the Government has never taken
seriously the provision of procedures through which individuals
may make complaint about service, services or activities of the
industries although these latter have a fundamental impact upon
our lives. We will see that opportunities to question the policies of
industry boards are even more noticeable by their absence. I will
move on to make some general points about the range of institutions discussed in the next section and I will pick a representative
sample of bodies to illustrate particular points to conclude the

[1] Poggi, *The Development of the Modern State* (1978).

chapter. This is a selective approach as the range of institutions is beguiling in its enormity and variety.

Definition of Terms

In 1981, the now defunct Civil Service Department drew up guidelines for government departments on the creation and control by a Minister of non-departmental bodies.[1a] The guidelines state that the objectives and structure of non-departmental bodies should be clearly defined and that future bodies should, where possible, be built on existing models. These are established by:

1. Act of Parliament where constitutionally necessary, *e.g.* public corporations for nationalised industries; or *e.g.* to transfer the assets of the Bank of England into public ownership, Bank of England Act 1946.
2. Incorporation under the Companies Acts (either directly or by share acquisitions or by a company limited by guarantee);
3. Royal Charter (B.B.C.; Arts Council; British Council; Research and Sports Councils; the Bank of England is a corporation under Royal Charter, though appointments to it are effected by statute; and see 1 *supra*;
4. Treasury Minute (University Grants Committee);
5. Informal creation of "shadow organisations" by the Minister before a proposed statutory body has been given official statutory authorisation;
6. Pure administrative *fiat* (*e.g.* for advisory or ad hoc bodies);
7. Royal Commissions established by the Royal Prerogative.

As we shall see in Chapter 6, the status of a body can determine whether its decisions or actions are subject to judicial review under R.S.C. Order 53. The guidelines advised that new members of such non-departmental bodies ought not to be civil servants of the Crown and that these bodies should not be Crown bodies. We should also note that our range of discussion is not confined to bodies established by any of the methods above which make them in some sense "official."

In 1979, the new Conservative Government was intent on reducing the number of non-departmental bodies and with that aim in mind it established a review under Sir. Leo Pliatzky.[2] The review did not cover all public sector bodies—"a single comprehensive

---

[1a] *Non-Departmental Public Bodies: A Guide for Departments* (1981).
[2] Cmnd. 7797 (1980).

review of this whole field" was "impracticable." Many of the more obvious candidates were excluded, such as nationalised industries, other public corporations, N.H.S. bodies, universities, etc. Even so, the bodies listed covered 48 pages of small print! These were as diverse as for instance under the Treasury: the Review Board for Government Contracts and the Treasure Trove Reviewing Committee! Sir Leo Pliatzky's suggestions for winding up were minimal,[3] and the Government has not been noticeably more voracious in its hunting of non-departmental bodies—in spite of the rhetoric to the contrary.[3a]

Non-departmental bodies are often referred to as QUANGOS, an acronym for quasi-autonomous non-governmental organisations, or QUAGOS which *are* governmental yet quasi-autonomous institutions. It has been commented that these widely used acronyms are virtually meaningless. Barker[4] has provided the following gradations which are useful, though contestable:

(1) *Government Departments* as described in Chapter 2;
(2) *Governmental Bodies*—established by one of the devices outlined in the C.S.D. guidelines; membership appointments made by the Government; Exchequer funding; varying levels of civil service or Parliamentary supervision, control or accountability. These include bodies hived off by government departments, and departmental agencies where responsibility to Ministers for management is intended to be different from the department itself; under this head I will include the Boards for nationalised industries;
(3) *Semi-private bodies*—a body not established by or dependent on the State but in a significant relation to it for the making and application of government policy (housing associations; National House-Building Council; National

---

[3] The review excluded nationalised industries, other corporations, major companies in which the Government has a shareholding, NHS bodies and Agricultural Marketing Boards, the Judiciary, local authorities, universities and certain professional registration bodies. The total of non-departmental bodies subject to his review were executive—489; Advisory—1,561; tribunals—67. In all 248 bodies were recommended for winding up saving £11,641,000. Executive bodies alone accounted for £5,800m expenditure. The administrative cost of the tribunals was £30m.

[3a] See the Prime Minister's statement, H.C. Deb., Vol. 68, cols. 57–58, November 19, 1984.

[4] Barker, *Quangos in Britain: Governments and the Networks of Public Policy Making* (Barker ed. 1982).

Federation of Housing Societies; the C.B.I.; Institute of Directors, or T.U.C.;

(4) *Private organisations* or "the surrounding society as a whole." About these, I will have little to say.

This is a categorisation which will be adopted for present purposes. The questions we are concerned with are: What kinds of accountability exist and should exist?[5] Are the procedures and processes adopted by such a wide variety of bodies as fair and open as is desirable in all the circumstances? Are there effective means for gaining redress of grievances? The general point will be made that the array of devices which operate are woefully inadequate for forms of redress or for participation by interests apart from the most powerful or influential, a theme emphasised by the fact that the bodies in question are not elected, but appointed, selected or approved, usually by Ministers.

Why Are Non-Departmental Bodies Resorted To?

Non-departmental bodies can be useful ways of facilitating government by utilising experts and advisers without employing them as civil servants. They can operate in highly politically charged areas over which a government department might assume responsibility but which is felt to be too contentious or sensitive an issue to be under the aegis of politicians and party politics—such might be race relations, or arts subsidies, university financing or running an industry. They can be established to placate demands of pressure groups in a particular area, so that the government can appear to be doing something although the body in question will be starved of appropriate resources, powers or procedures to achieve its statutory aims effectively—many claim the Commission for Racial Equality and Equal Opportunities Commission, or the Health and Safety at Work Executive are examples of this. A particular activity may require sensitive and independent judgment which it may be inappropriate to hand over to courts or specialised tribunals. A body may have to perform a variety of regulatory, supervisory, advisory or adjudicatory functions in a particular field of administration requiring a high degree of expertise and a broad

---

[5] Barker citing Hague *et. al*, (1975) mentioned vertical accountability (upward accountability to government); downward to clienteles by, *e.g.* participation; horizontal to peer groups. Accountability can also be *ex ante*; *ex post*; and "process accountability" (monitoring of the work). See also: Law Reform Commission of Canada *Independent Administrative Agencies* (1980); and *Parliament and Administrative Agencies* (1982).

range of skills. Using non-departmental bodies may be a convenient device to avoid control and accountability for decision-making or to achieve irreconcilable political ideologies[6]; or to spread more broadly the base of power. They can be used as an effective means to "get the business done" without labouring under the constraints which are imposed on departments of State.

The State in a Mixed Economy

The tasks of the State in a mixed economy—and it is worthwhile remembering that ours is still a mixed economy—were described by Wolfgang Friedmann[7] as the regulation of the economy and industrial relations, allocation of scarce and collective resources, regulation of potentially dangerous activities, and regulation of race relations to name but a few. Regulation can be achieved by a department directly or via an agency or quasi independent body appointed by Ministers or by central government allowing a degree of autonomy and self-regulation to particular institutions such as the Stock Exchange, the Press, Professional Bodies and to a decreasing extent Trade Unions. The State is further identified by Friedmann as a provider through its social welfare, health and educational programmes. The State is also an entrepreneur. It seeks to maximise profits in its provision of essential and basic services, and just as controversially through its ownership of business and commercial interests, most importantly nationalised industries.

The State is an umpire. It establishes the bodies to adjudicate in disputes, to regulate and arbitrate according to a body of precepts, principles, rules or exigencies to settle disputes. Limitation upon what the Courts could achieve led to the widespread creation of tribunals. General statutory complaints mechanisms might also fall under this head.

We might also add that the State is a protector through its provision of armed services and police forces. In fact, this role of the State is given pre-eminence in the current political philosophy of

---

[6] *e.g.* to further state control and intervention under a Labour Government and also to insist upon their utilisation as an alternative to direct intervention by the state, as was suggested by the Conservative Government in 1970. As Davies, *What's wrong with Quangos?* (1979) says, "This ambivalence derives from their *quasi*-governmental nature." For further reasons behind their creation see *Public Policy and Private Interests: the Institutions of Compromise* (Hague, McKenzie and Barker ed. 1975), p. 362.

[7] Friedmann, *The Rule of Law in a Mixed Economy* (1971).

the right which espouses the notion of "The Strong State"[8] hand in hand, ambivalently, with "The Minimal State."

To a greater or lesser extent, the contemporary State is involved in making effective the above tasks. As a fact of our political existence, successive governments have found it convenient to rely upon bodies shortly to be described to assist in the various tasks just described. This has been problematical for a variety of reasons.

First, there is an increased and increasing risk of internal conflict within the State apparatus when the State engages in such a variety of roles. The State as umpire, for instance, may clash with the State as entrepreneur, or the State as regulator may clash with the State as provider.

Secondly, the above processes assisted and accompanied "corporatism"—a system of government organisation and control which brought with it particular problems for legitimation of public authority and power.

Corporatism

Corporatism is characterised by, *inter alia*, mutual agreement between interest groups in the private sphere such as employers, trade unions, business associations, banking and insurance groups and the government. The government bargains not to regulate the affairs of the particular interest groups directly, but allows a degree of self-regulation in return for mutual accommodation and support. Corporatism takes many forms, but along with the basic features outlined above may be increasing State direction of the economy to avoid the vicissitudes of unregulated market competition. Corporatism as a form of social organisation differs markedly from competitive market capitalism. In the latter mode of production, the central features are, in theory, a limited State, a clear separation between the public and private sectors—sectors which corporatism helps to confuse—a neutral and autonomous body of law and a free and open market in which private individuals exchange their privately produced goods or commodities or services. It has been persuasively argued that in twentieth century Britain–and this merely built upon previous developments—corporatism effected a movement from government by law to government by administration.[9] The extent of State control and exercise

---

[8] A term used by Margaret Thatcher in a forthright manner: see "The First Airey Neave Memorial Lecture," London, March 3, 1980.

[9] For a leading comment on the situation in the 1970s, see Winkler, "Law, State and the Economy: The Industry Act 1975 in Perspective" (1975) B.J.L.S. 103.

of power was not made explicit in law, but had to be located in Circulars, Codes of Guidance, Planning Agreements,[10] informal bargained relationships and consultative processes, ministerial letters and internal departmental rules. Law has long since undergone a transformation so that it is no longer an autonomous device to control government, where that is possible in our constitutional theory, and help establish along with universal franchise and market mechanisms the basis of State legitimation claims. It became a tool to achieve specific ends; to be used increasingly instrumentally, *i.e.* for partial purposes, to such an extent that the Rule of Law ideal itself became undermined. There is a movement away from the formal institutions of law and politics to informal and administrative *fora* for the making of important governmental decisions. Very often, what is happening is not open to public scrutiny or debate and therefore escapes orthodox political or legal forms of accountability. The resort to non-departmental bodies offers an opportunity for governments to control without being seen to control.

It needs to be emphasised that there are good and legitimate reasons why resort has been made to non-departmental bodies. Outright hostility is often ill-informed and tendentious.[11] The present chapter will detail pressing concern about the use of non-departmental bodies in a governmental framework which considers itself democratic. Many of the declared aims of the present government are directly opposed to corporatist tendencies and seek a reversion to pure market capitalism by privatisation of state assets and deregulation of administrative control. Be that as it may, the structure and institutions which were the product of the nineteenth and twentieth centuries still remain, and the problems associated with their development will still confront those who wish to see democratic ideals given greater realisation.

While the model of corporatism which saw the trade unions as an incorporated group of central significance in governmental policies relating to industrial peace, wage settlements, health and safety at work, etc., has been considerably dismantled, we should be far from complacent that corporatism has disappeared. Recent work has detailed how different interests have moved more promi-

---

[10] These took the form of non-legal guarantees by a Department—first the Department of Industry, then Energy—for assistance to a company in return for extensive disclosure to government and, *e.g.* unions on corporate development and activities.

[11] For some of the good reasons, see Fulton, *Report of the Committee on the Civil Service* Cmnd. 3638 (1968) and "hiving off" to non-civil servants of administrative decision-making, especially at p. 18. For less measured comments, see Holland and Fallon, *The Quango Explosion* (1978).

nently into the charmed circle, especially finance capital and to a lesser extent advisors and philosophers of a free-market, right-wing disposition.[12] More subliminal has been the emergence of "welfare corporatism" whereby interests and interest groups such as the insurance world, private health organisations, building societies and professional groups attain fiscal and welfare advantages denied to poorer groups not as a result of *direct* State hand-out, but after informal and sometimes protracted negotiation.[13] Their resultant advantages are not seen as the consequence of public welfare, but as the product of private wealth and private negotiation and thus in some sense apolitical and uncontroversial.

Privatisation and Deregulation

Privatisation of State assets has included the widespread selling off of publicly owned industries and de-nationalisation, as well as selling off public sector housing. Deregulation has included the movement towards enterprise zones (discussed in Chapter 3), "free ports" and relaxation of planning controls.

The aims of privatisation and deregulation are the contraction of the public sector, the expansion of the private sector and the jettisoning of as many non-departmental bodies as possible. One of the objectives is the hope that the private and the public sectors will become more easily distinguishable. It has been plausibly argued that such developments will not unequivocally separate the two sectors but may well increase the opportunity for informal networks and relationships to develop between them, even in the absence of formal regulatory mechanisms.[14] The methods which governments have employed in the past to achieve policies which have relied upon the power of the public purse and placing of government contracts without appropriate scrutiny from Parliament have been well documented.[15] In the United States a great deal of attention has been devoted to the methods whereby large private corporations render the government favourable to the interests of the former and whereby the United States government and its agencies effectively delegate to private interests policy-

[12] Lewis and Wiles, "The Post-Corporatist State" (1984) 11 J.L.S. 65.
[13] Harrison, *Welfare Corporatism* (1984).
[14] Lewis and Harden, "Privatisation, De-regulation, etc." (1983) 34 N.I.L.Q. 207.
[15] Daintith, "Legal Analysis of Economic Policy" (1983) J.L.S. 191; Ganz, *Government and Industry* (1977). And it is interesting to note the emergence of "planning agreements" in local government whereby authorities are offering financial assistance to firms who sign such agreements. On quasi-government in local government see Cousins in Barker (ed.) *op. cit.* n. 4, *supra*.

making of a public nature.[16] Where the Federal Government relies upon regulatory agencies to regulate the private sector, there are well catalogued studies of the agencies being "captured" by the interests they are supposed to be regulating. The Administrative Procedure Act of the United States and judicial interpretation of that Act have sought to protect procedurally and fairly all interests within these informal and *ex parte* developments. Many of the bodies I am going to examine in the United Kingdom are involved in management or regulation on behalf of the government and therefore in some respect on behalf of the "public interest." This chapter will attempt to show how they have often performed their duties in an undemocratic and unaccountable manner. It is idle to suppose that terminating the life of non-departmental bodies which peform regulatory or managerial tasks, or privatising industries or utilities and returning them to a "neutral" framework of an open competitive market will reduce the degree of State influence in the private sector. It is more likely to make the degree of that influence more covert and secretive, more informal and negotiated as the episode of the Stock Exchange, the Director General of Fair Trading and the Department of Trade and Industry illustrated in 1983.[17]

The Public Corporation and Nationalised Industries (N.I.s)

The public corporation device is not peculiar to N.I.s but the general pattern of public ownership in the United Kingdom has been to vest the assets of an industry or utility in a public corporation. This is not an agency of the Crown, although various statutory powers and duties are attached to it. Since 1945, power of appointment to the boards of public corporations has tended to lay with ministers.

Herbert Morrison, who had a central role in popularising the public corporation concept for commercial and public purposes, emphasised not only the board's commercial responsibilities but

[16] *The Dilemma of Accountability in Modern Government: Independence versus Control* (Smith and Hague ed. 1971); *The New Political Economy: the Public Use of the Private Sector* (Smith ed. 1975); Hague *et al*, *Public Policy and Private Interests: The Institutions of Compromise* (1975).

[17] The Government instructed the Director General of Fair Trading to cease proceedings before the Restrictive Practices Court under the Fair Trading Act, 1973 against the Stock Exchange in return for a promise by the Stock Exchange to regulate certain "restrictive practices" out of existence if the institution were exempted from the restrictive practices legislation. See Restrictive Trade Practices (Stock Exchange) Act 1984.

also its wider social responsibilities. The board was not merely engaged in "capitalist business; the board and its officers must regard themselves as the high custodians of the public interest."[18]

(a) Boards' duties and relationships with Ministers

There were ambivalences in these dual approaches which still inhere in the legal framework of the N.I.s. The duties of each corporation are set out in separate statutes, though there are plans to unify these in one statute. The 1976 NEDO report says "They are usually described in general terms with little guidance on relative priorities or means of reconciliation when conflicts arise," *e.g.* whether to be profitable or simply "break-even." The ambiguity of the statutes reflects much of the inherent conflict in the purposes of nationalisation[19] and often renders the statutes for all practical purposes non-justiciable before a court of law.[20]

The Morrisonian concept was widely seen as representing an "arms length" relationship between the corporation and the government. Ministers were given power to issue general directions, but the day to day management was to be the concern of the board. Ministers, however, have preferred not to direct N.I.s formally to comply with wider political objectives, but to impose influence by informal means. "Government by nudge and fudge" according to a former board chairman.[20a] Recent litigation and practices would suggest that the degree of ministerial intervention

---

[18] Morrison, *Socialisation and Transport* (1933).

[19] *A Study of U.K. Nationalised Industries*, National Economic Development Office (1976) and Cmnd. 7131 for the Government Reply. The Government wishes to introduce legislation which will establish the primacy of external financing limits and financial targets over "break-even" requirements, render dismissal of board chairmen easier and facilitate privatisation.

[20] *Charles Roberts and Co.* v. *British Railways Board* [1965] 1 W.L.R. 396; though cf. *British Oxygen Co.* v. *South of Scotland Electricity Board* [1959] 1 W.L.R. 587 (H.L.). Note also *Booth and Co. Ltd.*, v. *National Enterprise Board* [1978] 3 All E.R. 624. Statutory duties have been expressly excluded from judicial review in some cases, and because they are couched in exhortatory language are not usually susceptible to judicial review in others. In *Booth*, the plaintiff had an interest which was specific enough to test by litigation where there was an alleged breach of duty. Might there be more chance of judicial review of such duties under the revised Order 53? See Chap. 6. The London Electricity Consumer Consultative Committee has argued that the Government's use of Financial Targets and External Financing Limits to achieve wider economic objectives *viz* the increase of the price of electricity by 2 per cent. to achieve a reduction in the public sector borrowing requirement was outside the powers of the Electricity Acts 1947 and 1957; (1983–84; H.C. 215, ii) pp. 57–59.

[20a] Sir Peter Parker, ex chairman of British Rail Board.

is really quite substantial.[21] The present Government in its 1983 election manifesto emphasised the need to work closely with "top class" managers whom it would appoint to tackle each industry's problems. Letters of objectives were sent out to most chairmen by the Government. In spite of the existence of a Select Committee for N.I.s until 1979,[22] the "arms length" relationship between boards and Ministers posed obvious problems for the achievement of ministerial accountability to Parliament, and there was an absence of structured debate about long term plans in Parliament. Since 1979, responsibility for review of the general performance of nationalised industries has lain with the relevant departmental select committee. The National Audit Act 1983, expressly excludes N.I.s along with various other public bodies, from the supervision and scrutiny of the Comptroller and Auditor General. General financial control by the Treasury over N.I.s has been described as "characterised by confused thinking, unsound practice and unfortunate consequences."[23] The Treasury has maintained that in cases of conflict between the commercial interests of a particular corporation and the Government's economic objectives the former would not necessarily outweigh the latter. External financing limits—the amount an industry can borrow from external sources in any one year—and financial targets are claimed by consumer groups to have a severe impact on the prices consumers have to pay for goods and services, yet the limit set by the Treasury is beyond effective consumer challenge.

Generally the statutory duties of N.I.s are couched in exhortatory language and do not create legal rights for individuals. There is no Ombudsman for N.I.s though the creation of such has been advocated.[24] A frequent complaint has been that the monopoly or near monopoly position of N.I.s has created both a power akin to taxation by the State in the provision of essential services and unfair competition for competitors. For the latter domestic law offers little by way of redress, though the impact of European law has yet to be fully gauged.[25] The Competition Act 1980 contains a power for the Secretary of State to refer to the Monopolies and

---

[21] *B.S.C.* v. *Granada T.V.* [1982] A.C. 1096: *Air Canada* v. *Secretary of State for Trade* (No. 2) [1983] 1 All E.R. 910, H.L.

[22] It was established in 1952.

[23] And see the Treasury and Civil Service Committee *Financing of the N.I.s* (1980–81; H.C. 348, I, etc.); and recently the Public Accounts Committee (1983–84; H.C. 139).

[24] *Infra.*

[25] Art. 86 of EEC Treaty and "dominant position." See *Garden Cottage Foods* v. *Milk Marketing Board* [1983] 2 All E.R. 770.

Mergers Commission activities of N.I.s on questions relating to efficiency and monopoly position.[26] The government sees the panacea for the consumer and private businessman in privatisation, and a free competitive market.

(b) The 1976 National Economic Development Council Report

The NEDO report of 1976 on N.I.s described the mutual distrust between ministers and civil servants on one hand and the managers of N.I.s on the other, as well as the absence of criteria to assess performance, managerial competence and an absence of open structures to make long term plans and objectives. NEDO identified a feature of N.I.s which is central to our present concern. In advocating a new approach for N.I.s, the report recommended a democratic framework for the making of rolling plans and important decision-making which is worth quoting:

> "(T)he evolution of strategic plans for N.I.s must be a combined operation. Experience here and abroad shows that interest groups which are closely concerned with the content and implementation of the industries strategies . . . need to be involved in their formalities at an early stage. This is particularly true of government and trade unions but it applies more widely—for example to industrial users and other consumers."

Statements of corporate aims are usually set out in corporate plans, though these are not agreed with Government in any formal sense and are rarely made public. Even Select Committees have found it difficult to see them. Calls for greater efficiency and accountability in N.I.s and in their relationships with sponsoring departments would be more realistic if there were a body such as the Policy Council for each industry as recommended by NEDO, comprising *all* the representative interests above.[27] The report was not precise about the ways in which domination by more powerful interests might be avoided at such councils, however.

The failure of N.I.s and government to develop democratic and open processes of decision-making to reflect fully the "public" conception of state enterprise has left N.I.s vulnerable and open to attack, with little public good-will to call upon. The attack came by

---

[26] Competition Act 1980, ss.11 and 12.

[27] The Report argued for a Corporation Board which would manage the industry within the framework of objectives established by the Policy Council. See further, Sir A. Knight (1982) P.Q. 24, and Redwood and Hatch, *Controlling Public Industries* (1982).

the appointment of chairmen fully in line with government thinking and a systematic rundown of industries which were not to be
sold off. In British Steel for instance, the rundown of the industry
was achieved with minimal consultation with unions, a feature
which the Select Committee on Trade and Industry criticised. The
future planning of the steel industry began to take place through
bargaining with the private sector and the creation of subsidiaries
owned jointly by British Steel and private companies. Competition
between private companies and state owned producers resulted in
an informal arbitration mechanism to the then Department of
Industry for complaints of unfair pricing.[28] In other words corporatism writ large. For those individuals who cannot bargain or hag-
gle with state industries reliance must be placed upon the
grievance mechanisms provided by the State for such industries—
the NICCs.

Nationalised Industry Consumer Councils (NICCs)

The Secretary of State for Trade stated in December 1981[29] that
NICCs "need to provide an expert and effective complaints handling service easily accessible and known to and trusted by consumers." They were urged to "spend more of their available time
and resources on pursuing the concrete problems of customers and
less on broad policy issues." The effect of policy decisions on consumers, however, is very often at the heart of complaints by
NICCs about service, quality or pricing.

(*a*) *General Structure and Powers*

There were 44 NICCs in 1981 covering the gas, electricity, coal,
rail and ferry transport, posts and telecommunications. With the
Energy Act 1983, all are now statutory bodies.[30] The details of
organisation differ, but both gas and electricity have a national,
regional and local presence. NICCs involve almost 1,000 ministerial appointments, and are independent of their respective industries.

> "All NICCs . . . have statutory functions, certain of which
> are broadly similar. In general they are required to consider

---

[28] I am grateful to Norman Lewis for knowledge of this point.

[29] *Consumers' Interests and the Nationalised Industries*, December 1981. The document was one of the first reviews of non-departmental bodies performed after
the Pliatzky Report, *supra*.

[30] The Water industry has, since 1983, consumer consultative committees. There
are no consumer "watchdogs" for the oil and nuclear industries.

any matter raised by consumers, Ministers or the industries themselves concerning the service and facilities provided by their respective industries—only two[31] are excluded from considering charges; they can pursue matters which appear to them to be worthy of consideration . . . and they are required to notify their conclusions to the industry and/or Minister.''

Although generally national councils deal primarily with policy matters, regional councils with policy and individual complaints and local councils with complaints, the practice can vary considerably; even within the same industry there are wide variations between regional and local practice. NICCs deal collectively with about 70,000 complaints a year. This number represents a steady increase, although many complaints are made to Citizens Advice Bureaux and other agencies and there is widespread evidence suggesting that many consumers do not complain because they consider it futile. NICCs have a limited role for London Regional Transport services[32] (*i.e.* permanent closure of lines), and do not cover buses, aviation, or the oil or nuclear industries which are state owned. These usually have other devices through which the consumers' interests can be raised and which are notable for their complexity, anonymity and general lack of efficiency.

The recommendations of the 1981 Paper will, as far as they are still relevant, be examined later. It should be said, however, that the paper was a disappointment because it blandly ignored the weaknesses of NICCs to press home a complaint successfully against an industry.

(b) Policy and Individual Complaints

It should be made clear that there is often a clear relationship between wider questions of policy and consumer complaints—a point which seems to have been ignored or misunderstood in the *Justice* Report which advocated the creation of an Ombudsman for N.I.s though it showed little interest in making the voice of consumers more effective in policy or strategic matters.[33] Electricity Consumers' Council Annual reports, for instance, reveal the woeful inadequacy of statutory consultation with Area Boards of the Electricity Industry over fixing of tariffs. Eighty per cent. of the final price of electricity is determined by the Generating Boards'

---

[31] Central Transport Consultative Committee and Transport Users' Consultative Committees.
[32] *Infra.*
[33] *Justice* (1976) *The Citizen and the Public Agencies.*

Bulk Supply Tariff (the price charged by Generating Boards for the electricity used by Area Boards). The Bulk Supply Tariff for 1982/83 was not formally published until March 25, 1982. "This was not only several weeks *after* consultative councils had considered detailed retail tariff proposals from their Boards, but in most cases *after* the individual Area Boards had published their own tariffs." Government financial targets have an economic impact on the charge ultimately passed on to the consumer, yet such matters are *terra prohibita* for the councils. There is also a valuable interaction between policy and complaints work, since the national councils are anxious to see how certain industry policies actually affect consumers and are also keen to monitor trends of complaints so that they might make suggestions for reform, *e.g.* electricity or gas "cut-offs," relationships with social security agencies, the position of the elderly and appropriate methods for payment of bills. In short, the individual complaint often cannot be isolated from general policy considerations.[34]

The National Consumer Council (N.C.C.), in a valuable discussion about NICCs in 1976, made the following points: it was usually impossible for them to apply pressure at the important decision-making processes; NICCs made inadequate use of data on complaints' analysis—it was unknown for instance how N.I.s dealt with complaints themselves and it is still true to say that there is little idea of how complaints are dealt with at the local non-statutory council level; lastly, the flow of necessary information to NICCs from N.I.s was almost universally inadequate for the formers' duties, with too much relying upon concession and personal initiative rather than "comprehensive arrangements for full disclosure."[35]

The 1976 report of the N.C.C. recommended that NICCs should have more effective opportunities to force a Minister to account to Parliament for his decision where he disagreed with a NICC's proposal. It is interesting to compare such a recommendation with

---

[34] In fact there seems to be a conflation of wider issues of a policy nature and individual grievances in the statutory procedure by which a Regional Electricity Consumer Council can bring a representation to the Electricity Council (of the industry); *infra*. This has caused confusion as to what subjects are appropriate for a representation.

[35] N.C.C. *Consumers and the Nationalised Industries* (1976). It has been claimed that there were 11 different security or privacy headings for classifying information held by the Electricity Council and the Central Electricity Generating Board. This excluded "personal" headings. It was believed that there could be 14 compared with six for central government: see Delbridge and Smith in *Consuming Secrets: How Official Secrecy Affects Everyday Life in Britain* (Delbridge and Smith ed. 1982).

the procedure obtaining in one industy, again electricity, where area (regional) councils can make a representation to the Electricity Council under the Electricity Act 1947 about an Area Board, whenever area councils believe a "defect is disclosed in that Board's general plans and arrangements."[36] No representation was made by a council until 1978—it simply never occurred to councils to invoke the procedure. It was also felt that sections 7(6) and (7) of the 1947 Act offered little assistance in describing what issues could properly be raised on a representation by the council, and there is no provision for a council to make a representation on a subject which is not a defect in the "Board's general plans and arrangements" but which the council feels is against the consumer interest. The Electricity Council, to whom representations are made, is not an independent body but an integral feature of the electricity industry. If it appears to the Electricity Council (E.C.) that a "defect, etc.," is disclosed they "may give to the Board such advice as they think fit for remedying the defect."[37] The Secretary of State is also empowered, after representations have been made to him by the council, and various other safeguards, to "give such direction to the Board as he thinks necessary for remedying the defect."[38] It is all rather anodyne and vacuous.

No procedure is laid down in the statute for the making of representations, though the council must consult with the Area Board before making the representation to the E.C., which in turn must consult with the other two bodies when a representation is made. By the beginning of 1980, none of the councils had approached the E.C. "for information on any procedural matter either with respect to presentation of their case or the form that consultation should take." In fact, the E.C. had internal guidelines aimed at ensuring "good administrative practice" in such issues, though the Electricity Consumers' Council had not been informed of their existence. The *practice* of the E.C. was to offer "an informal" (non-statutory) hearing to councils *as well as* individual complainants where they existed. The E.C. opened every proceeding by emphasising that they were not "judicial proceedings." Councils had found the decisions of the E.C. to be sparse and disheartening "and rarely were there reasoned decisions."[39] Improvement of these procedures is currently being canvassed and it should be mentioned that the Electricity Consumers' Council has drafted

---

[36] Electricity Act 1947, s.7(6).
[37] *Ibid.*, s.7(7).
[38] *Ibid.*, s.7(8).
[39] Electricity Consumers' Council *Research Report No. 1*, Alice Ayerst (1980).

Codes of Guidance for conciliation and arbitration on repairs and services of electrical appliances sold by Area Board outlets. The industry's Code of Guidance on payment of gas and electricity bills has been criticised by the Electricity Consumers' Council which observed that some Boards still need to refine "their procedures and communications with consumers." The Code was vague on procedures before and after "cut-off" and on consumer redress after possible unfair action by Boards.[40]

(c) Complaints about Public Transport—Answer Privatisation

In 1981, the N.C.C. stated that the three most immediate problems for consumers were: prices, declining standards and unresolved complaints or disputes between consumers and N.I.s. Public transport systems have been the object of much attention by the N.C.C. recently. Various reports have noted widespread public disquiet and the indifferent quality of county council annual transport plans.[40a] Transport Users' organisations, *inter alia*, must be consulted in the making of these plans under the Transport Act 1978 and consultation generally has been described as "disappointing." The plans are often badly produced, frequently changed, cover too large a geographical area, are often considered irrelevant and arouse little curiosity or interest, in spite of complaints about public transport being one of the most frequently aired grievances of consumers. The plan-making exercise reveals the usual faults of the absence of a duty to report comments received and an inability to insist that councils produce adequate plans. Much criticised though these exercises have been, it is interesting to compare them to the Transport Act 1983 which increases Government control over revenue grants paid by metropolitan counties to transport executives.[41] The executives are under a duty

---

[40] Electricity Consumers' Council *Code of Practice on the Payment of Domestic Electricity and Gas Bills* (1984). For the 12 month period ending June 30, 1983, 88,124 households were disconnected from gas and electricity supply—almost 93 per cent. were low income or "vulnerable" households.

[40a] Winfield, *Public Transport Plans And All That* (1981) and *Public Transport Planning, The End of An Era* (1982); National Consumer Council *Public Transport* (1982). The Monopolies and Mergers Commission has carried out investigations and reported on public transport undertakings under the Competition Act, 1980. The Secretary of State has announced that guidelines will be produced for the M.M.C. which place emphasis on the competitive impact of *all* merger proposals, rather than reference to the broad "public interest," *The Guardian* February 1, 1984.

[41] Following the "Fares Fair," etc., litigation: *Bromley L.B.C.* v. *G.L.C.* [1982] 1 All E.R. 129; and also *R.* v. *Merseyside C.C. ex p. Great Universal Stores* (1982) 80 L.G.R. 639.

to prepare annual plans covering a three year period concerning proposals relating to the provision of transport services and fares. Nowhere in the statute is there reference to consultation with groups representing consumer interests when preparing plans.

With transport, information on performance criteria is generally poor, particularly in the bus industry and a draft code of practice published by the D.o.E. in 1981 for bus operators on the provision of information was not circulated in draft to user or consumer representatives.[42] London Transport had a better record than many operators. Transport Users' Consultative Committees only cover trains, and cannot deal with complaints about fares or charges.[43] Transport Commissioners can hear complaints from the public about bus operators, though this role is even more secluded from public knowledge than comparable functions of other NICCs. There were complaints' procedures in the London Transport system for Greater London, as well as for metropolitan county systems, and in fact these authorities featured better than average in N.C.C. reports. The Transport Act 1980 encouraged a greater degree of competition from private operators by easing or restricting regulation by licensing, but for "short stop" services the introduction of private capital has been minimal. For long-haul routes there was far greater private activity, though that has largely been restricted to the more popular routes. Privatisation has not precipitated greater accountability to the extent that was predicted and has done little to obviate the anachronistic and byzantine procedures for redress of grievances or to encourage constructive participation in decision-making. There is little publication of the details as to how public bodies spend subsidies and it is as well to remember that private operators are often in receipt of public subsidies. In July 1984, the Government published plans to privatise the National Bus Company, remove the road transport licensing system, privatise the municipal bus industry, and pay grants to local authorities to be provided to private contractors to subsidise rural and less popular routes.[44] London anticipated this development when the GLC lost their responsibility for London Transport

---

[42] The British Rail Board published a *Commuters Charter* in 1981, setting out its performance targets.

[43] Transport Users' Consultative Committees can only make recommendations on whether the closure of a passenger carrying railway line would cause hardship or not. They lost the right to consider the financial case for closure in 1962. The Government has rejected the case for Transport Users' Consultative Committees for the bus industry.

[44] *Buses*, Cmnd. 9300.

to London Regional Transport,[44a] amid plans to allow greater
competition from private transport operators in the metropolis,
but without any considered reference to consumer participation or
complaints procedures.[45] The London Regional Passengers' Committee has no power to investigate charges for services or facilities,
and only limited powers in relation to railway closures.

The Future

In 1982, the N.C.C. submitted a discussion document to the
Department of Trade on NICCs, suggesting that they should fulfil
two basic functions.

First, to represent the interests of consumers in general in the
formation and monitoring of the policies of the industries; monitoring the effectiveness with which N.I.s meet the needs of consumers in terms of both standards of service and value for money;
and helping to formulate and monitor consumer performance targets for N.I.s against which their performances could be assessed.

Secondly, the provision of an effective complaints mechanism
for individual complaints about standards of service, etc.

(a) Consumer Performance Targets

There should be a rationalisation and clarification of performance criteria—"on numerous aspects of daily operations of N.I.s
there are no explicit standards of performance which individual
customers can expect. Such few standards as there are—frequently
cast in general terms—are scattered through obscure statutes, isolated codes of practice and internal management policies . . . It is
perhaps because of the lack of explicit standards that consumer
dissatisfaction with N.I.s is so disturbingly widespread."[46]

Success or failure in meeting consumer performance targets
which NICCs would help establish would be reported in annual
reports, accompanied by explanations if they had not been met
and NICCs should have a power to report to Ministers if not satisfied with the explanation. If the department agrees that an industry was making insufficient effort to meet its consumer
performance targets, this should be considered against the public
interest and could possibly be remedied by ministerial order directing the industry to prepare a plan which would be laid before

---

[44a] Appointed by the Secretary of State.
[45] London Regional Transport Act 1984, ss.40–41 and Sched. 3.
[46] N.C.C., *Response to Consumers' Interests and the N.I.s* (1982).

Parliament. Reports of NICCs would be available to Select Committees to assist them in ensuring the performance of all remedial action. It should be open to the councils to consider other policy issues: "Proposals for privatisation also have important implications for consumers. It is, therefore, essential that councils should be able to express their views on *any* (emphasis added) policy proposals affecting consumers." It is improbable that government would ever allow NICCs to comment upon macroeconomic policy as it affects N.I.s.

(b) "Effective Grievance Procedures"

On the second point, all NICCs are currently conducting exercises to establish "effective grievance procedures." The most constructive contribution has come from the N.C.C.[47] They have made the powerful point that grievance procedures can only be effective where there are recognised standards—consumer performance targets—laid down in Codes of Practice under statute for each industry. These would set out a clear and detailed set of principal performance standards which the industry would have to maintain in relation to each consumer. It was envisaged that they would be subject to judicial review.[48] The Codes would be the products of participatory exercises between NICCs, N.I.s and "other interested parties" and feedback would establish whether standards are adequate. It is only when standards have been established "that it becomes possible to devise a sensible system for testing the legitimacy of grievances" and ensuring the enforcement of standards. The general proposals were: effective publicity for the codes; establishment of clear and accessible procedures for grievances to be considered within the industries; investigation and conciliation of complaints by NICCs; appropriate procedures for the independent determination of the more resistant disputes; the availability of adequate advice services to advise and assist consumers with the case at each stage as is relevant. The N.C.C. recommended that an Ombudsman or localised system of small panels jointly set up by industries and NICCs could provide the "independent determination"—and I would add the necessity of an independent chairman.

[47] N.C.C. (1982). There has been widespread disagreement between N.I.s and *within* each industry as to the appropriate procedure.
[48] Whether they would or would not create individual rights is not so straightforward: see *Booth and Co. Ltd.* v. *N.E.B.* [1978] 3 All E.R. 624. The N.C.C. speak of Enforcement Procedures being laid down in the Codes, and this could complicate an application for review unless the procedure itself was not being followed.

In advocating procedures for grievances and possible hearings the N.C.C. drew heavily on models negotiated by the Office of Fair Trading with trade associations in the private sector and which were contained in codes of practice on conciliation and arbitration procedures. These include common redress procedures; personal hearings and use of a pre-hearing interview; strict time limits for the conciliation and arbitration stages; giving reasons for decisions; availability of technical inspection facilities; publicity for decisions and an explanatory leaflet on code arbitrations. It should be emphasised that these models have emerged, with public prompting, from the private sector. Further, the privatisation of British Telecommunications will not bring to a demise the arrangements for consumer representation and grievance handling which can ultimately involve an Independent Complaints Panel drawn from members of the Chartered Institute of Arbitrators.[49] After the privatisation of British Telecommunications there will be opportunities provided in the Act for interested parties to put their views and comment upon others before telecommunication licences are awarded by the Secretary of State or Director-General of Telecommunications, together with licence investigatory hearings (by the M.M.C.) and ultimate possibility of resort to the courts. The Telecommunications Act 1984 provides that the Director-General for Telecommunications[49a] is subject to the jurisdiction of the Parliamentary Commissioner for Administration. The Director will assume the relevant functions of the existing consumer councils on privatisation, and consumer advisory bodies will assist him. He will also be responsible for investigation of anti-competitive practices, although apprehension has been expressed about the adequacy of his powers.

(c) *Government Reaction*

The most recent Department of Trade publication on NICCs[50] stated that although the Government was hoping to subject N.I.s more effectively to market forces "most industries will remain monopolies or near monopolies." The Department was basically supportive of the N.C.C. proposals, though it was distinctly cool about NICC contribution to policy decisions and rejected a statutory power for NICCs to demand relevant information from industries as "the cost would be out of proportion to the benefit." It

---

[49] *Code of Practice for Telecommunications* (1983).
[49a] Who will head the Office of Telecommunications.
[50] *N.I.C.C.s—A Strategy for Reform* (1982).

might be asked: whose cost and whose benefit? The Department did not favour the creation of sectoral NICCs,[51] preferring to keep one NICC per industry. It is difficult to avoid the conclusion that NICCs engaged in a lot of special pleading to maintain their present existence and status quo! Surely the game was given away by the Department when they said that following up adverse reports by NICCs should be a matter for industries themselves! Little is going to be conceded, a point realised by the Gas Consumers' Council who, in commenting upon the Department's Draft Guidelines for Consumer Councils, regretted the Government's failure to consult the Council on the Government's role in defining the framework of financial and performance requirements within which the British Gas Corporation operates; they could not discuss the price of gas or the performance of the gas industry! The Council made familiar complaints about a lack of information from the industry and inadequate funding.

(d) The Water Industry

The Water Act 1983 imposes upon water authorities a duty to submit to the Secretary of State a report on the arrangements they propose to make for the representation of the interests of consumers in their areas,[52] having regard to guidelines issued by the Secretary of State.[53] These state that arrangements should provide a forum to discuss, with wide terms of reference, policies and actions. Consumer consultative committees should form the basis of the arrangements—one for each division within each authority. Members of these committees are to be appointed by authorities themselves on the nomination of other bodies, the authority itself selecting the nominating bodies.[54]

A consumer consultative committee would only deal with a complaint that the authority could not settle itself. A council should be "consulted well in advance" of decisions with "significant implications" for their consumers. This is not a matter of hard right but "grace and favour," and the council will be virtually powerless in the absence of good intention within authorities. Under the Act, water authority meetings have been withdrawn from those public meetings which are covered by the Public Bodies (Admission to Meetings) Act 1960, so that the public and press are

---

[51] As favoured by the N.C.C. This would involve separate N.I.C.C.s for the energy, industry, the communications industry and the transport industry.
[52] Water Act 1983, s.7.
[53] *Water Authorities and the Representation of Consumers' Interests* D.o.E. (1983).
[54] And would include such obvious candidates as local authorities.

given no automatic right to be present. Within weeks of enactment, authority meetings were being held *in camera*.

Non-Departmental Bodies and Regulatory Activity

I now intend looking at specific examples of regulation by particular bodies, and I will attempt to explain why or why not, they offer examples of fair, efficient and open administration. The range extends from public corporations operating in a formal manner to the semi-official bodies in Barker's third category. The method of regulation adopted by government over particular bodies or activities will often reflect the degree of trust with which a body or institution is held by government. One political outlook will place faith in the ability of professional bodies, the Stock Exchange or the commercial world to regulate themselves. The same outlook will often distrust forces of labour represented by trade unions, which are seen as posing a threat to national unity and stability without displaying any commensurate sense of responsibility. In this case direct and detailed regulation by legislation and judicial involvement is the order of the day. It serves to remind us that not only is the choice of those areas which require regulation often highly politically motivated, but the *method* adopted by the government is often equally political. A relatively successful mode of regulation will now be examined. It should be noted that the interests it regulates are often powerful and extremely influential.

(a) Civil Aviation Authority (C.A.A.)[55]

It would be hard to imagine aviation to-day, national or international being free of regulatory controls. Fitness of pilots, aeroplanes and operators; passenger safety; international implications of traffic rights' negotiations to name a few points dictate the necessity. In the United Kingdom the problem has been what kind of regulation, how much, and by whom? Baldwin has presented a convincing argument that the body charged with this task until 1971—the Air Transport Licensing Board—operated in too judicial and inflexible a manner in its licensing and other functions. Its decisions were frequently overruled by the Board of Trade thereby creating a good deal of uncertainty for flight operators. The Civil Aviation Authority[56] has a wide variety of statutory

---

[55] Baldwin, (1978) P.L. 57; (1980) *Public Administration* 287. The C.A.A. is financed by the aviation industry.
[56] Established by the Civil Aviation Act 1971. Now the Civil Aviation Act 1982.

duties and powers to regulate the aviation industry, realising certain objectives including: securing that British airlines (so far as they reasonably can) provide air transport services satisfying "all substantial categories of public demand," etc.,[57] and "the reasonable interests of air transport users." It is an "independent" agency of the Department of Trade and Industry responsible for economic and safety regulation.

It was envisaged that the C.A.A. would regulate, make decisions in a judicial manner in trial-like proceedings and issue policy statements and guidance notes to operators and prospective operators under the ultimate Policy Guidance of the Minister, who can also issue directions on specific grounds. This relationship envisaged independence for the C.A.A. and exercise of its own expertise in technical matters, while the Government retained the residuary power to shape policy after its own political objectives. It has been plausibly argued that this relationship was misunderstood by the Court of Appeal which saw the C.A.A. as a totally independent judicial body, not a body exercising a subtle blend of administrative, judicial and executive functions under a residuary government direction.[57a] Since 1971, the C.A.A. has consistently moved away from judicial hearings to engage in "consultative proceedings in combination with public hearings" thereby producing guides for future licensing decisions. Formal hearings have been used in conjunction with other formal and informal proceedings and by utilising its research knowledge, it has frequently been able to set down its policy for future decisions in some detail, achieving a fair balance between the creation of policy and the exercise of its discretion. The C.A.A. was distinctive because of its combination of functions and skills in a highly technical area—judicial, regulatory, executive and advisory. What was also distinctive was the wide variety of approaches it adopted to suit different decisional *milieux*.

The Civil Aviation Act 1980 abolished the powers of the Secretary of State to issue Policy Guidance to the C.A.A. There is still a right of appeal to the Secretary of State from C.A.A. decisions; in 1980–81 to 1982–83 there were 28 appeals, in most of which the C.A.A.'s decision was upheld, though the last year saw three

---

[57] "[A]t the lowest charges consistent with a high standard of safety in operating the services and economic return to efficient operators . . . and with securing the sound development of the civil air transport industry of the U.K." s.4(1) of the Civil Aviation Act 1982.

[57a] *Laker Airways* v. *Department of Trade* [1977] Q.B. 643, C.A.; and Baldwin *op.cit.* n. 55, *supra*.

decisions of the C.A.A. reversed. There were 88 public hearings related to air transport licensing in the same period. Procedures for the hearings and appeals are contained in the C.A.A. Regulations 1983.[58] The C.A.A. also publishes an Official Record which describes classes of licences and the procedure for applying for a licence, making objections and representations, procedure at public hearings, etc. Before granting, refusing, revoking, suspending or varying an air transport licence, bodies representing the views of users may be heard as well as environmental groups (if the latter have made objections or representations). The C.A.A. can hear other parties, who have entered an objection, at their discretion. No person shall be heard where the Secretary of State has directed the C.A.A. to grant or refuse *etc.* a licence. Legal representation is allowed; evidence may be presented orally or in writing. At hearings, mutual examination of cases of the interested parties is allowed. Appeals to the Secretary of State cannot be made by the user or environmental bodies, or by parties appearing at the hearing at the C.A.A.'s discretion, though all these parties will be served with transcripts of the appeal. Appeals are in writing "though if heard orally, the other parties at the first hearing would presumably have the right to make oral representation" the C.A.A. believed.

The 1980 Act preserved the power of the Secretary of State to issue directions upon specific grounds to the C.A.A. but it also imposed a duty upon the C.A.A. to publish the policies which it intends to adopt in relation to its duties. Prior to the Act, the C.A.A. had published copious booklets outlining its policy intentions, and it engaged in detailed programmes of consultation and research with operators and users to produce such statements. These documents did not constitute "law," yet they helped applicants marshall their cases at the licence application hearings.

There can be little doubt that the record of the C.A.A. is impressive and it has achieved much to provide predictability and consistency of standard in a flexible and dynamic field of administration. There were however, two perceived problems associated with the removal of the Secretary of State's power to issue Policy Guidance to the C.A.A. How was the C.A.A. to be made politically accountable for the exercise of public power? Secondly, if accountability was to be achieved by a right of appeal to the Secretary of State, would the lessons of the Air Transport Licensing Board experience be forgotten? Would there be a temptation for the Secretary of State to overrule the C.A.A. more frequently,

---

[58] S.I. 1983 No. 550.

causing incoherence and inconsistency where such decisions went against policy statements and research by the C.A.A.? There were three reversals of C.A.A. decisions in 1982–83. The danger is that the government will be tempted to achieve its ends by informal pressures and private persuasion without appropriate public and Parliamentary scrutiny.[59] A powerful committee, for instance, which included the Prime Minister, was established to decide on the outcome of a review by the C.A.A. on the privatisation of British Airways and its impact upon the United Kingdom airline industry.[60]

(b) The Commission for Racial Equality (C.R.E.)

The C.A.A. has generally been acknowledged as an efficient and effective regulatory body. Less successful has been the C.R.E., though of course it has attempted to regulate human relationships in an area which many still believe is best left to personal choice rather than public opinion or public regulation. The C.R.E. attempts to advance the interests of those groups who have not attained standing or influence in public life, and it frequently runs counter to deeply ingrained prejudices, not least in Government and governmental bodies.

The C.R.E. is a "multi-faceted" statutory agency of government, combining grievance remedial, advisory, investigatory, promotional and regulatory functions in pursuit of its statutory objectives to eliminate racial discrimination and to promote equality of opportunity and good race relations. The Race Relations Act 1976 was the third legislative attempt since 1965 to tackle the problems of racial discrimination and division. Official publications and the C.R.E.'s own researches show that not only is racial discrimination still widespread, if in a more covert form, but that public and government bodies at *all* levels had failed to respond adequately to discrimination and disadvantage of a racial nature.[61] "A major constraint has been a lack of support from

---

[59] Especially when, for instance, the C.A.A. was instructed by the Transport Secretary to review completely its airline routes policy after lobbying by private airline operators concerned about the "unfair competition" from British Airways on the latter's privatisation; H.C. Deb., Vol. 50, cols. 686–694, December 12, 1983.

[60] *Airline Competition Policy*, C.A.A. (1984). This recommended divesting British Airways of various routes and the report was felt in many quarters to be below the standard of previous C.A.A. reports.

[61] For central and local government see the Memorandum of the Commission to the Home Affairs Committee (Race Relations and Immigration sub-committee) (1981–82, H.C. 46). Recent reports of the C.R.E. cover the NHS and the Metropolitan Police; and Racial Disadvantage (1980–81; H.C. 424). Also: *Immigration Control Procedures: Report of a Formal Investigation*, C.R.E. (1985).

government" failing to demonstrate "a firm commitment to equal opportunity" and the Home Office itself has been investigated for alleged discriminatory practice in its immigration control. Its administration and the system of immigration control were criticised.[62]

The C.R.E. has power to conduct formal investigations for "any purpose connected with its statutory duties." These have been described as "general" investigations where there is no allegation of discrimination and "belief" investigations where an individual or organisation is suspected of discriminatory practices and is named.[63] It possesses powers to issue non-discrimination notices; to give assistance to individuals seeking redress against unlawful discrimination; to provide grants to bodies promoting equality of opportunity and to conduct research to influence policy. It alone has power to investigate formally allegations of systematic indirect discrimination and instigate certain proceedings. It also issues Codes of Guidance and has various *sub poena* powers.

All applications for assistance by individuals are considered by the complaints' committee; if the C.R.E. does not bring the case to the industrial tribunal or county court but leaves it to the individual, the record of success is very poor. It frequently attempts to settle complaints informally—especially in advertising cases.

The powers of the C.R.E. to conduct formal investigations have been the object of much judicial scrutiny recently. The C.R.E.'s procedures are prolix—"So complicated that I will not attempt to explain it" said Lord Denning. Their proceedings are administrative, and though they must be conducted fairly, C.R.E. witnesses cannot be compelled by respondents to undergo cross-examination.[64] The Court of Appeal has held that the whole of the investigatory proceedings can be re-opened upon appeal to an industrial tribunal, involving a full re-hearing of the facts—even though proceedings had taken four years and the respondent had two opportunities to submit his representations through counsel to the Commission.[65] The House of Lords has held that allegations of direct racial discrimination had to specify the acts in the notice where a person was named, and have insisted upon strict compliance with the preliminary hearing under section 49(4) before

---

[62] *Home Office* v. *C.R.E.* [1981] 1 All E.R. 865; though *cf. Amin* v. *Entry Clearance Officer* [1983] 2 All E.R. 865, H.L. N. 61, *supra* for the report.

[63] See Griffiths L.J., *R.* v. *Commission for Racial Equality, ex p. Hillingdon L.B.C.* [1981] 1 Q.B. 276.

[64] *R.* v. *Commission for Racial Equality, ex p. Cottrell and Rothon* [1980] 3 All E.R. 265.

[65] *C.R.E.* v. *Amari Plastics* [1982] 2 All E.R. 499. This means an examination and re-examination on *all* the issues of fact on appeal before an industrial tribunal or county court.

the investigation. Section 49(4) in fact, appears to have been the result of a Parliamentary misunderstanding.[66] The judges have inhibited quite drastically an already prolix procedure.

These decisions have made much of the "draconian" "inquisitorial" and "criminal" nature of the allegations, and that accordingly it is only right that the respondent must have the protection of adversarial proceedings.[67] There can be no other expression for it: "judicial hostility" to the C.R.E. has been widespread and not infrequently outspoken. Some of this hostility, no doubt, relates to the existence of the C.R.E. itself and its aims; other judges doubtless distrust the novel framework of an agency created to tackle collective and systemic manifestations of prejudice—by word of mouth employment opportunities or cultural attitudes for instance.

If there is a judicial hint that the C.R.E. procedures should be more legalistic and technically precise, then this would seem to have the support of the Home Affairs Select Committee in its report on the C.R.E.[68] It recommended that the C.R.E. employ more lawyers for complaints' handling and investigations and it placed an unjustifiably high premium on lawyers and legal processes, although the report was published without reference to the cases discussed above. The C.R.E. it argued should concentrate on promoting its victories and investigations, rather than general promotional work which should be the responsibility of the Home Office and local government.[69] The Committee was in fact highly critical of the C.R.E.'s commitment to law enforcement *and* promotional work. Judged by "victories," the C.R.E. has not been a notable success.[70] The ambitions of the C.R.E. have also been over expansive and sometimes incoherent. In their defence can be placed the fact that their weaponry has been ill conceived and pro-

---

[66] *C.R.E.* v. *Hillingdon L.B.C.* [1982] A.C. 779; *R.* v. *C.R.E., ex p. Prestige Group plc* [1984] 1 W.L.R. 335.

[67] Non discrimination notices can ultimately be enforced by an injunction. The former *per* Griffiths L.J., "condemn."

[68] H.C. 46 (1981–82).

[69] The C.R.E. was not meant to be a shadow Race Relations Department, believed the Home Affairs Committee. The Home Office itself has been the subject of a C.R.E. formal investigation, and for local government's record on race relations, see Young and Connelly, *Policy and Practice in the Multi-Racial City* (1981).

[70] At the time of the committees's report, the C.R.E. had only completed 10 of its 45 formal investigations. For a famous "victory" however, see *Mandla* v. *Dowell Lee* [1983] 1 All E.R. 1062 (H.L.) and a wide interpretation of "ethnic." For an appraisal of the C.R.E. and the Equal Opportunities Commission, see Appleby and Ellis, (1984) P.L. 236.

lix, that there has been widespread antipathy to its existence and techniques and that there has been little attempt by Government or Parliament to provide leadership on what is meant by "good race relations." Support from the Government has not generally been forthcoming—it refused to extend legal aid to industrial tribunals on discrimination cases in its reply to the Select Committee.[71] Community Relations Councils often have indifferent relationships with the C.R.E.[72]

The C.R.E. are clear as to how they would like to see their role being made more effective. In a 1983 consultative document, they have recommended 10 changes which would *inter alia* shift the onus of proof onto the respondent once less favourable treatment has been established; render "indirect discrimination" less technical; impose stronger obligations on *all* public authorities to combat racial prejudice; improve and shorten their investigatory procedures; and the creation of a Discrimination Tribunal. Reaction from public bodies has been hostile and it remains unlikely that these recommendations will see the statute book. Opponents of the C.R.E. argue that the Commission, in its present role and through its suggested reforms, is attempting to transmute into legal duties what are more appropriately left to moral aspiration.[73]

(c) *The Housing Corporation (H.C.)*

The C.A.A. and the C.R.E. both possess a degree of formality and openness in the manner in which they perform their duties. Formality and openness do not characterise the working of the next corporation, not because of any obvious specific intention that these should be absent, but rather because of the unstructured development of the body. The consequence has been a degree of informality which has invariably operated against the general interests of those whom the body regulates.

The Housing Corporation was created by the Housing Act 1961 and gradually emerged in preference to other bodies as the overseer and registrar of housing associations, bodies which provide housing to sections of the public. These latter bodies date from the nineteenth century and by 1981 there were about 3,000 registered with the H.C. Finance for associations comes from central government and loans from the H.C. The Corporation has statutory rulemaking powers which are exercised after consultation with the

---

[71] Cmnd. 8547.
[72] These are often the contact and referral point for complaints and complainants.
[73] Fuller, *The Morality of Law* (1972).

Housing Association Registration Advisory Committee. In fact published criteria were largely ignored in favour of individual bargaining between the H.C. and associations. Details of the relationship between the D.o.E. and the H.C. were not spelled out in statute. Nor was the relationship between these two and the National Federation of Housing Associations (N.F.H.A.), a representative body of associations which in fact diminished in importance when the H.C. became the supervisory body of associations at the D.o.E.'s instigation. All three bodies have a regional presence. The relationship between the D.o.E. and the H.C. has little by way of a public or open dimension.

The history of the H.C. since the early seventies has revealed obvious shortcomings in its oversight of associations. There has been an emphasis upon informality of relationship between the D.o.E., H.C. and N.F.H.A. at central and regional levels. For tenants of shoddy housing, this had often resulted in the absence of a forum through which to complain, especially about some repairs which are the responsibility of the D.o.E. Bad feeling has existed about the allocation of housing units to associations on a generally presumed "grace and favour" basis by regional offices of the H.C. The N.F.H.A. has achieved some informal improvements at regional level and is pressing for procedural and substantive reform covering unit allocations and the H.C.'s disciplinary functions, open criteria for H.C. decision-making and reasoned justification for allocations. There has also been pressure for an internal appeals mechanism for aggrieved associations. The D.o.E. has done little to encourage their development in the past.

On the associations' accountability to their tenants, the H.C. have issued a circular enjoining openness and broadening of membership of associations, but it is doubtful whether the Circular or sections 43 and 44 of the Housing Act 1980,[74] where the statute applies to associations, really provide enough to obtain genuine progress towards participation and grievance redress.

(d) Regulation of Commercial Broadcasting and Cable Television

Even when a formal statutory body is established to regulate a particular activity by licensing or disposing of franchises, there is often a relegation of wider interests apart from the contracting parties to the sidelines. It might be instructive to look at the Independent Broadcasting Authority, a statutory body charged with the task of issuing broadcasting and sound franchises to pro-

---

[74] See Chap. 3.

gramme contractors, as well as regulating and supervising the provision of television and sound broadcasting in the independent sector while ensuring standards of good taste and decency. Its powers are loosely drafted and broad-ranging, evoking the criticism that it does not operate "within a framework of legal control consonant with its powers of patronage and consonant with . . . the control customarily exercised by Western governments when dispensing valuable community prizes."[75] When reviewing broadcasting franchises, the I.B.A. is under a duty "to take such steps as appear to them to be appropriate (including if they think fit the holding of public meetings)

  (i) to ascertain the opinion of the public . . . about the service to be provided there

 (ii) to encourage the making of comments and suggestions about that service by members of the public . . . and shall take into account those opinions and comments and suggestions.[76]

This did little more than statutorily approve the I.B.A.'s existing practice and there was a rejection at the committee stage of the Bill of a proposal to make the holding of public meetings compulsory and to provide a procedural code augmenting opportunities to participate. The statute is silent on the procedure to be followed by the I.B.A. and applicants, nor is there a duty to give reasons for decisions.[76a] While the licence allocation stage is devoid of procedural protection, it is interesting to note that there is a statutory Broadcasting Complaints Commission which has jurisdiction over complaints of unfair and unjust treatment and unwarranted infringements of privacy by the BBC as well as the independent sector. Going by the Commission's 1982 Report the body is singularly unimportant if one judges by the number of complaints received and investigated. Until March 1983, it received 234 complaints, 188 of which were outside its jurisdiction. 9 were subject to full adjudication and three of those were upheld.[77] In its annual report for 1982, on the other hand, the I.B.A. stated that it received 2,471 complaints, many concerned with Channel 4.

Looking at the I.B.A. itself, complaints about that body centre around two aspects. Television companies regard it as supererogatory and expensive. Why can they not deal directly with the Home Office rather than through a regulatory body which they have to

[75] Lewis N. (1975) P.L. 317.
[76] Broadcasting Act 1981, s.19.
[76a] All these points are made by Elliott M. (1981) M.L.R. 683.
[77] See also, *R.* v. *B.C.C. ex p. BBC, The Times*, May 17, 1984.

finance? Secondly, why regulate at all? There is wide agreement that conferment of airwaves or similar broadcasting opportunities are activities requiring *ex ante* controls rather than simply relying upon the law of defamation, the criminal law[77a] and informal or formal relationships between government and broadcasters whereby the latter comply with government wishes on censorship. But if the I.B.A. is part of a legitimating process, so that it has to go through consultative and participatory exercises to accord with democratic and responsible forms of decision-making, why are its exercises so anaemic in this regard? Critics suggest that it has not widened the nature of the debate about the policy of broadcasting, but performs acts of tokenism. Responsibility for this state of affairs must lie with the Government.[78]

Cable television was introduced in something of a frantic manner. The Home Secretary announced that he would establish the "financial and regulatory framework with which customer satisfaction and economic progress can be achieved while the public interest is safeguarded (and) those prepared to invest should be encouraged rather than prohibited." Minimum standards of decency would be established and safeguards to prevent abuse ensured.[79] The actual inquiry into Cable television and the consultative process were conducted at break-neck speed and constituted an extremely thin participatory exercise;

> "There were no public hearings at which competing views could be tested, no chance of a second round of comments in response . . . no opportunity to argue that the separation of broadcasting policy from economic and technological issues was misconceived."[80]

A franchise authority was envisaged by the 1983 White Paper which would operate a formal competitive licensing system for cable operators on criteria largely under the control of the authority though the procedural matters are not dealt with in detail in the 1982 or 1983 White Papers, nor in the eventual Act. Local authorities are considered worthy of consultation in each case, and the authority will be required to make such other arrangements as appears to it to be expedient to enable the public generally to make their views known. And this duty only applies to franchises, not to wider issues of policy adopted by the authority. It was decided to introduce 12 pilot cable schemes in November 1983

[77a] See *e.g.* Cable and Broadcasting Act 1984, ss.25–27.
[78] See in particular the Annan Report, Cmnd. 6753.
[79] H.C. Deb., Vol. 43, (June 1, 1983). See n. 77a, *supra*.
[80] Lewis and Harden, "Privatisation, De-Regulation, etc." (1983) 34 N.I.L.Q. 207.

(only 11 applicants were considered suitable) and *before* any of the above minimal safeguards were introduced.

(e) The "Unofficial" End of Officialdom—The University Grants Committee

To recapitulate an earlier point, the nebulous constitutional position of many non-departmental bodies, even within Barker's second category, and the denial by Government that such bodies are really governmental, allow the Government to avoid an appropriate level of responsibility for the bodies, be it constitutional, legal or political. The vagueness helps to conceal the range of "public" activity; it helps to conceal what the State is actually doing and through which instruments it operates, and *a fortiori* what it ought to be doing. The University Grants Committee (U.G.C.), for instance, is a body established by Treasury Minute[81] to inquire into the financial needs of universities, to advise the Secretary of State on the allocation of public grants, to assist in the preparation and execution of plans for the development of universities and to collect, examine and make available information about university education. It is often claimed that the U.G.C. acts as a "buffer" standing between the Government and universities to maintain independence and academic freedom. Since 1981, universities have faced severe cuts in expenditure. Ministers have responded in Parliament to questions about cuts by saying that this is a matter for the U.G.C. alone. All the members of the U.G.C. are appointed by the Secretary of State. When the U.G.C. has been questioned about certain of its recommendations by the Select Committee on Education or the Public Accounts Committee, it has replied that its advice to the Secretary of State is confidential and must remain so. Universities which complained because they suffered financial penalties for not complying with what they felt to be unspecified criteria in general policies laid down by the U.G.C., had to engage in negotiations and a process akin to roulette to disengage themselves from the penalties. The end result was one of uncertainty, ambivalence and outright discretion. The criteria changed as Government attitudes to expenditure on universities unfolded, requiring further cuts in expenditure. The Universities, and indeed the U.G.C. were placed in a very uncertain position, the latter taking much of the criticism that may have been more appropriately directed towards the D.E.S.

---

[81] Are the actions of bodies thus created judicially reviewable under Order 53?

(f) *"Semi-Official" Relationships*

The degree of informality between Government and those non-departmental bodies, which Barker placed in category 3, hinders even more completely the public knowledge of, and accountability for, such quasi-governmental decision-making processes. Hood has shown for instance how the relationship between government and football pools' operators developed to protect a few of them "by carefully maintained loopholes in the gambling laws" (while also becoming the Post Office's largest customer). Pools' operators acquired a position akin to tax farmers, and further protection was afforded by tax legislation which made it impracticable for competitors to enter the market.[82] He argues further that the desire to avoid a "Ministry of Culture" resulted in a series of semi-official arrangements for censorship and "oblique methods of finance," *e.g.* the Press Council, British Board of Film Censors, the Arts Council, local authorities, tourist promotion bodies, universities, etc. Government contracts in the field of armaments, drugs, telephones, computers, and micro technology have helped to create giant "private building and engineering firms" within what is largely a public sector context.[83] Caution should be invoked before arguing that because a body contracts with the State, it should be considered quasi-governmental; when, however, the contract is a way of achieving government policy on unrelated themes such as: extension of collective bargaining, health and safety at work or de-unionisation; price controls, wage controls or de-regulation, a quasi-governmental framework is difficult to eschew.

(g) *Self-Regulation*

A greater trend towards self-regulation by trusted private bodies is unlikely to decrease the opportunities for such informal relationships between Government and "private" concerns. Self-regulation means quite simply that the body is left to regulate itself, either in the absence of any statutory controls or under a loose statutory framework operated by civil servants or an intermediary commission. There is no detailed regulation or control under statutory power by a Government department or mediating agency. If any variant of governmentally approved or authorised

---

[82] Hood "The Rise and Rise of the British Quango," *New Society*, August 16, 1973.

[83] And notice the recent outcry over the effective monopoly of the British Oxygen Company to supply gas to health authorities in a contract with the DHSS.

self-regulation for such bodies becomes the norm,[84] the exclusion of representation of interests apart from the Government and the private body has undesirable and undemocratic consequences, especially where such interests stand to be vitally affected. Yet there is rarely any formal or informal opportunity for such interests to be heard in the private bartering processes, let alone the existence of grievance procedures—apart from expensive legal, or remote political arenas. This is true for bodies in Barker's second group, as well as the third group. The attraction for government to achieve its desired ends by "hidden persuasion" and the implications for democratic standards are obvious and insidious. Some of the bodies referred to in sections (e) and (f) above are self-regulatory, *e.g.* the Press Council,[85] the Stock Exchange, the U.G.C. to some extent, the professional bodies such as the Law Society, Bar Council, General Medical Council or Lloyds, and the T.U.C. Many of these bodies have featured in recent "upsets" where it has been widely felt that there are inappropriate controls over and inadequate information about, their privileged exercise of power and influence as well as an absence of impartial grievance procedures through which to pursue effectively a justified grievance.

Conclusion

Few non-departmental bodies have published grievance procedures for those aggrieved by their decisions. Throughout the whole spectrum of such bodies, the informal processing of complaints by the relevant bodies was repeatedly discovered to be a common event. There is little recorded about such processes—witness the internal procedures of N.I.s for instance. There is a frequent absence of provision allowing public participation in decisions—the C.A.A. is in this company a striking exception. Where it is permitted in a structured manner, participation is invariably too late in the process to allow any opportunity to influence the nature of a decision.

If the Government chooses to disbandon or lessen the impact of bodies in Barker's group 2, then there is every justification for believing that it will resort more widely to the "semi-official" bodies in group 3, the status of many of which is indeterminate. Regulation will be achieved by co-operation built around mutual self-respect and informality, making it more difficult for public law

---

[84] See Gower, *Review of Investor Protection* (1982) and Cmnd. 9125 (1984) on the regulation of the investment business. See now Cmnd. 9432 (1985).
[85] Robertson, *People Against the Press*, (1983).

techniques to foster the ideals which law is supposed to convey—openness, accountability, responsiveness, efficiency, participation by the governed in the process of government. Our public law has done little to advance the ideals through the wide-range of networks which this chapter examined. At least in the United States the process of regulation, and de-regulation,[86] is more open and allows greater procedural opportunity for participation of interested parties in rule-making, de-regulation and other decisions having a substantial impact upon the public interest. And of course in the United States there is legislative provision for freedom of information and "government in the sunshine."

Privatisation has proceeded by conferring on Ministers the widest possible powers of sale. Sale of public assets has in many cases resulted in a monumental financial loss to the tax-payer, or has been detrimental to the interests of industries still remaining within the public sphere. The methods of sale have attracted criticism from a non-partisan Public Accounts Committee. The Government has accepted that the privatisation programme is no longer about a long-term rational plan, but is simply "ideology": the private sector is *always* better, *always* more efficent. There has, of course, to be Parliamentary sanction and approval of privatisation proposals enshrined in legislation. The details of these developments are left largely to non-departmental bodies and informal networks. After Parliamentary discussion of the shell, there is an absence of a clear regulatory framework, operating through democratic and open processes assisted by a public law which was sensitive to interest representation, open and fair procedures, fully reasoned arguments. This is hardly surprising as it continues the tradition of secrecy, informality and non involvement of the public which characterised, and still characterises, the working of the British State and in particular its quasi-governmental setting.

---

[86] See Chap. 2, *supra.*

Chapter 5

OMBUDSMEN AND OTHERS

This chapter discusses those bodies, invariably statutory, whose major task is to obtain satisfaction from public authorities for individuals who are aggrieved by decisions, non-decisions, actions or non-actions which amount to maladministration or culpable behaviour. The generic title of most of these grievance-remedial agencies is "Ombudsman" and they exist in relation to central government departments and some other specified agencies linked to central government[1]; local government and water authorities and the hospital service of the NHS; Northern Ireland has its own Ombudsman. In this chapter there will also be examination of the procedures for registering complaints against the police *via* the recently formed Police Complaints Authority (formerly Police Complaints Board).

The bodies examined in this chapter have all been provided by Parliament to attempt to make good the failures of our political and legal institutions in their respective efforts to rectify the shortcomings of, or assist individuals with grievances against State activities. The form of the institution which I will discuss, the "Ombudsman," is being extended into the private sphere, and the chapter will conclude with discussion of an agency whose statutory responsibilities reflect a phenomenon of both public and private bureaucracy, namely, information held about individuals in the form of vast computerised data banks.

The emergence of Ombudsmen in central and local government, the NHS and the appointment of the Police Complaints Board in 1976 illustrated a growing awareness within Government of public disquiet over the ability of those institutions to handle and respond to complaints about their activities in a fair and responsible manner. The Ombudsmen for central and local government and the Health Service are the most developed independent grievance-

---

[1] See the Parliamentary Commissioner Act 1967, Sched. 2 (as extended) for details. The range of bodies listed includes many which are not government departments as described in Chap. 2. Complaints must be brought within 12 months.

remedial devices we possess in the administrative as opposed to the legal or political realms. The Police Complaints Authority differs, as only the most serious complaints will receive its direct attention. These factors make them important subjects for our study. But Governmental concessions in providing these bodies were given at a price as all the bodies are considerably limited in what they can investigate. There were to be no investigations of complaints about policy and its impact. Only complaints of an individual and otherwise restricted nature were to be examined, though we shall see how Parliament has provided for the special position of the police.

The Philosophical Underpinnings of the British Ombudsman

It is of interest to note that the introduction of the Parliamentary Commissioner for Administration (P.C.A.) or the Commissioner for Local Administration (C.L.A.), established to remedy injustice caused by administrative defects in what are generally relatively mundane causes, should have provoked such opposition. This is all the more curious when one considers that Ombudsmen in the United Kingdom are primarily directed towards righting the individual wrong—only secondarily are they concerned with improving *general* administrative regimes or systems, though it is not difficult to cite general improvements in the quality of administrative practices and decision-making as a result of P.C.A. and C.L.A. reports. Further, any criticism of the "merits" or departmental policy of a decision—as opposed to governmental or party political policy dimensions which are outside the jurisdiction of the P.C.A. in their entirety—is expressly excluded by the legislation establishing the P.C.A. and C.L.A.[2] unless the decision contains maladministration. And then of course it is the maladministration which is to be the object of inquiry, not the merits. In matters concerning the NHS, the clinical judgment of doctors and consultants was excluded from the investigatory powers of the Health Commissioner. Lastly, just in case the concessions made by political

---

[2] Parliamentary Commissioner Act, s.12(3); Local Government Act 1974, s.34(3).On "departmental policy," *i.e.* what departments are responsible for on a day to day basis, as opposed to "policy questions of political significance" for which ministers were responsible individually and collectively, see the *Fourth Report from the Select Committee on Procedure* (1964–65; H.C. 303). While the essence of the distinction may be clear *in abstracto*, are ministers not responsible for *all* policy factors? Both the P.C.A. and Commissioners are appointed by the Crown, *i.e.* the Government and hold office "during good behaviour" subject to various provisions.

and administrative powers proved to be too much of a *faux pas*, their decisions, with the sole exception of the Northern Ireland Commissioner for Complaints, cannot be enforced by law against the bodies falling under their jurisdiction. Acceptance of an adverse decision has to be "negotiated" where there is reluctance to accept it.

The office of the P.C.A. owed its origin to Ombudsmen who had operated in Scandinavia for well over a century and a half, and in New Zealand.[3] The original British model—the P.C.A.—differed from its Scandinavian forbears and Gregory associates this difference with the influence of the Whyatt Report which saw the Ombudsman being an adjunct to Parliament as opposed to an agency independent of the political and administrative regimes.[4] Unlike Scandinavian models, the Whyatt Report recommended that a distinction should be drawn between complaints about the merits of discretionary decisions and those about bad administration such as delay, rudeness or inefficiency, and as we saw, this distinction was maintained in the legislation. Finally Whyatt introduced what has been referred to as the "filter," *i.e.* complaints would first have to be made to a Member of Parliament (or councillor in local government) and then handed on to the Ombudsman. For the P.C.A., and C.L.A. there was to be no direct access and this was a novel feature of the Ombudsman idea. "Whether the Labour Government were right or wrong to cast their P.C. scheme in the form they did, there can be no doubt that . . . planted in their proposals were the seeds of a great deal of misunderstanding and discontent."[5] The P.C.A.'s job was to strengthen the position of Parliament in the resolution of grievances against departments. In spite of this official line, the previous P.C.A. has doubted the wisdom of the filter[6] and has recommended that he should be invited by a complainant to review the M.P.'s handling of a complaint without the complainant formally requesting the M.P. to pass it on to him.

Policy was to be the concern of Parliament. In the words of Richard Crossman, maladministration was to cover "bias, neglect, inattention, delay, incompetence, ineptitude, perversity, turpitude, arbitrariness and so on." It would have been "a long interesting list." Effort was to be made to avoid legalistic overtones in

[3] Whyatt Report (1961); Gregory and Hutchesson, *The Parliamentary Ombudsman* (1975); for a general comparative study see Anderson, "The Ombudsman Research etc." University of Cal., Santa Barbara (1982).
[4] Gregory and Hutchesson, *op. cit.*
[5] Gregory and Hutchesson, *op. cit.* (1975), p. 86.
[6] H.C. 322 (1983–84).

the phrase "injustice as a consequence of maladministration"; the meanings of both terms would be "filled out by the practical processes of case work."[7] His concern was not to be with the technical correctness of a decision but whether a public power had been used properly, misused, or abused, *i.e.* with the administrative quality of a decision. If there was an appropriate remedy in a court of law or a tribunal, and it was reasonable to pursue it, then the P.C.A. would decline jurisdiction.[8] Complaints had to be made to the M.P. within 12 months of notice of the matter constituting the complaint—though this period can be waived.

(1) THE PARLIAMENTARY COMMISSIONER FOR ADMINISTRATION

Lawyers writing about the P.C.A. have described how he has been a useful adjunct to a system of administrative law[9]; how he has developed a body of case precedents which he can use informally to guide his discretion in future cases in a judicial like manner[10]; or that he should not be a court substitute or poor man's lawyer and that lawyers did him a disservice if they cast him in their own image.[11] Certainly the previous incumbent of the office was the first to be a lawyer and he has stated that his legal background had not made a conscious contribution to his approach.[12]

(a) *Some Facts and Figures*

P.C.A. annual reports have revealed how there is considerable confusion in the public eye as to the position and powers of the P.C.A. As well as receiving many complaints directly from the public, he also receives a significant number which are under the jurisdiction of the C.L.A., or concern the police, N.I.s or other public authority. The P.C.A. himself has voiced disquiet as to what happens to complainants whose complaints are returned to them, though since 1978 he has operated a system whereby if the complainant is willing, he will refer the complaint, if notionally within his jurisdiction, to the relevant M.P. asking him or her to re-refer it. Certainly the office appears to be poorly publicised and in a population of over 55 million, it does seem strange that in 1983

[7] H.C.Deb., Vol. 734, cols. 51–2 (1966–67).
[8] Parliamentary Commissioner Act 1967, s.5(2).
[9] Wade, *Administrative Law* (1982) p. 85.
[10] Bradley (1980) *C.L.J.* 304.
[11] Harlow (1978) *M.L.R.* 446.
[12] *Annual Report*, 1979.

he had only 751 complaints referred to him[13] (compared with 838 in 1982, 917 in 1981 and 1031 in 1980). Of the complaints referred in 1982, he accepted 27 per cent. for investigation. In 1981, 24 per cent. were investigated, and of 202 cases where an investigation was completed, he concluded that:

33·2 per cent. were wholly justified (67);
31·7 per cent. were partly justified (64);
35·1 per cent. were not justified (71).

"The 'market shares' of the departments complained against have not changed very much in recent years" although the Department of Employment had seen an increase in complaints against it, while the Department of Education and Science had, surprisingly, seen a decline. Top of the list was the DHSS, complaints against which constituted 29 per cent. of total referrals for 1982, followed by the Inland Revenue at 18 per cent., D.o.E. with 7·5 per cent., Department of Employerment with 6 per cent. and the Home Office with a surprisingly small number of 3·5 per cent. The Ministry of Defence and Department of Transport shared 2·5 per cent. All that these figures reveal is that those departments whose administration brings them into direct contact with the public are more likely to be the subject of a complaint than those which do not have contact such as the Treasury. Decisions of the latter while ultimately having a far greater impact on the community or classes of the community, do not have a direct and immediate impact on individuals in a personal form thereby rendering them unlikely to be the subject of a complaint of maladministration.

(b) Investigations and Jurisdiction

Set out below is the P.C.A.'s own account of his method of investigation. He has often described his informal connections and representations to departments operating outside the formal procedure.

"I decide whether the complaint is *prima facie* within my jurisdiction to investigate; if it is, I must next afford the department against whom the complaint is made the opportunity to comment; any officials named in the complaint, or identifiable

---

[13] It was envisaged that the P.C.A. would receive about 6,000–7,000 complaints per annum. In 1974, the P.C.A. investigated 252 cases. In Sweden, the Ombudsman investigated 2,638 complaints from a population of 8 million for the same year. A survey by an M.P. revealed that only 7 per cent. of M.P.s sampled knew that they could approach the P.C.A. on prison matters; see Birkinshaw, "The Closed Society: Complaints Procedures and Disciplinary Hearings in Prisons" (1981) N.I.L.Q. 117.

from details given, must similarly be afforded that opportunity. Only very rarely am I able to come to a conclusion on this evidence alone. In the majority of cases all the department's relevant papers have to be obtained and carefully examined by my investigators; officials in local, regional and headquarters offices may have to be questioned for further evidence or explanations; and complainants and other witnesses may have to be interviewed. And the time consuming process does not of course end with the interviews. They may throw up fresh points to be argued or remedies to be settled. In the end everything must be tied up to my satisfaction before I can send my report to the Member of Parliament. However, while still operating this same broad procedure, I hope to reduce the number of cases in the pipeline without sacrificing the quality of either investigations or reports to Members."[14]

The P.C.A. has been accommodating in his interpretations of standing of complainants and has allowed representative groups to bring complaints via their M.P. Public bodies are prohibited from making a complaint against departments[15] thus helping to ensure that the P.C.A. concerns himself with complaints of an *individual* nature as opposed to becoming involved in disputes about relationships between organs of the state. Schedule 3 lists the "Matters" which are not subject to his investigation and as well as covering international relations,[16] extradition, investigation of crime and state security, legal proceedings and courts martial, the prerogative of mercy etc. there are also excluded from investigation personnel matters, in the broadest sense, of members of the armed services, civil service or employees of those bodies within the jurisdiction of the P.C.A.[16a] This last exclusion has probably over the years caused the greatest agitation, though the most important exclusion generally is that in paragraph 9 of the Schedule: "Action taken in matters relating to contractual or other commercial transactions, whether within the U.K. or elsewhere, being transactions of a government department or authority to which this Act applies" or other public authority except those "concerning the compulsory purchase of land or its disposal as surplus land."

---

[14] (1981–82; H.C. 258), para. 28.
[15] *Loc. cit.* n. 8 s.6(1)(*a*) and (*b*).
[16] See, however, Parliamentary Commissioner (Consular Complaints) Act. 1981.
[16a] See, however, S.I. 1983, No. 1707. Personnel matters are not excluded in Northern Ireland.

(c) Commercial and Contractual Transactions

This latter exclusion has been criticised *inter alia* by *Justice*, a Royal Commission and the Select Committee on the P.C.A. as well as by Sir Cecil Clothier himself in his final report as P.C.A.[17] The Select Committee has recommended that the P.C.A. should investigate complaints "that a department had been improperly influenced in deciding which firms to include among those entitled to tender for contracts, or had made such a decision in an arbitrary manner, or that a department had acted improperly in connection with the withdrawal of a firm's name from the list of approved tenderers." Where companies had been omitted because they had contravened Government policy the P.C.A. has opined that this is not an appropriate matter for his investigation, but should be left to the representations of M.P.s. The Select Committee believed that if such an omission operated inequitably, or not in a uniform manner then this should be appropriate for investigation.

The Government in its reply[18] argued that commercial relationships and grants to industry where there was a use of "statutory powers involving a wide measure of commercial discretion" should not be subject to review by the P.C.A. Clearly there are contractual matters which could be more appropriately dealt with by litigation, but the whole administrative side of buying and selling, and the patronage and extent of government pursuit of its objectives by contractual devices attending such activity, are outside the P.C.A.'s jurisdiction. These matters are extremely unlikely to come before a court in any justiciable manner.[19] Some of the hair-splitting judgments on what is within or without the jurisdiction of the P.C.A. border on casuistry—complaints about the communication of confidential information by one department to another he could investigage as they are "administrative" but if the information is used to remove a contractor from a list of tenderers, as it has been, that is a commercial matter and excluded by paragraph 9. The limitation of the functions of the P.C.A. as perceived by the Government was brought home clearly when discussing the award of regional development grants to industry under the Industry Act 1972.[20] Grant is provided in the form of a contract, based upon

---

[17] In respective order: Justice (1977); Cmnd. 6524 (1976); Fourth Report from the Select Committee on P.C.A. (1977–78; H.C. 615 and 444) and *ibid.* (1979–80; H.C. 593); (1983–84; H.C. 322).

[18] Cmnd. 7449 (1979).

[19] They might relate, for instance, to the receipt of "confidential information" by a department.

[20] Now Industrial Development Act 1982, and Cooperative Development Agency, etc., Act 1984. *NB.* Chap. 2.

commercial considerations and advice from bodies which are not subject to investigation by the P.C.A.: "The Minister of State did not believe that it would be possible for the P.C.A. to discover whether any improper consideration had entered into the use of the Department's discretion in the period leading up to the award of a contract."

Government is unwilling to have its contractual relationships and powers subjected to scrutiny by the P.C.A. because it does not consider that commercial affairs are "of the very nature of government." The Government's activities as a buyer of goods and services were "quite different from those of its operations which were subject to the P.C.A.'s scrutiny."[21] The point is that it *is* exercise of power of government that is in question, but a power that is exercised through the medium of contract, not necessarily statutory command or authorisation, and it is this very power which is inadequately supervised. It is true that the revamped Comptroller and Auditor General can investigate that value for money is achieved in Government contracts but this constitutes a very different exercise from an investigation into the fairness and propriety of their allocation or non-allocation. The Select Committee made the point tellingly: "The Government has a duty to administer its purchasing policies fairly and equitably, and if these policies are the subject of complaint then the complaints should be investigated; this is particularly important if any future Government were again to use the award of contracts as a political weapon." This would not entail the questioning of the merits of allocation of contracts, the Committee believed.

There is some ambiguity here in the Select Committee's approach, forced upon it no doubt by the constraints imposed upon the P.C.A.'s constitutional limitations. He cannot question the merits of a decision; there is an area of governmental activity where it is felt that because of inadequate accountability devices, unjust activities may ensue; the real threat comes when the Government uses its powers to achieve political objectives without adequate accountability, and yet political matters are, as the Select

---

[21] The argument that some tasks of government are "governmental" and others are not and that the latter ought not to be subject to the same accountability devices as the former, really does open the door for non-governmental government. A converse argument is used to avoid investigation by the Commission for Racial Equality or Equal Opportunities Commission into government activities which are peculiar to government, or "governmental": Race Relations Act 1976, s.75 and *Home Office* v. *C.R.E.* [1981] 1 All E.R. 1042 and Sex Discrimination Act 1975, s.29 and s.85(1) and *Amin* v. *Entry Clearance Officer* [1983] 2 All E.R. 865, H.L.

Committee themselves said, more appropriately the concern of M.P.s. If policies themselves are unfair, why should the P.C.A. not be able to criticise them?

(d) Maladministration and Bad Rules

Although it has rejected a broader definition of "maladministration" as suggested by *Justice*,[22] the committee has encouraged the P.C.A. to extend the parameters of his own definition. It was felt originally that the P.C.A. could not question statutory rules or departmental administrative rules (primary legislation is not action taken in the course of administrative functions and is *per se* outside the P.C.A.'s competence). The rationale of this exclusion was that rule-making was a legislative not an administrative function. *Individual* decisions under statutory, or delegated legislative authority or under departmental rules were an appropriate subject of investigation if a complaint was made. The Committee has distinguished between statutory instruments and other forms of delegated legislation. If the former, the P.C.A. cannot question their form, content or merits, though he may examine the effects of an instrument allegedly causing hardship to a complainant and he may ask the department to review its operation and inquire into the steps taken by the department. For the latter category, non-statutory instruments, he may not question their form, content or merits, but his powers to investigate maladministration in the stages leading to the making of the order, or its review, seem to be broader. For departmental rules, the P.C.A. was initially wary of becoming concerned with what are often expressions of department policy. The Select Committee urged the P.C.A. that when a rule was causing hardship or injustice in a particular case under investigation, he should inquire as to what action had been taken to review the rule, and if the rule were found defective, what action had been taken to remedy the particular hardship sustained by the complainant. If the rule had not been revised, it would be open to the P.C.A. to find maladministration in the individual case if there had been deficiencies in the departmental review of the rule.

There have been numerous occasions when the P.C.A. has asked a department to review its policy rules but has subsequently found nothing on which to bring a finding of maladministration. A department would have to be very inept to carry out a review of a

---

[22] Who recommended that he be empowered to investigate any "unreasonable, unjust or oppressive action," *Our Fettered Ombudsman* (1977).

rule which was so inadequate that it amounted to maladministration. If deficiencies are not present in the review, there is little that the P.C.A. can do if the department persevere with the rule.[22a] It is interesting to note that the P.C.A. has investigated the Prison Rules, Rule 33(1) and the departmental rules supplementing it, and which are concerned with correspondence between a prisoner and other persons. He found nothing to criticise, although in *Silver* v. *U.K.*[23] censorship under this rule, and the departmental rules in particular, was found to be in breach of Art. 8 of the European Convention of Human Rights. Further as the P.C.A. did not constitute an "effective remedy" under Art. 13 for breaches of the Convention, the British Government was found to be in breach of Art. 13. This is to apply international standards to our domestic administration, a task which was never envisaged for the P.C.A. His task is not to question the content of legality, but to ensure administrative propriety within a given framework of legality.

(e) *Good Administration and Maladministration*

What standards of administrative propriety has he insisted upon? Gregory and Hutchesson list the following shortcomings which have been criticised:

(1) Assorted mistakes, errors and oversights.
(2) Failing to impart information or provide an adequate explanation.
(3) Giving inaccurate information and misleading advice.
(4) Misapplication of departmental rules and instructions.
(5) Peremptory or inconsiderate behaviour on the part of officials.
(6) Unjustifiable delay.
(7) One might add not treating, so far as possible, like cases alike.

Further, the P.C.A. has long established that he can question the *quality* of the exercise of discretion in a decision, though it was argued that exercise of discretion was *per se* a judgment upon the

---

[22a] Though the Select Committee may put pressure on the department: see *e.g. Knechtl*, 2nd. Report, Select Committee on P.C.A. (1970–1971) p. XII and Cmnd. 4846.

[23] Judgment of the Court, March 25, 1983 and see Birkinshaw, "Legal Order and Prison Administration" (1983) N.I.L.Q. 269.

merits of a decision. The common fault has been a failure by officials to consider all relevant factors in the case in question, and the circumstances in which such failures have occurred have been varied. The P.C.A. has criticised departments for not following all necessary procedures to elicit relevant information, including sometimes the holding of interviews on an informal basis or not allowing appropriate cross examination at a public inquiry, even if the inquiry was conducted within the strict letter of the Inquiries Procedure Rules. The P.C.A. has criticised discrepancies between the information collected by officials, and the way this differs from the advice which they hand on to their Ministers when such advice constitutes the reasons afforded to a complainant for a decision.

The P.C.A. is given wide powers to obtain information,[24] the only exclusion being Cabinet documents.[25] Access to documents is not available to Members of Parliament individually[26]; the P.C.A. can ask officials questions which individual M.P.s cannot; he can get more answers and as his investigation unfolds, more information comes to light. He is the acknowledged expert on what constitutes "maladministration" and there has been little doubt that he has been far more effective in remedying routine grievances than M.P.s. As the office was established to further the role of Parliament *vis-à-vis* the executive's administrative activities, the relationship of the office with the Select Committee and the role of the Select Committee were seen as essential.

(f) The Role of the Select Committee

The Select Committee was left largely to establish its own role. It discusses the reports of the P.C.A. all of which are laid before both Houses and it may apply pressure to departments to provide remedies. In 1969 it declared its interests as being: examination of the remedies for aggrieved persons, particularly in cases where the P.C.A. has made a special report under section 10(3) (failure to

---

[24] Though this will not necessarily be handed over to the complainant. Under s.68 of the Education Act 1944, when complaints are made to the Secretary of State about an education authority "The Department . . . when confronted with requests to see information obtained from authorities . . . starts with the predisposition not to give it," though they might if circumstances merit it. The P.C.A. agreed with this predisposition, C 90/82.

[25] Is this still justifiable given the decisions in recent Public Interest Immunity litigation? See Chap. 6 and *Burmah Oil* v. *Bank of England* [1979] 3 All E.R. 700, H.L. and *Air Canada* v. *Secretary of State* [1983] 1 All E.R. 910, H.L. and Parliamentary Commissioner Act 1967, s.8.

[26] For the position of M.P.s on Select Committees, see Chap. 2.

remedy after a finding of injustice caused by maladministration) and secondly the remedial action within departments when his investigations brought to light defects in a *system* of administration. Gregory and Hutchesson describe how out of these two emerged a concern with "administrative policy"—"what departments are responsible for by way of day to day administration, as opposed to policy questions of political significance for which Ministers were responsible."[27]

The sense of the distinction is reasonably clear, though there is a characteristic ambivalence here as Ministers are notionally responsible for *all* policy.[28] It is possible to indicate changes in administrative practice within departments as a result of Select Committee pressure, and the Government did accept that changes in administrative rules should be announced in Parliament when the original rules had been announced there. What of rules not announced? The record of the Select Committee is tinged with some diffidence as it has tended to concentrate on procedural points rather than substantive points of policy. The Select Committee has recommended that the P.C.A. should review legislation where it is not producing the results Parliament intended, though only when M.P.s were unaware of the consequences of the legislation. They rejected proposals by *Justice* that the P.C.A. could conduct investigations on his own initiative without a complaint from an M.P., though it favoured a follow up inquiry after a complaint had been lodged where the P.C.A. believed that a department, or section of a department, was not dealing efficiently with its business. The previous P.C.A. has been bolder and while noting that he was the only national Ombudsman not to have the power to investigate on his own initiative, suggested that such an investigation with the Committee or its chairman might be in the public interest.[29] I examined the Select Committee's arguments in favour of extending the jurisdiction of the P.C.A. into commercial matters, and on its proposals to have jurisdiction extended the Government has adamantly and generally refused to cede ground.[30] What success the Select Committee has enjoyed has not been achieved after heroic struggles with the executive, though the legislative extension of the limitation period for claims relating to depreciation of land

[27] See n. 2, *supra*.
[28] Though they do not always accept the implications of such responsibility, again Chap. 2.
[29] (1983–84; H.C. 322), para. 8.
[30] *Cf.* the change introduced by the legislation at n. 16, *supra*, and in relation to personnel matters, S.I. 1983 No. 1707.

values caused by public works which resulted after a critical special report of the P.C.A. on the time limits and publication of the scheme by the Department of Transport was an outstanding "victory."[31] Two of the biggest Governmental "defeats" at the hands of the P.C.A.—*Sachsenhausen* and *Court Line* did not follow Select Committee Reports but inept Ministerial addresses to the House of Commons. The "success" of the Select Committee has been achieved by its very presence; it instils in senior civil servants the knowledge that they might have to answer embarrassing questions and it has allowed a continuing dialogue to be established, formally and informally, between M.P.s and civil servants.

It would be germane to highlight the lack of publicity associated with his office, the paucity of coverage given to his reports—he publishes quarterly "selections" of his investigations—and that he remains an object of obscurity in the public eye. Allied to that is the fact that he cannot enforce his findings upon a reluctant department, and though outright refusal to accept a decision is rare, only on *one* occasion has the Select Committee constrained a department to remedy an individual injustice caused by maladministration. In 1981, the P.C.A. in his annual report started to list the remedies awarded by departments beyond a mere apology, and some of the individual sums are quite significant, *e.g.* £57,000 compensation because of a mishandling of an application for regional selective assistance.[32] Of course, the amount of compensation awarded, if any is awarded at all, is based upon *ex gratia* considerations by the department, not legal right. Where individual cases raise precedents for a whole *class* of case which it would be difficult to deny, the constitutional principle that significant amounts of public expenditure must be authorised by *specific* legislative authority has been invoked to evade compensation. In the land compensation cases referred to above, for instance, an estimated amount of £8 million was involved in compensation. In a field characterised by negotiation, discretion and political sensitivity, much no doubt depends upon the attitude and temperament of a particular Commissioner. It would be unfair to lay at his door the shortcomings which ensue from limitations inherent in his powers and office. Those limitations were deliberately imposed because of constitutional sensitivities and political jealousies. It is a wonder, perhaps, that the P.C.A. has been accepted and

---

[31] Amendments to the scheme were effected by Pt. 13 of the Local Government Planning and Land Act 1980 and followed the first "special report" of the P.C.A. under s.10(3) of the 1967 Act (1977–78; H.C. 666).

[32] C. 1004/80.

achieved what he has, which probably means that he has not been an unduly burdensome thorn in any important flesh.[33]

(2) COMMISSIONERS FOR LOCAL ADMINISTRATION

(a) *General Issues*

The Commission for Local Administration was established by Part 3 of the Local Government Act 1974. There are three Commissioners covering three regions in England and there is a Commissioner for Wales and one for Scotland. The Act required the Secretary of State to designate representative bodies for the Commission in England and for Wales and the English body comprises the local authority Representative Bodies, the GLC and the National Water Council. These bodies publish the annual reports of each Commissioner and the Commission. The Commission is under a duty to review the operation of the Act each year in relation to investigation of complaints. This review is passed to the representative body when the Commission wishes particular views to be passed on to local authorities or government departments. The Representative Body, constituting interests that are the subject of possible criticism note, can add "such comments to those recommendations or conclusions as they think appropriate." The Representative Body can also add their comments to the Commission Report in an Annex.

Complaints are made in writing to any member of the authority complained against, though Commissioners have discretion to waive the necessity where any member of the authority is requested to refer a complaint to a Commissioner and does not do so. Complaints do not have to particularise the nature of the grievance and the Court of Appeal has been generous in its inter-

---

[33] Shortly after writing this, the P.C.A. issued the report of an investigation into the Home Office after a complaint by Mr. John Preece who was convicted on the evidence of a forensic scientist whose competence was subsequently questioned. Mr. Preece was sentenced to life imprisonment. The complaint revealed, according to Mr. Jack Ashley M.P. "stunning complacency; incompetence and major errors of judgment" on behalf of Home Office officials. The Commissioner criticised the episode as "a pollution of justice at its source." My basic view remains unchanged; (1983–84; H.C. 191) for the report. This is not meant as criticism of the previous incumbent whose name "is synonymous with long and very thorough investigations." (*The Guardian*, January 27, 1984). It is to acknowledge the constraints imposed upon the office by its legislative and *constitutional* framework. In Sweden, for instance, reform of the penal system was due in large measure to the Ombudsman. It is also noticeable that the Ombudsman has had a more significant impact on administrative *systems* in New Zealand.

pretation of the discretion of a Commissioner to accept complaints which are not specifically pleaded, which have by-passed the member and which are outside the 12 month time limit.[34]

The C.L.A. has always advocated that it should have the power to receive complaints directly rather than through the member, providing that the authority is given the chance to put its own house in order before an investigation began. In its 1978 Report, the C.L.A. described a research project which showed that if complainants were interviewed *before* their complaints were rejected, such interviews often produced evidence not apparent from the written submission resulting in the investigation of complaints which would otherwise have been rejected. Nevertheless, the Representative Body has persistently refused to countenance the abolition of the "filter," and indeed its insistence that the nature of a complaint be made specific and in writing is far more demanding than the Court of Appeal's.[34a] The Representative Body has consistently refused to support requests by the C.L.A. to extend their jurisdiction and to render more precise what is meant by maladministration—a phrase the C.L.A. does not like. The annual reports show that there is generally mutual trust and co-operation between authorities and the Commissioners though there are some notable exceptions creating problems as we shall see. Commissioners refer to frequent informal contacts with authorities under investigation and this frequently leads to the production of more information. The C.L.A. now possesses power to demand information from authorities which is on a par with that possessed by the P.C.A. in relation to departments.[35] When complaints are not rejected at an early stage, *e.g.* outside jurisdiction, the usual practice is for the Chief Executive to comment on the understanding that these may be sent to the complainant; if the Commissioner feels that after consideration of the complaint and comments, it should not be pursued further, his decision and the Chief Executive's comments will be sent to the complainant. If the investigation does continue, files will be examined, interviews conducted, and then it may become apparent that the investigation should proceed no further. If it does proceed, it will only at the final stage lead to a formal report which is sent to the member, to the auth-

---

[34] *R. v. Local Commissioner, etc., ex p. Bradford M.B.C.* [1979] 2 All E.R. 881, Q.B.D. and C.A.

[34a] *Ibid.*

[35] A power effected by s.184 of the Local Government Planning and Land Act 1980, which in turn reversed a restrictive interpretation of the C.L.A.'s powers by the Divisional Court in *Re A Complaint Against Liverpool C.C.* [1977] 2 All E.R. 650.

ority and to the complainant.[35a] The C.L.A. can make three findings as appropriate: no maladministration; maladministration but no injustice suffered as a consequence; maladministration causing injustice for which the C.L.A. can recommend *ex gratia* compensation from the authority, but only *after* he has investigated and reported. No legal power exists for the authority to make a payment after their own *internal* investigation alone.

(b) The C.L.A. Bailiwick

There are prohibitions on what the C.L.A. can investigate and these include: contractual and commercial matters excluding land acquisition–disposal; personnel matters; internal matters of school management or administration; and where the complainant has an alternative avenue of legal or administrative redress unless in the circumstances it would not be reasonable to insist upon the complainant pursuing such relief. Legal proceedings and criminal matters are outside his jurisdiction as are complaints "affecting all or most of the inhabitants of the Authority's area." From 1981 housing complaints have topped planning complaints as the leading subject matter of complaints properly referred.

(c) Access to the C.L.A., Direct Complaints and the Representative Body

The Commissioners generally speak well of their relationship with authorities, but their reports do indicate that a significant number of authorities are displaying a hostile reaction to the C.L.A. It is also noticeable that the Representative Body has not been forthcoming in its support of the C.L.A. The Representative Body has refused to support an extension of the C.L.A.'s jurisdiction into contractual or commercial matters, which when one considers the Salmon Commission Report[36] and notorious events in local authority administration is a surprising omission. It has insisted that matters of internal school management should remain beyond the investigatory powers of the C.L.A. as should personnel matters. Most importantly, it has refused to countenance a removal of the "filter" reference through a member: "the present system was not an obstacle to complainants. The instructions on the complaints' form are quite clear as to procedure."[37] The Body

---

[35a] The authority has to publicise the existence of the report which must be available at its offices.

[36] Cmnd. 6524 (1976).

[37] 1982/83 Report.

argues that it is essential that the member receives a complaint so that the authority can investigate the matter itself before the intervention of the C.L.A. *Justice*, in its 1980 Report on the Local Ombudsman, said that the most thorough investigation of a complaint takes place not when it is referred by the complainant to a member or to the council, but when, under the Local Government Act 1974 s.26(5), the Commissioner brings it to the attention of the authority before beginning his formal investigation. It should be noted, however, that every year, more complaints come in direct than through members of authorities. In 1981/82 there were 1,953 direct complaints (1982/83 saw a 5 per cent. increase) and 1,729 complaints referred through members which had not first come direct. Direct complaints tend not to be frivolous or trivial and about 40 per cent. of full investigations each year are into complaints which were initially made direct. All of this means extra time and expense for the C.L.A. and complainants. About one half of direct complaints disappear once they are referred back to the complainant, and the feeling in the C.L.A. is that they lose heart and as these are often the most vulnerable members of the community some of those most in need of assistance do not receive it. The *Justice* Report showed how the upper socio-economic brackets were more likely to use the C.L.A., though it pointed out that treatment was the same for all groups once the complaint was properly referred. Over 90 per cent. of direct complaints sampled by the C.L.A. had complained initially to the authority, and because they received no joy came to the C.L.A. Some 60 per cent. gave up when told "to go back to square one." In short "complainants *do* try to have their complaints settled locally." Incidentally, in Scotland and Wales direct complaints amount to about two thirds of complaints.[38] These figures speak for themselves.

The Representative Body has also rejected a proposal that the C.L.A. should conduct investigations on his own initiative—either without a complaint (as is possible with the Ombudsman in Sweden, Finland, Canadian Provinces, and New Zealand) or on the request of an authority where no complaint has been made.

(d) *The Representative Body—Time for a Change?*

Two specific issues have revealed the unsupportive nature of the Representative Body especially when one compares it with the Select Committee on the P.C.A. and how the latter body has

---

[38] *Ibid.*

assisted the P.C.A. Under the Local Government Planning and Land Act 1980, the Secretary of State was empowered to issue or approve Code(s) of Practice concerning the publication by authorities of information about their functions for their community. The C.L.A. requested the D.o.E. that the Code on Rate Demands should contain information about authorities' *own* grievance procedures and the C.L.A. In the event, the information was restricted to "possible supplementary information that might be published in association with rate demand notes" and a C.L.A. survey showed that very few authorities gave any information at all on these topics. The Representative Body, supported by the local authority associations, doubted whether the Code of Guidance should contain such information[39] and the D.o.E. did not meet with the C.L.A. to discuss their review of the exercise.

The second problem has concerned the minority of authorities which do not comply with a Commissioner's final report. The only sanction for a Commissioner is to publish a "further report" setting out the facts and giving it maximum publicity.[40] In 1982/83, 20 further reports were issued. Since 1974, 103 reports have been issued and the C.L.A. has reported 78 "unsatisfactory outcomes." It is also noticeable that Commissioners are becoming more vehement in their denunciation of those authorities which do not comply with their recommendations. The C.L.A. arranged a meeting with the Representative Body to discuss this problem which the latter body accepted was unfortunate, but it felt that outside pressure was "unnecessary and ill-founded." It agreed, instead, to recommend to all their member associations that they should write to all their members urging them to respond "positively and speedily" to the C.L.A.'s findings. This recommendation did not prove acceptable, however. This is hardly surprising in view of the fact that the Association of District Councils had advised its members to avoid making formal resolutions committing the authority to undertake specified non-statutory neighbour or general public consultations in connection with planning applications, but that such consultative exercises should remain a matter of informal exercise of discretion by planning officers.[41] This advice arose from cases where an authority had a policy of public consultation on such applications—but had not consulted in a par-

---

[39] In its 1982 Report a C.L.A. survey showed that few authorities gave any information about local procedures for considering complaints or about the C.L.A. in their rate demands and supporting literature. The GLC had a good record in this respect, publishing information in its paper "The Londoner."

[40] Local Government Act 1974, ss.30(4), (5) and (6) and 31.

[41] See D.o.E. Circ. 71/73.

ticular case. Even though not statutorily bound to consult it had found itself the subject of an investigation into maladministration. The motive of the Association of District Councils is understandable, if highly undesirable—after all if an authority has a policy it should stick to it unless there are good reasons for not doing so. What is regrettable is that the Association issued its advice without consulting the C.L.A. or the Representative Body! When, on another occasion, the C.L.A. recommended that it should produce Codes of Practice for authorities on good administrative practice based on their findings and investigations—and C.L.A. reports offer a mine of useful information on such practices—the Representative Body spurned the idea, saying it was a matter for authorities and their associations.

It may well be that the C.L.A. will have to be invested with powers to seek enforcement of his recommendations through court orders as exists for the Northern Ireland Complaints' Commissioner, where courts can also quantify the complainant's loss. *Justice* supported this proposal, though the C.L.A. obviously is unwilling to prejudice its relationship with authorities generally by resorting to legal enforcement. There are some signs that the C.L.A. is beginning to recognise this possibility, however.[42] *Justice* also recommended that the Representative Body should be abolished, and one is tempted to say that this would be no great loss and it would certainly assist the C.L.A. if a new body were obviously more impartial and carried more impact. On one matter, the *Justice* report was disappointing. It saw the C.L.A. as a remedy for individual grievances essentially, and underplayed the role it could perform in improving standards of general administration. A reading of Commissioners' Reports has brought home the sensitivity of individual commissioners to the balance to be struck between the requirements of administrative efficiency, administrative necessity and individual justice, not only for the complainant but for whole classes of complainants. There is often a skill displayed by particular local commissioners, I feel, that is not often repeated elsewhere in our public administration. The skill is in achieving a balance between public efficiency and individual justice. It has been reprehensible that the Commission has not been taken too seriously in certain quarters of local authority administration.

(e) Impact upon Administration

It is notable how in Commissioners' investigations a broader range of subject matter is beginning to appear. In 1982/83 the

[42] See the 1983 Report and, *e.g.* Inv. 994/C/81.

Commissioners received 2,753 complaints on reference from members; formal investigation reports were issued in 316 cases. One hundred and seventy cases of maladministration causing injustice were established and 388 cases were settled locally (at all stages). In spite of the significant number of local settlements, the C.L.A. does not want to be under a *duty* to be a "conciliation officer." The average length of time in investigations where there is a formal report is 43 weeks; the average time between a first report and a further report is 37 weeks—quite a time-consuming business where an authority is recalcitrant.

The C.L.A. has insisted that authorities give reasons for decisions which are clear and precise and informative; provide correct information and accurate advice; obtain and give access to all relevant information in the making of a decision[43]; allow interviews and representations to be made; and have insisted on "fair play" in administration, to a far greater extent than would be insisted upon by law,[44] and that authorities generally get their procedures right for the future[45] by drawing up their own Codes of Practice[46] or establishing more obvious domestic grievance procedures.[47] Some of their recommendations have involved expenditure of large sums of money, *e.g.* £100,000 to a community group, although three-quarters of the sum would be provided by central government.[48] The C.L.A. has come much closer to questioning the merits of a decision than has the P.C.A., though the statement: "The decision was taken with maladministration and I therefore am able to question the merits,"[49] is unusually sanguine.[50] Generous accommodation for "standing" has been afforded to representative groups bringing complaints. The C.L.A. and individual Commissioners have done far more to publicise their service than has the P.C.A. One would feel happier if

---

[43] It is interesting to notice this point in relation to local authority appeal procedures under the Education Acts 1980 and 1981—see Chap. 3 and 1983 Report and Invs. 466/C/82 and 388/C/82.

[44] "An Ombudsman's task is not to decide whether authorities were entitled to take particular decisions as a matter of law, but to establish whether their decisions were taken with or without maladministration. Compliance with the law gives no immunity from maladministration. Acceptable administrative action lies within the frame of a wider (and less precise) concept than action within the law": Pat Cook, 1983 Report, Inv. 387/77.

[45] Inv. 158/C/81.

[46] Inv. 404/H/81.

[47] Inv. 945/C/81.

[48] Inv. 13/C/80.

[49] Inv. 9/5/82.

[50] On an attempt to establish the distinction between the role of the C.L.A. and the use of the ballot box to change a decision, see Inv. 11/S/82.

the full council or full committee with overall responsibility for the service in question were legally obliged to consider the report, rather than fobbing it off to sub-committees as is sometimes done.[51] A greater use of interviews, especially for members of poorer groups would clearly be worthwhile to help those who have difficulty cutting through the thickets of public administration.

(3) COMPLAINING ABOUT HEALTH TREATMENT

The Health Service Commissioner (H.S.C.)—who is in fact the P.C.A.—was created by the National Health Services Reorganisation Act 1973.[52] He reports on complaints made to him from complainants, their relatives or other suitable person who can make a complaint on behalf of somebody who has died or is unable to act for himself. There *is* direct access to the Commissioner and a health authority can ask the H.S.C. to investigate a complaint which it has referred to him. The H.S.C. reports to the appropriate Secretary of State rather than to Parliament, though his reports are laid before both Houses. The most important matter excluded from investigation is a complaint which in his opinion concerns "the exercise of some person's clinical judgment" in the provision of diagnosis, care or treatment. His remit covers "any failure in the services provided by the various health service authorites listed in the Act, or any other action taken by them or on their behalf." There must be an allegation of hardship or injustice in consequence of the failure, or in consequence of maladministration connected with the other action.

(a) *Complaints About Policy*

Many complaints are concerned with features which relate to reduction of government expenditure and which are outside the competence of the H.S.C. Recent plans to assist the privatisation of the NHS; or to render it "more efficient" upon criteria accept-

---

[51] One Commissioner has suggested that a small representative panel of members should be empowered to give immediate attention, on the advice of the chief executive, to any case which the Ombudsman is investigating and where a remedy seems required. This would apply whether there was a formal report, or an "informal suggestion" after preliminary enquiries. Only in the event of failure to agree by the panel, would it be necessary to involve the whole council and relevant committees. The Ombudsman and panel could discuss "informal settlement of grievances." There are obvious advantages in this suggestion if it works to the benefit of the complainants and providing that it does not deflect the responsible committee's attention from any lessons to be learned.

[52] See now the National Health Service Act 1977.

able to the tenets of private industry; the furthering of centralisation by the creation of a Health Service Supervisory Board and a full-time NHS Management Board[52a]; and cash restrictions will all doubtless contribute to widespread disaffection and grievance about the future of the National Health Service. Such grievances will generally have to be expressed through the ballot box, the media or the streets. Where the Government has encountered stout resistance from District Health Authorities to their proposals, Government appointments on Regional Authorities have reacted in a highhanded manner.[53] Community Health Councils which are not overly popular with the Government, have a statutory duty to represent the interests of the public in the health service in their districts "and this could include commenting on District Health Authority plans for developing or changing services, assessing how local facilities compare with recommended national standards, investigating facilities for patients or monitoring complaints."[54] A frequent complaint from Community Health Councils is that they are provided with inadequate information. Before the reorganisation in 1981 for instance, they had sometimes been denied access to relevant papers on, *e.g.* proposed hospital closures prepared for Area Health Authorities. The future will seem to witness growing pressure to cut down on community consultation and participation, and a growing trend towards "business efficiency" where everything has a price, though not necessarily a value. Some District Health Authorities have organised "local meetings" to coordinate health and social services planning. Emphasis has been upon informality and coordination with parallel exercises conducted by Community Health Councils.[55]

[52a] Bodies with an "informal, non-legal status" so as not to formalise unnecessarily their role "*vis à vis* the Secretary of State"—a classic reason for establishing a quango: R. Griffiths, *NHS Management Inquiry* (October 1983).

[53] Causing a High Court judge to express "disquiet" over the manner in which the powers under statutory regulations were exercised by a regional authority which indicated that dismissal of district authority members would follow any objections to proposed cuts in public expenditure, *R.* v. *North West Thames Regional Health Authority, ex p. Neva, The Times*, October 20, 1983.

[54] N.C.C. (1979). The position is still rather confused: *Information Needs of Community Health Councils*, N.C.C. 1984. Prior to 1981, District Authorities were called Area Health Authorities.

[55] See *The Health Services*, October 29, 1982. The Griffiths Report, *supra*, spoke of a review of all *consultation* arrangements required by legislation or administrative order, *e.g.* "closure or changes of use of health buildings . . . to speed up and simplify the essential consultation required." The Management Board and Chairmen should "promote realistic public and professional perceptions of what the NHS can and should provide"—is this the official construction of reality?

(b) Complaints by Individuals and Clinical Judgment

On the question of individual complaints, a central feature has been the inability of the H.S.C. to question decisions based upon "clinical judgment." Various official and Select Committee reports urged the Government to reconsider this exclusion, especially as about 50 per cent. of complaints related to aspects solely concerned with clinical judgment, and what complainants wanted was "an explanatory mechanism" not compensation.[56] As the Select Committee put it, it was a failure causing widespread public dissatisfaction. "There is a danger that people who only want to establish what happened to them . . . will be driven to expensive and unnecessary litigation." The medical profession was opposed to such an extension, as were their insurers, but after pro-tracted negotiation between the DHSS and medical representative bodies, a complaints procedure for complaints other than those relating to family practitioners' services was introduced by H.C. Circular (81)5. In the memorandum accompanying this circular was a procedure to be introduced on a trial basis to deal with com-plaints relating to the exercise of clinical judgment by hospital medical and dental staff. The Circular has, then, the dual purpose of providing a complaints procedure before the H.S.C. is resorted to, and more importantly allowing a complainant the opportunity of obtaining a "second opinion" on clinical judgment. For the first part, there are exhortations to provide adequate information to patients, good communication between staff and patients and sym-pathetic reception of complaints which if made formally in writing or orally, are to be investigated by senior staff. Authorities are encouraged to monitor complaints and to "introduce a systematic and effective method of reviewing complaints to identify signifi-cant trends . . . to enable improvements." The procedure for complaints is detailed, and can end up with the District Manage-ment Team or the Chairman of the authority replying, though nowhere is the presence of the patient at a discussion of the com-plaint advocated.

Complaints about clinical judgment involve the consultant (or doctor) in question who can discuss the matter with the patient, a reply from the consultant or District Administrator and if the com-plainant is not satisfied, the Regional Medical Officer will discuss the matter with the consultant, the complainant and colleagues.

---

[56] A recent C.I.P.F.A. report, *Health Care U.K. 1984* (1984) has painted a detri-mental impression of the health complaints system. See (1977–78; H.C. 45) and (1979–80; H.C. 465) for the comments of the Select Committee on independent investigation of "clinical judgment."

The penultimate stage brings into play two independent consultants who can meet the patient, leading where necessary to an Independent Professional Review by two consultants nominated by the Joint Consultants' Committee. The complainant can be accompanied at the discussion by a friend, or relative, and a G.P. The Independent Professional Review provides the "second opinion." The complainant receives a formal reply from the District Administrator stating what action is to be taken, and the issue will generally remain confidential.

Uncontroversial as these provisions are, the medical profession was extremely unhappy about the "second opinion" provision and the prospects of "double jeopardy," *i.e.* the procedure would be used by a complainant to elicit information to bring an action in negligence against the authority.[57] A recent report by the DHSS has stated the procedure is eligible for complaints "which are substantial, but which do not seem likely to lead to litigation."[58] One hundred and eighty-four complaints were referred to Regional Medical Officers in England in the 16 month period to December 1982. By that date, there had been 63 independent reviews. Wales and Scotland have a slightly different procedure. Some of the English cases have taken up to 10 months to complete. It seems that the procedure is aiming essentially to be a prophylactic device for the future, so that lessons may be learned from past mistakes and adequate explanations offered. However in about a quarter of the concluded cases, the complaint was not resolved to the satisfaction of the complainant. Out of 48 cases rejected as unsuitable for review, 20 were considered to be by complainants who were information gathering for future litigation. Nearly 50 per cent. of all hospital complaints in writing in England are about clinical judgment (1981, total of complaints 14,649, clinical judgment 6,341 (43·3 per cent.). The number coming through to Regional Medical Officers represents 3 per cent. of all complaints about clinical judgment.[59]

(c) General Practitioners

For family practitioners who are on the NHS lists, there have been special complaints provisions since 1912, when the State first

---

[57] The law has become more accommodating in recent years in allowing greater scope for pre-action discovery in accident cases, *Waugh* v. *British Railways Board* [1980] A.C. 521. Only 4 per cent of complaints about medical negligence are litigated.

[58] DHSS *Report On Operation Of Procedure For Independent Review Of Complaints Involving The Clinical Judgment Of Hospital Doctors and Dentists* (1983).

[59] *Ibid.*

contracted with private practitioners for the latter to provide their services to the public at public expense. These emerged as ancillary features of "value for money" mechanisms and complaints can be dealt with by service committees whose procedures, duties and powers are prescribed in statutory regulations.[60] Appeals, held *in camera*, go to the Secretary of State. Parties and witnesses may attend, and legal representation is allowed on appeal to the Secretary of State though it is excluded at hearings before service committees.[61] The presence of the complainant or a legal representative seems to make a crucial difference at appeal level, even though the procedure is supposed to be informal.[62]

Local Family Practitioner Committees[62a]—who contract with the practitioners—can investigate the complaint informally if the parties agree, without prejudice to the right to a formal hearing. These procedures are used to achieve a compromise or consensual settlement, whereas the formal procedure is concerned with the proper performance of the terms of a practitioner's contract.

(4) COMPLAINTS AGAINST THE POLICE

There has been widespread public disquiet over a range of issues covering relationships between police and the local community. These include: total distrust by deprived urban communities especially black communities, of the police and the exercise of their powers; allegations of police corruption; allegations of police violence and deaths due to violence while in police custody; police tactics at, or against those travelling to, demonstrations and pickets; "fire brigade" and other contemporary forms of policing such as the use of Special Patrol Groups, mutual aid and Support Units; the role of special divisions in "political" investigations; and the subject of police powers recently enacted on a uniform statutory basis in the much criticised, and seldom applauded Police and Criminal Evidence Act 1984. Nor should we overlook the role of the police National Reporting Centre which coordinated police administration nationally in the miners' picketing of 1984–1985, and the Police National Computer. It is always too easy, and

---

[60] NHS (Service Committee and Tribunal) Regs. 1974 (S.I. 1974 No. 455).

[61] See Reg. 7 which is a little ambiguous in this respect.

[62] In 1981, 706 cases were investigated by the General Medical Services Committee. Breaches of duty were found in 122 cases from which there were 64 appeals (34 made orally), 49 of which were brought by the complainant. The complainant was successful at 11 of the appeals, at ten of which he or a representative was present. Hearsay evidence may be heard, though *cp. R.* v. *Board of Visitors of Hull Prison ex p. St. Germain* [1979] 1 W.L.R. 1401, D.C.

[62a] See Health and Social Security Act 1984, s.5.

therefore simplistic to cast the police as the repressive arm of a "strong state," enforcing a class system of justice at the expense of working or lower classes under the guise of maintaining the "rule of law." It cannot be overlooked, however, that authoritarian elements in the police may be afforded unnecessary encouragement to abuse their extensive powers if the methods of obtaining accountability, complaint resolution and relations with local communities are inadequate. Increasing informal centralisation of administration is often cited as a factor encouraging such tendencies.

(a) Control Over and Accountability of the Police

It is often remarked that the police are accountable to the community in two respects. First, by the law itself in as much as they are charged with enforcing the law impartially in the name of the community, though in reality it would be virtually impossible to obtain a mandamus directed against a Chief Constable directing him to perform his duties[63]; and in as much as the police are answerable to the ordinary criminal and civil law of the land for their actions. Secondly, the police are accountable under Acts of Parliament to *local* police authorities which are special committees of local authorities, with variations for "combined forces."[64] Though "officers of the Crown," the police are paid by local authorities, but they are "servants" of neither.[65] Responsibility lies to central government through H.M. Inspectors of Constabulary and, ultimately to the Home Secretary or relevant Secretary of State though he is not empowered to issue specific directions to Chief Constables on policing policy or operations.[66] In London the police authority is the Home Secretary.

---

[63] *R. v. Commissioner of Police of the Metropolis ex p. Blackburn* [1968] 2 Q.B. 118 (C.A.); *R. v. Chief Constable of Devon and Cornwall ex p. Central Electricity Generating Board* [1981] 3 W.L.R. 867 (C.A.).

[64] Often referred to as police committees, membership comprises two-thirds county councillors and one-third magistrates. Prior to 1964, they were referred to as "Watch Committees." For combined forces they are referred to as police authorities.

[65] A police officer is liable individually for any torts committed on duty and by virtue of s.48 of the Police Act 1964, the Chief Constable is liable vicariously for any tort committed by an officer in the course of his employment. If such an action is successful, damages are paid out of the police fund. See n. 66, *infra*.

[66] *e.g.* for Scotland, Secretary of State for Scotland. The Home Secretary has power to award, and withhold 50 per cent. of a force's expenditure. It has been argued that the Home Secretary can direct the Metropolitan Commissioner more specifically than he can Chief Constables of other forces by virtue of Metropolitan Police Act 1829, s.1, though *cf.* Lord Denning in *ex p. Blackburn* [1968] 2 Q.B. 118 (Hartley and Griffith, *Government and Law* 1981). And *cf.* Marshall *Constitutional Conventions* (1984) pp. 120–121.

The argument has often been advanced that from the nineteenth century onwards, police forces outside London have been subject to centralisation of administration at both a formal and informal level and that local accountability to the "watch committee," as it was called, gradually diminished in significance and efficiency. In England and Wales in 1857, there were 239 separate forces; today there are 43. With increasing informal control over police activities from the Home Office and increasing resort to highly technological aids, the *Royal Commission on the Police*[67] in 1962 stated that in exercise of his power over general policy matters and policing activities of an operational nature, the Chief Constable "should be free from the conventional processes of democratic control and influence." Police authorities in England, Wales and Northern Ireland are charged, however, with the duty of ensuring "the maintenance of an adequate and efficient police force"—the physical side of policing. The Chief Constable is statutorily responsible for the "direction and control" of forces. In Scotland the role of the police authority is similar, though it has a different composition. In Northern Ireland, the authority is appointed by the Secretary of State.

Chief Constables present annual reports to the authorities— these vary enormously in utility and content as their subject matter is within the discretion of the Chief Constable. A survey in 1976 found that only 10 authorities in England and Wales regularly used their power to call for special reports from the Chief Constable. As regards public access to meetings of the authorities, a recent survey[68] established that just over 50 per cent. of the authorities in England, Wales and Scotland allow the public into their meetings. Not all regarded this as a public right and most of them qualified the degree of access given even though it would appear that the Public Bodies (Admission to Meetings) Act applies to police committees. London has no police authority apart from the Home Secretary and this has been a cause of grave concern for many London Boroughs which have felt that there has been inadequate accountability to local communities in the Boroughs.

Finally, the police authority has power to ask for, if the Home Secretary approves, the resignation of the Chief Constable in the interests of efficiency.[69] The power of the authority to suspend chief officers under the Police Regulations will be restricted by

---

[67] *Royal Commission on Police Report* (1962) para. 87.
[68] *State Research Bulletin* (1982) Vol. 5, No. 29, p. 29.
[69] Police Act 1964, s.5(4).

regulations which will necessitate the approval of the Police Complaints Authority before suspension.[70]

(b) Complaints Against the Police

The method for registering complaints against the police was revamped in 1976 by the Police Act of that year. These reforms, which took 10 years to find their way onto the statute book,[71] purportedly increased the role of the public in the investigation of complaints by the creation of the Police Complaints Board (P.C.B.). It has been suggested that the 1976 Act, despite police protestations "did little more than confirm the long standing right of police to investigate themselves."[72] The P.C.B. could ask for information from the police about a complaint and could ultimately direct that disciplinary proceedings be brought against an officer. Essentially investigation was to be by the police themselves. The details of the procedure involved 37 separate stages.[73]

Criticism of the procedure and the philosophy underpinning it was widespread. Looking at the figures, there was a dramatic fall in complaints with the introduction of the P.C.B. The number of complaints which resulted in disciplinary charges does seem to be slight and the feeling was pervasive that the system was slanted against the complainant.[74] Sir Cyril Phillips, chairman of the

---

[70] *The Times*, October 10, 1984.

[71] The Police Federation and the then Metropolitan Police Commissioner, Sir Robert Mark bitterly opposed reform. Sir Robert said he could not work with the new system and announced his retirement—though he admitted that his pension rights were more beneficial at his then age of 60, *The Times*, March 5, 1976 and see Humphrey's article, in *Policing the Police* (Hain ed. 1979).

[72] Under s.49(1) of the Police Act 1964. There is a code of discipline for all policemen laid down in statutory instrument. The quotation is from Humphrey *op. cit.* n. 71, *supra*.

[73] Humphrey *op. cit.* Again the procedure was in a statutory instrument.

[74] Who would face the criminal standard of proof. "Double jeopardy" and the D.P.P.'s 51 per cent. rule are examined in the text and in n. 79a *infra*, but often those complaining are invidivuals on the receiving end of enforcement of the law. Use of prosecution powers for tactical purposes and making complaints likewise, cannot be ignored (1979–80; H.C. 631). The Home Office had anticipated about 25,000 complaints per annum. In the P.C.B.'s report for 1978, the first full year of the P.C.B.'s operation, 7,358 complaint cases were received. Of 3,079 matters of complaint dealt with 107 resulted in disciplinary charges, with 15 recommended for such by the P.C.B. Figures on charges upheld are found in annual reports of H.M. Inspector of Constabulary. In 1982, the P.C.B. dealt with 17,514 matters of complaint. Disciplinary charges were made by the police in 247 instances, the P.C.B. recommended a further 46, and 1,604 officers received "constructive advice." The P.C.B. used its powers to *direct* that disciplinary proceedings be brought on *one* occasion after 1977.

P.C.B. rejected the idea of a totally independent complaints system: "Much would be lost if responsibility for receiving and investigating complaints were removed from the police . . . The system, by and large, is working well."[75]

(c) *Brixton, Lord Scarman and the Police and Criminal Evidence Act*

Lord Scarman did not concur. Outlining the factors behind the violent rioting in Brixton in 1981, he focused upon a collapse of the police liaison committee in 1979; "hard" policing methods; an absence of consultation with the community and a deep distrust by the community of the independence of the complaints procedure.[76] "Unless and until there is a system for judging complaints against the police, which commands the support of the public, there will be no way in which the atmosphere of distrust and suspicion between the police and the community in places like Brixton can be dispelled." A point that was repeated in Liverpool and Manchester. His recommendations for a more sensitive and racially enlightened training of police officers (including eventually his recommendation that racially discriminatory or prejudicial behaviour should be a specific disciplinary offence),[76a] and his suggestion for a revamped complaints procedure and for the creation of a statutory duty upon Chief Officers of Police and police authorities to liaise through more localised committees have, to a greater or lesser degree experienced some realisation. Liaison in London, he recommended, should be at borough or district level. On the complaints system generally, he expressed the belief that the existing procedure was more concerned with internal disciplinary matters rather than satisfying the complainant and that it lacked "a sufficiently convincing independent element." His specific recommendations were for a conciliation procedure for less serious complaints which would operate informally, greater use of outside police officers to investigate more serious complaints and the use of an "independent" supervisor, *e.g.* the chairman of the P.C.B.

---

[75] 1981 Report.
[76] Scarman, Cmnd. 8427 (1981). The cessation of the liaison committee was not the direct fault of the police. He did refer generally to the absence of channels through which black members of the community could articulate their grievances.
[76a] Police and Criminal Evidence Act 1984, s.101(1)(*b*). See: *Racism Awareness Training for the Police* (1984) Home Office Research and Planning Unit, Paper 29.

After various reports and replies and one aborted Bill,[77] the Government elected for a three tier system of complaints-handling. These procedures were outlined in the same Bill which significantly extended the powers of the police in England and Wales, aspects of the Bill which had attracted criticism from the Church, the legal, medical and journalist professions. The drafters of the second Bill do, on the surface, appear to have made more of a conscious effort to make the procedure more autonomous and "independent." For example, the P.C.B. is to be renamed the Police Complaints Authority and the clause introducing the new procedures no longer states that the Police Act 1976 "shall take effect subject to the amendments specified in this section" as did the first Bill. It has the appearance of a more self-contained procedure. The Authority is to consist of a chairman, appointed by Her Majesty, *i.e.* the Prime Minister in reality, and eight other members appointed by the Secretary of State. No former "constable" may be a member, members can be whole-time or part-time and there will be two deputy chairmen of the Authority which is to be a body corporate. Schedule 4 deals with length of office, removal from office, remuneration, appointment of staff and establishing regional offices with the consent of the Secretary of State and the Treasury.

(d) The Complaints Procedure

Turning to complaints made by member(s) of the public, or made on their behalf and with their written consent against a member of the police force, the chief officer of police for the area is under a duty "to take any steps that appear to him to be desirable for the purposes of obtaining or preserving evidence relating to the conduct complained of;" and to record the making of the complaint if he considers he is the "appropriate authority" to deal with it. If he is not, he has to send the complaint, or particulars of it if not in writing, to the "appropriate authority." The chief officer or appropriate authority determines whether the complaint can be dealt with informally or formally and a chief inspector or superior officer may inquire to assist in the making of such a decision. If the chief officer, etc., determines that it shall be investigated formally, he has to appoint an officer to investigate, and he may request a chief officer from another area to supply an investigating officer. If

---

[77] The Triennial Report of the P.C.B., Cmnd. 7966; the Plowden Report, Cmnd. 8193; the Home Affairs Committee, (1981–82 H.C. 98, 1) and the Government reply, Cmnd. 8681 (1982).

the request is made, an officer must be provided. Informal investigation requires the consent of the complainant and concerns complaints that would not justify a criminal or disciplinary charge if proved. There are separate provisions for complaints against officers above the rank of chief superintendent. The last tier concerns those complaints which the chief officer has to refer to the Authority and these include complaints concerning death or serious injury and those covered by statutory regulations; the chief officer also has power to refer to the Authority any complaint which is not required to be referred. The Authority has power to require submission of a complaint which has not been referred by the chief officer, etc., and the latter may refer any *indication* of commission of a criminal or disciplinary offence by officers of chief superintendent rank or below not contained in a complaint to the Authority because of their gravity or exceptional circumstances. The Authority shall supervise investigations which they receive on a mandatory reference and they must supervise other investigations, including those into specific allegations, etc., where they consider it "desirable in the public interest" that they should do so. The Authority has power to approve the appointment of investigating officers for supervised investigations. Supervised inquiry reports are sent to the Authority and the chief officer, etc., and the complainant may receive "if practicable to do so," a copy of the Authority's "appropriate statement" to the chief officer, etc., stating whether the Authority is satisfied with the investigation, or if not why not. If the complaint is not supervised, only the chief officer, etc., receives a copy of the investigating officer's report. Regulations are to provide for supply of a copy of the complaint to the complainant and the officer investigated. Complaints about "direction or control" *viz.* policy are not covered by the procedure, and nor are complaints about conduct which have been, or are, the subject of criminal or disciplinary proceedings.

The chief officer decides whether the investigation has revealed a criminal offence appropriate for disciplinary charges or serious enough to refer to the Director of Public Prosecutions (D.P.P.). The Authority has to be informed, after the D.P.P. has decided upon the criminal issue if referred to him, whether disciplinary charges are being brought; if not why not and, if brought, whether as a consequence of criminal or disciplinary offences, and other matters. The Authority can direct a chief officer to refer a report to the D.P.P., or to bring disciplinary charges himself and may ask for "such information as they may reasonably require" to discharge this last function. Disciplinary tribunals held pursuant to the direction of the Authority will comprise the chief officer (the Commissioner or his nominee in London) as chairman and two members of the Authority who have not been involved in the case. Police committees must keep themselves informed of the manner in which complaints against members of the force are dealt with. The Authority must not disclose information received, though they do make various reports to the Secretary of State.[78] Regulations are to provide for an informal complaints procedure and provision of information to the Authority. Significantly "double jeopardy" has been amended. This was where the P.C.B. had interpreted the decision of the D.P.P. not to prosecute a criminal charge,[79] to necessitate that disciplinary charges should not be directed to be brought where the same issues had to be proved in a disciplinary charge as in the criminal charge. This had caused great controversy and a ruling from the High Court that a fixed practice by the P.C.B. was *ultra vires*.[79a] Doubtless the details of the new arrangements will be contained in guidance to be issued by the Secretary of State.

The P.C.A. is not an independent Ombudsman, although considerable effort has been invested to present the Authority as a truly impartial entity. It is true to say that the police will still investigate the vast majority of complaints themselves without supervision from the P.C.A. and that apart from the informal procedure, the likelihood in practice is that the formal investigations will be considered as internal disciplinary matters; and it is interesting to note that the disciplinary rules have been amended.[80] That apart, one wonders how open and perspicuous the new procedures and accountability devices will be, given the fact that police criticism of Lord Scarman's report was so scathing at one stage, that the Law Lord felt obliged to call a press confer-

---

[78] When requested to do so; when the "gravity or exceptional circumstances" of a subject necessitates, in their opinion, a report; and a triennial report on the working of the complaints machinery, and an annual report.

[79] As well as considering the Police Act 1976, s.3(8) and Home Office Guidelines.

[79a] In exercising his discretion to prosecute or not, the D.P.P. sought a degree of probability of success of at least 51 per cent. *i.e.* higher than a normal prosecution. See *R.* v. *P.C.B. ex p. Madden* [1983] 2 All E.R. 353 and the fettering of discretion by the P.C.B. *The Guardian* estimated that 20,000 cases could possibly be affected, December 23, 1982.

[80] Indeed, the Legend to Pt. 9 of the Act is "Complaints and Discipline." Officers are to be given the opportunity to comment on complaints processed informally. A police officer found guilty of a disciplinary charge can appeal to the Secretary of State, who will issue guidance to chief officers on complaints and discipline. The Home Secretary has bowed to pressure from the Police Federation to allow officers facing disciplinary charges involving a possibility of dismissal, demotion or resignation, to be legally represented; *cf. Maynard* v. *Osmond* [1977] 1 All E.R. 64, and s.102.

ence to reply to criticisms that he had undermined police authority. The Police Federation vacillated in its attitude to an independent complaints authority and on the general theme of accountability, the Commissioner of the Metropolitan Police issued a report on that force in January 1983. Great stress was placed by the Commissioner on accountability to the public, yet the 50 page report was not shown to the public—they, the press and M.P.s received a 10 page summary.[81]

(e) Local Consultation

General accountability is to be provided by the statutory duty upon the police authority, after consulting the chief constable, to make arrangements which they are under a duty to review "from time to time," in each police area to obtain "the views of the people in that area about matters concerning the policing of the area" and for obtaining cooperation in crime prevention. Separate arrangements are to be made for London centering on each borough or each district as appropriate. The Commissioner has to take account of guidance issued by the Secretary of State, and "shall consult" the council of each London borough or district about the appropriate arrangements. The Secretary of State has a general power to ask for reports on the arrangements and to require a review of the arrangements.

One should immediately note the vacuousness of many of these provisions. What, for instance, will the bodies be allowed to discuss? How will the subjects be chosen? How will membership be comprised? There is a good amount of discretion suffusing statutory duties, which will no doubt be supplemented by well-intended administrative guidelines urging full consultation. There is no provision ensuring that the chief constable, or commissioner, takes a "serious look" at the views of the bodies. Non-statutory interim procedures had been available for such consultation prior to the enactment of the duty described above, and the Home Office issued *Guidelines on Consultation with the Community*.[82] This provided little detail on: the points of membership and administration outlined at the beginning of the paragraph; law enforcement; and those operational aspects of policing which it would be wrong to

---

[81] A study commissioned by the Metropolitan Police upon themselves revealed widespread misuse of stop and search powers; pervasive racialism; and ingrained "sexist management practices" in the appointment of women police officers which contravened the Sex Discrimination Act (Policy Studies Institute, 1983).

[82] June 1982.

make the subject of local consultation. Clearly, there are policy and investigatory matters which it would be inappropriate to discuss if it hindered criminal investigation. But policy is a term which many feel has been invoked to ensure no discussion with the community or their representatives on aspects of policing that affect the local community in a general fashion, and it is difficult to believe that there will be a widespread change in police attitudes on this topic. Even Lord Scarman believed that not all operational matters should be ruled out of discussion, so that the community could be heard "not only in the development of policing policy, but in the planning of many, though not all, operations against crime."

The actual practices of police forces under the non-statutory liaison schemes varied enormously from those which had appeared to do "nothing except comply with the Home Office guidelines" or which appeared non-existent, to one urban authority which had spelt out the topics for discussion, constitution, membership, etc. . . . Such administrative details were common in the examples, but the Terms of Reference for discussion were almost uniquely detailed. These included:

(1) Provision of a forum for police and community representatives to discuss local policing problems and other matters of mutual concern;
(2) to promote feedback from the community on particular and general policy strategies and modes of operation;
(3) to enable the community to appreciate problems faced by the police in enforcing the law in that community;
(4) to encourage cooperation between the police and the community in the determination of priorities and the development of agreed strategies to deal with particular local problems;
(5) to discuss the effects of past police operations;
(6) to discuss the general implications of any pattern of complaints in the area and the provision of practical advice and assistance to members of the community in dealing with the police;
(7) lay visits to police stations.

At the time of writing, much is in a state of flux, though the above items do represent important issues which it would be appropriate to set down as statutory *minima*. The Home Secretary has for instance, instigated a trial scheme of lay visits to stations as have the Metropolitan Police. On the other hand, by the spring of 1983, it was reported that most London Boroughs had not met the basic criteria set out in the Home Office guidelines.[83] The wide disparity reveals the worst features of loose exhortatory provisions appealing to public authorities' better nature. Will the statutory provisions prove to be more successful?

(5) DATA PROTECTION

The Data Protection Act 1984 which seeks to "protect individuals against potential misuse of personal information held about them on computers" was enacted in July 1984. The Government opted for a Data Protection Registrar to establish the public register of data users and computer bureaux which the public may examine. It will be his responsibility to ensure that all data users and computer bureaux fulfil their statutory obligations and comply with the eight data protection principles. The Home Office press release described the Data Protection Registrar acting as "an Ombudsman for data subjects [who] will investigate complaints from individuals who believe that data relating to them are being held in breach of the principles." Representative groups of data users will be encouraged by him to draw up codes of good practice. Data users have a right of appeal against the Data Protection Registrar's decisions to a Data Protection Tribunal. Certain data will remain outside the protection of the Act. This includes data exempted for the purpose of safeguarding national security when a senior cabinet minister certifies to that effect, data used for payroll and accounting, law enforcement or revenue purposes and health and social work data. The extent of various exemptions has to be finalised. Apart from the exemptions the basic aim is that data subjects will be able to establish what data users have collected on the former. It has to be emphasised that the Act does not cover information which is not the subject of computerised data, such as ordinary files or paper documents.[84]

Conclusion

The development of Ombudsmen, statutory, non-statutory, autonomous or executive[85] knows no bounds in the common law world and beyond. He has been seen as a panacea for the wrongs of central government; local government; city government; health

---

[83] London Association of Community Relations Councils, *The Times*, March 17, 1983. Some boroughs, and the GLC, established their *own* police committees.

[84] The DHSS has asked social service departments to disclose information to individuals on their files, DHSS Circ. No. LAC (83) 14.

[85] That is an internal or "in-house" model.

care; the press[86]; prisons[87]; data collection; retention of official information; and the police, to name but a few. Yet it has to be questioned whether the Ombudsman in a British context is an important legitimating factor; whether in a functional sense, as a matter of constitutional reality or whether from the perspective which the public gains of the various offices. Many authorities have come to view the various Ombudsmen as safe, if something of a nuisance, because after all his office in a British context is carefully constructed to avoid asking the most searching or the most important of questions. This does not mean that the various offices are irrelevant or of no utility—rather perhaps that they do not do enough. It is remarkable how frequently complainants direct their complaints to the wrong Ombudsman.[88] This might fuel the case for those who would wish to see a general Ombudsman Commission covering all Ombudsmen in one office or a Commission for Public Administration as the Social Democratic Party suggested.[89] My own preference is to see the various offices given far greater publicity, expecially the P.C.A. and to increase their powers, especially in relation to enforcement of their decisions against recalcitrant bodies, and to give them power to criticise bad or unfair rules and policies.

Ombudsmen have invariably been attached to institutions which are formally part of our public administration, bodies or institutions that are accountable not through the market, but through the political arena. An interesting extension of the Ombudsman concept has recently occurred in the insurance business in the United Kingdom. An Insurance Ombudsman Bureau opened in 1981, and the scheme operates on a voluntary basis. His decision is not binding unless accepted by the policy holder and he is independent of the companies concerned. His remit includes "handling, investigating and resolving inquiries, complaints, disputes and claims between companies and their members." He can conciliate and arbitrate and make an award of up to £100,000. Member companies have grown considerably in number from his inauguration. There have been recent calls by the N.C.C. for an independent Ombudsman for the banking community in the United Kingdom,[90] to be financed by the banks and which would be based upon the insurance model.

---

[86] Robertson G. *People Against the Press* (1983).
[87] A recent recommendation for a prisons ombudsman has been made by *Justice* (1983).
[88] See (1979–80; H.C. 254) para. 12.
[89] *Taming Leviathan* (1983).
[90] *Banking Services and The Consumer* (1983).

Chapter 6

REMEDIES, AN OVERVIEW AND THE COURTS

It was common-place, recently, to read about the movement away from law, legal process and the representative institutions of government as effective control mechanisms over the exercise of power by the contemporary State. Writers argued that we had seen an increasing resort to administration and government intervention causing the development of a *bureaucratic-regulatory* form of law and government.[1]

This was characterised by the widest delegation of powers and conferral of discretion. The society in which such developments had taken place, it was argued, would have little need for a form of law that was based upon an individualistic outlook which placed freedom of the individual and individual property rights at the centre of its universe. The administrative state had swept aside the supremacy of the individual, and had placed its emphasis upon collective welfare, as interpreted by politicians and officials, and intervention. The current political rhetoric, however, emphasises privatisation, de-regulation, a minimal state and the supremacy of individualistic, or *gesellschaft* law.

I wish to conclude in this chapter by asking what has been learned from the lessons of Chapters 2–5? We still find ourselves in an administrative/regulatory state. It is a contradiction in terms to talk about the State without accepting a governmental and regulatory role, whether such roles are conducted through formal or informal processes. Such roles are still considerable and all pervasive. They have thrown up a host of opportunities, procedures and practices through which grievances may be redressed, opinions expressed and participation allowed. Some general points will follow on these matters.

I will then examine the role of our courts in controlling governmental power, allowing challenge by those aggrieved by administrative decisions and encouraging participation in public decision-

---

[1] Kamenka and Tay, "Beyond Bourgeois Individualism etc." in *Feudalism, Capitalism and Beyond* (Kamenka and Neale eds., 1975).

making. A detailed account of judicial review is not possible, but I will analyse the potential judicial contribution in relation to the practices discussed in preceding chapters.

What Lessons Are There For The Future?

(1) *Accessibility.* The practices and procedures which were examined were invariably precipitated by the need for government to legitimate the exercise of power where the traditional methods for providing or achieving control and accountability were either ineffective or too far removed from most members of society. In a general sense, and all these comments are general and not specific, procedures for remedying grievances must be accessible and open. We saw many examples of procedures which were neither accessible nor open and of whose existence most members of society are ignorant. Where this is the case, the utility of such procedures is singularly impaired. Where there is a real need for confidentiality, it should be respected.

(2) *Effective.* Procedures must be effective and must be shaped appropriately for the task in hand; their powers must be adequate and their objects clearly thought out and published. This may often necessitate a greater degree of clarity on the part of government and officials. This has sometimes been sadly lacking, as witness the Commission for Racial Equality.[2] Complainants must be informed at all stages how their complaint is progressing, and this must be processed as expeditiously as the circumstances allow. Enactment of codes of good administrative practice should be considered where desirable, and too much should not be left to good will and attitude, vital though these are. Grievance procedures must operate against an established set of published performance criteria of service to set realistic standards of performance for the body or area of activity against which complaints are made. In establishing such criteria, interested groups must be given fair and equal access to the process of setting the criteria involved.

(3) *Responsive.* Procedures and practices must operate in a responsive manner. This embraces qualities such as openness; giving of good reasons; providing interviews and explanations orally or in writing and in detail when requested. Complaints should be properly logged, and close liaison should take place between the policy divisions and those divisions where complaints are received so that where necessary policy can be framed, or programmes developed,

[2] See Chap. 4.

with the lessons of such complaints in mind. The degree of impartiality necessary to handle a grievance is obviously a factor of importance, as is the kind of procedure adopted.[3] Sometimes what is needed is an effective means of achieving conciliation. Sometimes independent arbitration after an informal hearing may be desirable or an independently chaired tribunal conducted on formal but not legalistic lines, or a public hearing to press one's case and challenge others. All currently exist; are they as effective and is good practice as widespread as it ought to be?

(4) *Policy.* It will be argued that all the above suggestions are directed towards complaints about the "administrative method" and its impact upon individuals or groups; there is nothing about real participation in shaping policy-making, *i.e.* the "political objectives" of governors.[4] We have seen how policy and merits have, expressly or effectively, been excluded from public discussion. It is the prerogative of Cabinet and respected advisers or designated officials such as Chief Constables. In some cases statements will be made to elected representatives. In other cases they are not made. I have discussed the arguments for revised procedures to act as "Big Inquiries" into major programmes[5] as well as consultation on policy proposals. Short of a decentralised and radically altered system of government[6] what reforms would be desirable to subject policy-making to independent and effective scrutiny. It is obvious that I am not satisfied with Parliament's ability to act as a continuing and effective overseer of policy by itself. It can deliver dramatic and effective rebukes for haughty government. But government is invariably too big, too professional and too adroit for Parliament. A balance has to be struck between government without effective restraint, and government which is in the hands of powerful minority interest groups and which cannot govern.

The former Permanent Secretary to the Treasury, Sir Douglas Wass, has argued for a large, single, permanent Royal Commission "from which panels would be drawn to carry out specific studies."[7] The Commission "would decide which issues to investigate, what terms of reference to give its panels and who should sit

---

[3] Ganz (1972) P.L. 215 and 299.

[4] See Wass, n.7, *infra.*

[5] Chap. 2.

[6] I do not intend this subject to be ruled out of consideration.

[7] Wass, *Government and the Governed* (1984), Chap. 6. He saw it possessing about 200 members. Appointment would be by the Crown on the recommendation of the Prime Minister. Clearly one must be alive to the dangers of patronage and this method of appointment is not adequate by itself.

on them." Appointed for a fixed period on the advice of the Prime Minister, it could co-opt specialist advisers and would appoint its own executive and Chairman. Where desirable "a dialogue could be established with appropriate Select Committees." It would possess a "limitless" remit into constitutional and major change, drawing membership from the professions, commerce, industry and banking, education, social work and so on. It would be an advisory and recommendatory body, not an executive one. This may not be quite a realisation of John Stuart Mill's:

> "Nothing less can be ultimately desirable than the admission of all to a share in the sovereign power of the State"

but it is an important idea and one that government cynicism ought not to be allowed to destroy.

What role can we expect the courts to play in the redress of grievances, as it is the courts that many regard as the overall quality control mechanism?

The Courts

The constitution settlement of the seventeenth century ensured that there would be no "independent" safeguard which was "somewhat fundamental" to act as a corrective to governmental excesses.[8] The supremacy of common law and its proprietary basis over other forms of law is well recorded,[9] as is the supremacy of Parliament over common law.[9a] What is of present interest are two developing themes in our public law.

The first has been the increasing reminders from the European Commission and Court of Human Rights of the failure of judicially

---

[8] Impeachment was the preserve of Parliament and it has not been used against an unpopular Minister since 1715. Criminal impeachment was last used in 1805: Roberts, *The Growth of Responsible Government in Stuart England* (1966); Berger, *Impeachment* (1973). For the development of ministerial responsibility, see Roberts *op. cit.*

[9] Both the *cursus scaccarii* of the Court of Exchequer—"the nearest approach to a body of administrative law that the English legal system has ever known" Holdsworth *A History of English Law* (Vol. 1)—and the Star Chamber and prerogative courts developed tendencies towards a public law *system* as opposed to distinct forms of relief. The seventeenth century ensured that the common law would succeed in having these developments interpreted as historical aberrations.

[9a] And see *Burmah Oil Co.* v. *Lord Advocate* [1965] A.C. 75 and War Damage Act 1965; *Shah* v. *Barnet L.B.C.* [1983] 1 All E.R. 226 H.L. and Education Fees and Awards Act 1983. Judicial decisions are frequently nullified by statutory regulations: Prosser, *The Test Case Strategy* (1983).

developed law in the United Kingdom to provide adequate protection for individuals in the field of human rights.[10] Even though the Convention is not part of our domestic law,[11] the areas affected by decisions of the Court and Commission and the prompting these have given to legislative reform and judicial development are becoming legion.[12] Less dramatic has been the impact of European law, which is a part of our domestic law,[13] though the field of equal pay has been directly and significantly affected by our Treaty obligations.[14]

The second theme is the much acclaimed[15] judicial development or creation of a "procedural public law" and a "coherent system of administrative law." The statement of Lord Diplock that there has been

"progress towards a *comprehensive system* of administrative law that I regard as having been *the greatest achievement of the English courts* in my judicial life-time"

[10] *Silver* v. *U.K.* Judgment, March 25, 1983 2/1981/41/60–66; *Malone* v. *U.K.* Judgment, August 2, 1984, 4/1983/60/94; *Campbell and Fell* v. *U.K.* Judgment, June 28, 1984 10/1982/52/85–86; *Dudgeon* v. *U.K.* 1982 4 E.H.R.R. 149; *X* v. *U.K.* (1982) 4 E.H.R.R. 181; *Ireland* v. *U.K.* Series A, Judgment, January 18, 1978; the *East Africans' case* (1981) 3 E.H.R.R. 76; *Tyrer* v. *U.K.* (1980) 2 E.H.R.R. I; *Campbell and Cosans* v. *U.K.* (1982) 4 E.H.R.R.

[11] Art. 25 of the Convention allows *individual* applications to be made to the Commission, although the Home Office has opposed ratification of Art. 25 in the past. In 1981 there were 132 applications under Art. 25 against the U.K., Germany was second with 109. The provisions of the Convention are not, apparently, "relevant considerations" to take into account in the exercise of a ministerial discretion: *R.* v. *Secretary of State ex p. Kirkwood* [1984] 1 W.L.R. 913. The Convention is employed by English judges as an aid to the interpretation of statutes, but not common law: *Malone* v. *Metropolitan Police Commissioner* [1979] 2 W.L.R. 700.

[12] One of the more famous pieces of legislation is the Contempt of Court Act 1981 following the *Sunday Times* v. *U.K.*: Judgment of April 26, 1979, Series A, Vol. 30. For judicial decisions on prison administration see *R.* v. *Governor of Wormwood Scrubs ex p. Tarrant* and *ex p. Anderson* [1984] 1 All E.R. 799 and 920; which held respectively that a prisoner may be entitled in appropriate circumstances to be represented before an adjudication heard by the board of visitors and that insistence that a prisoner ventilate his complaint of prison treatment internally before contacting a lawyer was *ultra vires*. Birkinshaw, "*Legal Order and Prison Administration*" (1983) 34 N.I.L.Q. 269. In *Golder* v. *U.K.*, Judgment of February 21, 1975, Series A, Vol. 18 the European Court of Human Rights held that a prisoner was entitled to see a lawyer to initiate legal proceedings. The Home Office effectively nullified this decision by an internal circular: C.I. 45/75. See now *Silver op. cit.* n. 10, *supra*.

[13] European Communities Act 1972, s.2(1).

[14] *McCarthys* v. *Smith* [1981] Q.B. 180, C.J.E.C. and C.A.; and *E.C. Commission* v. *U.K. and N. Ireland* (No. 165/82) [1984] 1 All E.R. 353 C.J.E.C.

[15] Especially by the judiciary.

captures the mood.[16] The recent decision of the Law Lords that executive action under the royal prerogative was reviewable in a court of law—at least in those subject areas which are appropriate for judicial review—is a landmark.[17] In that case, however, the Law Lords held that the Government ban on trade union membership at General Communications Head-Quarters was not unlawful *because* the Government had established that the ban was necessary in "the interests of national security."[18] The onus was upon the Government to establish such a ground. In other cases, courts have held that statutory language should be interpreted in a manner which necessitates that a factual basis is established before an executive discretion is exercised. In *Tameside, Khawaja, Guardian Newspapers* and the *G.C.H.Q.* decisions[19] the courts would not accept the bare assertion of the executive, or the *ex facie* reasonableness of executive discretionary action.[20] The *G.C.H.Q.* decision was also the occasion when Lord Diplock suggested a

[16] *I.R.C.* v. *National Federation of Self Employed and Small Businesses* [1982] A.C. 617.

[17] *Council of Civil Service Unions* v. *Minister for Civil Service* [1984] 3 All E.R. 935, H.L. There was doubt expressed by Lords Fraser and Brightman whether the Royal Prerogative itself as opposed to power delegated under it, was reviewable, though Lords Diplock, Scarman and Roskill suggested it was. See *R.* v. *Criminal Injuries Compensation Board ex p. Lain* [1967] 2 Q.B. 864 and *R.* v. *Secretary of State ex p. Hosenball* [1977] 3 All E.R. 452 at 459 where it was respectively held and suggested that prerogative procedures were subject to judicial review.

[18] There was apprehension that industrial disruption by unions would interfere with the security of the U.K. military and official communications and intelligence services at G.C.H.Q.

[19] *Secretary of State for Education and Science* v. *Tameside M.B.C.* [1977] A.C. 1014; *Khawaja* v. *Secretary of State for the Home Department* [1983] 2 W.L.R. 321, H.L.; *Secretary of State for Defence* v. *Guardian Newspapers* [1984] 3 W.L.R. 986, H.L.; G.C.H.Q. decision, *op. cit.* n. 17 *supra. Khawaja* established that the scope of review in habeas corpus was not confined to the "reasonableness" of the authority's *ex facie* case, but could establish the factual basis of the charge which the authorities would have to prove on a balance of probabilities. There was timely judicial support for Lord Atkin's dissenting judgment in *Liversidge* v. *Anderson* [1942] A.C. 206. *Cf. R.* v. *Secretary of State for the Home Department ex p. Ali* [1984] 1 W.L.R. 663.

[20] Though it would be too ambitious to suggest the development of a "substantial evidence" test as in the U.S.A. For the basic test on judicial treatment of facts, see *Edwards* v. *Bairstow* [1956] A.C. 14 and *Global Plant* v. *Secretary of State* [1972] 1 Q.B. 139. Statutory applications to quash under the Town and Country Planning Act 1971 have frequently been the occasion for a probing inquiry into facts supporting a decision: *Colleen Properties* v. *Minister of Housing and Local Government* [1971] 1 W.L.R. 433; *Niarchos (London)* v. *Secretary of State for the Environment* (1977) 76 L.G.R. 480; *Prest* v. *Secretary of State for Wales* (1983) 81 L.G.R. 193, C.A.

coherent categorisation of judicial review under the heads of: illegality (*ultra vires* proper); irrationality (abuse, etc., of discretion); "procedural impropriety" (breach of fair procedure/natural justice). He added "proportionality" as developed by French, German and EEC law. This is a review of the *merits* of a decision if it suggests "overkill" or is out of proportion to legitimate objectives.[21]

A development of singular importance was the reformulation of R.S.C. Order 53—the *Application of Judicial Review*.[22] This has made more coherent the procedure for application for judicial review so that *all* forms of relief: *viz*. certiorari, prohibition, mandamus[23] as well as declarations and injunctions[24] can be applied for in one proceeding, and can be coupled with each other and a claim for damages.[25] Relief under Order 53 is discretionary and is not given as of right.[25a] Recent decisions have insisted that review of a decision or action of a public body or official must be made by

---

[21] It is a far more probing test for the review of a discretion than provided by Lord Greene in *Associated Provincial Picture Houses* v. *Wednesbury Corporation* [1948] 1 K.B. 223, C.A. *cf. Padfield* v. *Minister of Agriculture, Fisheries and Food* [1968] A.C. 997.

[22] Now contained in statute: Supreme Court Act 1981, s.31; Order 53 is in S.I. 1977 No. 1955; and see S.I. 1980, No. 2000. It has recently been re-affirmed that Order 53 is a *procedural* and not a *substantive* reform, so that it cannot take away pre-existing rights: *Wandsworth L.B.C.* v. *Winder* [1984] 3 All E.R. 976, H.L.

[23] Certiorari is a device used to quash decisions of, originally, an inferior judicial body which were outside its jurisdictional powers or contained an error of law on the face of the record. Prohibition was an instruction to an inferior judicial body not to continue exceeding its jurisdiction. Their scope has long since transcended judicial or quasi-judicial bodies. Mandamus is an instruction ordering a public body or official to perform his lawful duties, *e.g.* exercise a discretion properly.

[24] The best treatment of public law remedies is in de Smith, *Judicial Review of Administrative Action* (1980). See Law Commission: Working Paper No. 40 (1970); Law Commission No. 73, Cmnd. 6407 (1976).

[25] A prerogative order could not be applied for in the same proceedings as a declaration or injunction prior to the reforms. Nor could a claim for damages be made with a prerogative order. Under Order 53, r.9(5) if proceedings are commenced by judicial review but it becomes apparent that they should have been commenced by writ the court hearing the application can treat the matter as if it commenced by writ.

[25a] It may be refused if, *e.g.* the applicant has behaved badly or is undeserving or the application is made after "undue delay" and if successful would be "likely to cause substantial hardship to, or substantially prejudice the rights of any person or would be detrimental to good administration": Order 53, r. 4; Supreme Court Act 1981, s.31(6). The time limit for application is three months, but this would not appear to be a right as "undue delay" *might* defeat the application on the grounds stated above even within three months: S.I. 1980 No. 2000. The three month period is subject to statutory or rule of court limitations upon seeking review, *e.g.* the six week rule in planning cases for an application to quash.

Order 53 procedure,[26] unless the applicant can show a breach of a private right,[27] in which case he may proceed by private action[28]; or he may raise the issue collaterally as a defence or attack in other proceedings.[29] A "Crown Office List" has been established which will be handled by judges who are, and who will become more expert in "procedural public law."[30]

All is not quite a picture of coherence. The public/private division is far from clear-cut in many situations.[31] The occasions when parties may challenge public decision-making by private action are unclear. Exercise by a public body of its contractual powers would appear not to be susceptible, generally, to Order 53 relief.[32] Withdrawal of licences would be.[33] The scope of the award of declarations and injunctions under Order 53 is still uncertain and has

---

[26] *O'Reilly* v. *Mackman* [1983] A.C. 120, H.L.; *Cocks* v. *Thanet D.C.* [1983] A.C. 286 H.L., *cf.* for Scotland *Brown* v. *Hamilton D.C.* (1983) *Scots Law Times* 397 (a working party was subsequently established to recommend a simple form of judicial review in Scotland); if an individual is seeking review of a private body's decision or action, private law procedure and not Order 53 is the necessary procedure: *Law* v. *National Greyhound Racing Club* [1983] 1 W.L.R. 1302, C.A. Public law tests of natural justice are applicable in many private relationships: *McInnes* v. *Onslow-Fane* [1978] 1 W.L.R. 1520; but tests of "reasonableness" in the exercise of a private discretion are rarely applicable unless a statute has introduced them, *e.g.* Unfair Contract Terms Act 1977; Employment Act 1980, s.4(2). See *Peabody Housing Association* v. *Green* (1978) 38 P. and C.R. 644; but see *Cheall* v. *Apex* [1982] 3 All E.R. 855 and review of a union rule-book *per* Lord Denning, and generally decisions on restraint of trade.

[27] Such as breach of contract, breach of duty of care, trespass or misfeasance of public office, etc., *i.e.* a "cause of action."

[28] *Davy* v. *Spelthorne B.C.* [1983] 3 W.L.R. 742, H.L. or as in *Cooper* v. *Wandsworth Board of Works* (1863) 14 C.B. (N.S.) 180; and *Ridge* v. *Baldwin* [1964] A.C. 40.

[29] *Wandsworth L.B.C.* v. *Winder* [1984] 3 W.L.R. 563, C.A. and [1984] 3 All E.R. 976, H.L. though *cf.* Lord Fraser at 980*b* (unreasonable termination of statutory security of tenure under contract. *NB* public sector tenancies at common law *Cannock Chase D.C.* v. *Kelly* [1978] 1 All E.R. 152.

[30] L. Blom Cooper (1982) P.L. 250.

[31] As witness for instance the discussion of quasi-government in Chapter 4 and the intermediate nature of many quasi-governmental institutions. See, *e.g. Peabody*, n. 26, *supra* for the position of housing associations. What of bodies established by Treasury Minute or "shadow" bodies set up informally? For review of recommendatory statutory bodies, see: *R.* v. *Boundary Commission for England ex p. Foot* [1983] Q.B. 600.

[32] *R.* v. *Post Office ex p. Byrne* [1975] I.C.R. 221; *R.* v. *B.B.C. ex p. Lavelle* [1983] 1 All E.R. 241; *R.* v. *East Berkshire Health Authority ex p. Walsh* [1984] 3 All E.R. 425, C.A., though failure to *incorporate* statutory contractual terms by public employers may be reviewable under Order 53, *sed quaere*? *R.* v. *Secretary of State ex p. Benwell* [1984] 3 W.L.R. 843 (Order 53 only remedy available on the facts).

[33] *R.* v. *Barnsley M.B.C. ex p. Hook* [1976] 3 All E.R. 452.

been hampered by conceptualisations pre-dating the reform of Order 53.[34] In their desire to protect public bodies from vexatious and tardy litigants, the courts have insisted that judicial review of a public body, etc., must be sought by Order 53. This requires leave and removes some of the procedural advantages of private action to establish the facts.[35]

One can speak more optimistically of the generous accommodation given to the interpretation of "sufficient interest" when determining which applicants may invoke the courts in judicial review.[36] The *National Federation* case suggests that each case will be dealt with with specific reference to its context and background.[37] If an applicant can raise a suspicion of unlawful activity in the exer-

---

[34] See Lord Scarman in *I.R.C.* v. *National Federation of the Self Employed and Small Businesses* [1982] A.C. 617 at 647–648 and Lord Wilberforce in *Davy* v. *Spelthorne B.C.* [1983] 3 All E.R. 278 at 287. The general tenor of these *dicta* is to the effect that the injunction and declaration may only be awarded where prerogative orders may be awarded. This would cut down the scope of Order 53 substantially and cannot be correct; see n. 22, *supra* and Lord Fraser. It seems that a declaration is the only method by which a statutory instrument can be impugned: *Hotel and Catering Industry Training Board* v. *Automobile Proprietary* [1969] 1 W.L.R. 697 (H.L.); *Hoffman La Roche* v. *Secretary of State for Trade and Industry* [1974] 2 All E.R. 1128, H.L. at 1153, 1159. For bye-laws see *Daymond* v. *Plymouth C.C.* [1976] A.C. 609. See Slade L.J. in *Law* v. *N.G.R.C.* note 26, *supra*. In *R.* v. *Secretary of State for the Environment ex p. Brent L.B.C.* [1982] Q.B. 593 D.C. and *R.* v. *Secretary of State for the Environment ex p. Hackney L.B.C.* [1983] 1 W.L.R. 524, D.C. both cases proceeded on the assumption that declarations could be awarded in circumstances where prerogative orders could not be awarded, or awarded only with difficulty. See further Woolf J. in *Ex p. Lavelle* [1983] 1 All E.R. 241, Q.B.D. and *R.* v. *Bromley L.B.C. ex p. Lambeth L.B.C., The Times* June 16, 1984. Injunctions may not be awarded against the Crown: Crown Proceedings Act 1947, s.21 and *cf. ex p. Kirkwood* [1984] 1 W.L.R. 913. For the difficulty in obtaining mandatory injunctions against public bodies see *De Falco* v. *Crawley B.C.* [1980] Q.B. 460, C.A. and *Smith* v. *I.L.E.A.* [1978] 1 All E.R. 411 at 418; *cf. American Cyanamid* v. *Ethicon* [1975] A.C. 396.

[35] Judicial review is a two-stage process; leave to apply followed by full hearing which can be expedited, see *R.* v. *Commissioner etc. ex p. Stipplechoice, The Times*, January 23, 1985, C.A. Review takes place in London. Cross examination, discovery, etc., can take place, but they are rare.

[36] *Barrs* v. *Bethell* [1982] Ch. 294 for a recent test under private law.

[37] *I.R.C.* v. *National Federation of the Self Employed and Small Businesses* [1982] A.C. 617 and Supreme Court Act 1981, s.31(3). For *locus standi* in private law litigation see: *Gouriet* v. *Union of Post Office Workers* [1978] A.C. 435. *Cf. Gillick* v. *West Norfolk and Wisbech Area Health Authority* [1984] Q.B. 581 where a parent sought a declaration in private law to declare that advice in a D.H.S.S. circular on prescription of contraceptives to a girl under 16 was *unlawful*; and *Att.-Gen* v. *Able* [1984] 3 W.L.R. 845. *Cp.* Local Government Act 1972, s.222 where local authorities can institute civil proceedings "protecting and promoting" the interests of local inhabitants: *Stoke-on-Trent C.C.* v. *B & Q Ltd.* [1983] 2 All E.R. 787.

cise of public power, no matter how recondite the power, sufficient interest may be established to make a challenge.[38] Whether
this will make a difference to the likelihood of success at the full
hearing is another issue.[39] I cannot, however, see the role of the
courts changing dramatically in assisting in the resolution of
grievances against the State.

In the United States, use of class actions, modified rules on *locus
standi* and the *Brandeis Brief*[40] together with the insistence that
regulatory agencies promulgate policy by rule-making and not
adjudication wherever possible, have all created far greater opportunities for legal process to be used as a starting point for the
mobilisation of collective rights and interests.[41] There are many
opportunities for interested parties to participate in varying
degrees of formality in agency rule-making which are far more
advanced than any British analogue. Doubtless, a constitutional
culture which emphasises the importance of due process of law and
equal protection of the law provides much of an impetus for law to

---

[38] In *R.* v. *Secretary of State for Social Services ex p. GLC, The Times* August 16,
1984 the Child Poverty Action Group, but not the GLC had sufficient interest to
bring an application under Order 53 on behalf of unidentified claimants wrong-
fully deprived supplementary benefit.

[39] See, *e.g. R.* v. *I.B.A. ex p. Whitehouse* (1984) 81 L.S.Gaz. 1992 and *R.* v. *Secretary of State for the Environment ex p. Ward* [1984] 1 W.L.R. 834. In *Ward's*
case, there is a statement to the effect that although a party may not have a private interest to found an action for breach of statutory duty, he may well have
"sufficient interest" for Order 53 review. What of situations where courts have
ruled that breach of a statute or statutory rules does not confer a right of action,
e.g. Prison Rules, and a prisoner claims that the rule is *ultra vires* seeking relief
under Order 53? He will have "sufficient interest" for Order 53 purposes when
seeking a declaration or mandamus. See *Williams* v. *Home Office No. 2* [1981] 1
All E.R. 1211, Q.B.D. *Raymond* v. *Honey* [1983] A.C. 1 and *NB. Ex p. Anderson* [1984] 1 All E.R. 920; *R.* v. *Secretary of State for the Home Department ex p.
Benwell* [1984] 3 W.L.R. 843; and *R.* v. *Deputy Governor of Camphill Prison ex
p. King* [1984] 3 All E.R. 897, C.A.

[40] The brain-child of Louis Brandeis (*Muller* v. *Oregon* 208 U.S. 412 (1908)) which
is a device for introducing social, economic and wider implications of a possible
decision before the court. His brief contained two pages of legal argument and
over 100 pages on the social and physiological benefits of reducing the working
hours of women. Similarly in the U.S.A. *amicus* briefs for interested groups are
a widely used device to widen the range of argument before courts in cases dealing with constitutional rights. *Amicus* briefs in the important case of *Regents of
University of California* v. *Bakke* 438 U.S. 265 (1978) which concerned reverse
discrimination, ran to three volumes. See Prosser, *The Test Case Strategy* (1983).

[41] Rule-making is prospective, collective and legislative as opposed to adjudication
which is usually but not exclusively retrospective and individualistic, *cf.* Shapiro
78 Harv. L.R. 921 (1965). On Executive delegated legislation and Congressional
"restraint," see: *Chadha* 51 U.S. Law Week 4907 (1983).

be used as a medium to raise issues of wide political concern in a manner which would be alien in British courts. It is also true to say that the American political and legislative processes had become so controlled by powerful vested interests, and the agencies alternated in their symbiotic relationships with the regulated so frequently that it was difficult to assess who was regulating whom; in these circumstances the courts became the only channel through which the small man, the "new propertied" man, could register his stake in the constitutional scheme of things. What can prevent courts, however, becoming the preserve of the mighty?

Let us examine how frequently Order 53 is invoked, and relief granted.[42]

Criminal		*Civil*	
1981 Leave granted	113	Leave granted	263
Leave refused	45	Leave refused	112
Relief granted	53	Relief granted	66
Applications dismissed	38	Applications dismissed	114
1982 Leave granted	121	Leave granted	347
Leave refused	49	Leave refused	168
Relief granted	61	Relief granted	87
Applications dismissed	39	Applications dismissed	111
1983 Leave granted	127	Leave granted	494 (sic!)
Leave refused	53	Leave refused	176
Relief granted	54	Relief granted	108
Applications dismissed	36	Applications dismissed	113

For *appeals* from bodies exercising statutory administrative, judicial or quasi-judicial functions, the issue of standing for an appellant is usually straightforward if a party has been involved in a two cornered encounter with an authority over the issue of a licence, grant, permission, etc. More difficult are those cases such as planning, compulsory purchase or environmental matters where statute allows a "person aggrieved" to apply to the High Court usually to have a decision by an authority or Minister quashed within a specified period (often six weeks) on the grounds that it was not within the powers of the Act.[43] Courts have given a wide berth to

---

[42] Judicial Statistics 1982 (Cmnd. 9065). See de Smith, *Judicial Review of Administrative Action* (4th ed., 1980), p. 31 for statistics on applications and awards under judicial review prior to 1978. Paucity of number should not be taken as an indicator of quality of decision.

[43] *e.g.* Town and Country Planning Act 1971, ss.242, 244 and 245. *See R. v. Secretary of State for the Environment ex.p. Ostler* [1977] Q.B. 122, and for the P.C.A. on the same case (1976–77 H.C. 524), pp. 16–18.

the grounds of "statutory quashing."[44] Conversely "person aggrieved" has been given a narrow interpretation in litigation and usually means a person with a *specific legal* interest in the issue.[45] In *Buxton* v. *Minister of Housing and Local Government,*[46] the plaintiff sought to set aside a grant of planning permission on the grounds of a blatant impropriety by the Ministry. Because in law the development proposed would not constitute a nuisance to his land, he had no legal grievance against the authority and, therefore, was not a "person aggrieved" entitled to seek an order to quash. Recent cases have, in their *obiter dicta,* not followed this narrow position suggesting that any person allowed to participate in the proceedings, *e.g.* a public inquiry, should have the right to make the application to the court.[47] An important development came in the *People Before Profit* litigation[48] where an action group had participated at a month long inquiry into a proposed local plan[49] of the local authority. The authority overrode the inspector's report which supported various objections made at the inquiry by the group against the plan, and rather peremptorily awarded planning permission in accordance with the plan. After the inquiry, the group became incorporated as a company limited by guarantee which meant technically it was a different legal entity from the group which objected at the inquiry and they sought to challenge the action of the authority. They sought relief by judicial review under Order 53. It was held that they were a body with "sufficient interest" as they were essentially the same group and legal technicalities ought not to defeat the merits. This seems to be a wider interpretation of standing than would be afforded by the "person aggrieved" formulation so common in specific statutory provisions allowing applications to quash. Nevertheless, the judge held with "very great regret" that their application failed on other grounds. Objectors had only a limited right of ultimate objection

---

[44] See n. 20, *supra* and also under different statutory schemes *Ashbridge Investments Ltd.* v. *Minister of Housing and Local Government* [1965] 1 W.L.R. 1320; *Robertson* v. *Secretary of State for the Environment* [1976] 1 All E.R. 689, Q.B.D. (application unsuccessful).

[45] The authorities for this proposition are cases dealing with the interests of creditors in bankruptcy proceedings in the 19th century; not quite the appropriate analogy of planning and environmental decisions of the late twentieth century.

[46] [1961] 1 Q.B. 278, Q.B.D.

[47] *Turner* v. *Secretary of State for the Environment* (1973) 28 P. and C.R. 123 and *Bizony* v. *Secretary of State for the Environment* (1975) 239 E.G. 281. The discussion of *Bushell* in Chap. 2 should be re-called at this point.

[48] *R.* v. *Hammersmith and Fulham L.B.C. ex p. People Before Profit* (1982) L.G.R. 322, Q.B.D.

[49] For local plans, see Chap. 3, *supra.*

even though the inquiry had come out almost entirely in their favour. Indeed, he thought "public inquiries very often may have no useful purpose at all . . . I am slightly perturbed that a public inquiry can take place and its findings be so favourable and yet the authority can dismiss it virtually out of hand . . . the objectors won after a month's inquiry and lost after a few minutes consideration by the (planning) committee." Had leave to proceed been granted, £5,000 security for costs would have been sought by the judge. And this brings us to the non-legal dimension restricting judicial relief against the State—money.

The State is its own financier—at our expense. In the field of litigation it is a "repeat player" while most litigants are "one-shotters."[50] To the latter, litigation is an unusual and often daunting experience. The former possess the expertise, the resources, the time; litigation is an occupational hazard and the costs do not fall on individual shoulders. Not all who litigate with the state are "one-shotters" of course, and to achieve some semblance of opportunity to use law as a device for protecting rights or interests, individuals often merge into groups advocating causes or issues and utilise devices such as the "Test Case" strategy.[51] Financing such litigation is nonetheless problemmatical unless privately funded. The award of legal aid displays a structural antipathy towards collective action[52-53] and posits whether the hypothetical individual would risk his own money on litigation. Public Interest law groups or neighbourhood law centres which provide a legal service to areas and issues which law has tended to neglect, rely upon public funding and charity. The latter are always at risk that public funding will cease if they act "politically" which is a fre-

---

[50] A phrase of Marc Galanter "Why the 'Haves' come out ahead: Speculations on the Limits of Legal Change." (1974) 9 *Law and Society Review* 95.

[51] See Prosser, *The Test Case Strategy* 1983.

[52-53] White "Lawyers and the Enforcement of Rights" in *Social Needs and Legal Action* (White, Morris and Lewis. ed. 1973); "The Distasteful Character of Litigation for Poor Persons" in *Lawyers in their Social Setting* (McCormick ed. 1976); Lewis, "Unmet Legal Need" in *Social Needs and Legal Action*. See also the Royal Commission on Legal Services (1979), *infra* and the Government Response Cmnd. 9077 (1983). The government places full emphasis upon the independent legal profession operating upon market principles and "legal aid from public funds should be available in appropriate cases for *individuals* who have inadequate resources." The Government "looks to the professions to maintain standards" of vitality and independence and to maintain "freedom under the law." It rejected a Council for Legal Services and Ministerial Responsibility for legal services in any particular area. Legal aid for "groups" was available in some cases (Legal Aid Handbook 1983) though individuals should learn to "pool their resources." All in all, it really is an apologia for the *status quo*.

quent complaint where they are challenging their paymasters for failing in public duties in housing, social services, public health, etc., or a government agency or influential institution. The problems encountered by the Community Development Project were referred to in Chapter 3. The Project's use of legal processes *inter alia* to ventilate collective grievances about inadequate housing policies; bureaucratic high-handedness; arbitrary management and allocation of capital were not tolerated. It was seen as being all the more offensive when the public purse was funding the activity. Is there something improper about the use of legal processes for such purposes? *The Law Centres Federation* in a criticism of the Royal Commission on Legal Services[54] stated 29 examples of work which they perform of a kind not catered for by private practitioners. These examples "should be uncontentious—each involved the provision of advice and assistance on matters relating to English law, albeit delivered in innovative fashion (and) have generated controversy and subjected the centres involved to outspoken attack. Regrettably, this seems bound up with the fact that law centre services are different from those traditionally provided, and because they are provided to different individuals and groups from those who had previously had access to legal resources . . . these novel ways of working involve acting on issues and against people or institutions who have previously been relatively immune from effective legal action."

Inevitably, reaction from frustrated campaigners included the belief that law, and legal process, is a sham, unable to live up to its rhetoric if asked to strike against vested interests of a public or private nature.[55] Certainly law has not assisted in the creation of a surrogate political process for those unable to utilise political mechanisms or influence political elites. Groups or individuals may be far more interested to influence the outcome of a decision by participating in its making rather than attacking it after the event. The United States has developed certain participatory procedures in public decision-making which offer more formal guarantees of opportunity for interested parties to contribute to decision-making than any British analogue. Agency rule-making is a clear example, and there are specific and general obligations in federal law for interested parties to be informed and provided with opportunity to make comment upon proposed rules, provide coun-

---

[54] The Law Centres' Federation, *Response to the Royal Commission on Legal Services* (1979).

[55] For an interesting account of the varying responses to the use of law and legal processes in the attempt to redress such social and economic imbalances, see Newham Rights Centre Report (1974–1975).

ter arguments to others' comments and for the agency to take a "hard look" at the comments. This process can be supplemented by hearings and oral presentation of argument.[56] Many government departments and local authorities in the United Kingdom make efforts to contact interested groups and individuals before bills, draft instruments, or bye-laws become law. A leading administrative lawyer Professor Wade, has spoken of the widespread practice of consultation by governmental bodies in relation to delegated legislation in the United Kingdom. It remains very often a discretionary and administrative practice, and even when duties to consult are enshrined in statute, they rarely provide opportunities which citizens can encash in terms of hard legal rights to participate.[57] In English law, there is no general presumption that parties will be consulted before legislative provisions or administrative rules are brought into effect, regardless of their ultimate importance or impact upon individuals.[58] When a general discretion to consult interested parties before making statutory orders or recommendations is present, the discretion is that of the designated official or politicians and though not unreviewable, it is extremely difficult to upset in practice. There has been little in the way of judicial insistence that a "hard look" is taken of views expressed where consultation does take place; that all parties are *fully* informed; and that reasons are provided as a matter of course even though there is no statutory duty to provide them.

The United States has afforded a more favourable climate in which law can be used as a method of mobilising political resources. This was achieved by liberalising the rules on standing and the development of class actions—a procedural device enabling a litigant whose claims are shared by, or similar to, numerous other individuals to litigate on behalf of their interests in court. If he wins, then remedial action and possibly large damages can be awarded to other members of the class. If he loses his individual claim, the court can deal with the class issue independently.[59] "Lawsuits involving the validity of governmental action

[56] The "hybrid" procedures. See Chap. 2.
[57] See Chaps. 2, 3 and 4, *supra. Cf. Aylesbury Mushrooms* v. *Agricultural, Horticultural and Forestry Industry Training Board* [1972] 1 All E.R. 280 (Q.B.D.) and *Lee* v. *Department of Education and Science* (1967) L.G.R. 211. *NB. R.* v. *Aylesbury Crown Court ex.p. Chahal* [1976] R.T.R. 489, D.C.; *Findlay* v. *Secretary of State for the Home Department* [1984] 3 W.L.R. 1159.
[58] *Bates* v. *Lord Hailsham of St. Marylebone* [1972] 1 W.L.R. 1373. It is different if there is an *individual decision* depriving somebody of something—either a right, a privilege or a "legitimate "expectation." And see: *Mahon* v. *Air N.Z. Ltd* [1984] 3 All E.R. 201, P.C., and Lord Roskill in the G.C.H.Q. litigation, n. 17.
[59] Chayes, "Developments in the Law-Class Actions" (1976) 89 Harv. L.R. 1318.

or inaction, rather than asserting private rights, have come to dominate Federal Civil Dockets."[60]

Throughout the 1970s, the Supreme Court sought to confine the wider interpretaton given to standing in the 1960s. This approach continues in the 1980's. Various cases have restricted the tests for standing[61] although *Duke Power Co.* v. *Carolina Environmental Study Group* has reaffirmed the sufficiency of environmental interests as a basis for standing. Freedom of Information legislation can be invoked by a "busy body" and specific Federal legislation can negative a restrictive interpretation of standing.[62]

Class actions have similarly been under judicial attack. Their use has been restricted in school segregation cases, civil rights, apportionment, environmental, consumer or other collective law suits aiming to vindicate rights of a more political and social nature.[63] The Supreme Court has treated the class as numerous individual claimants and claims and not as "a single jural entity capable of suing and being sued . . . constituted ad hoc for the very purpose of conducting a particular litigation and that its principal or only unifying characteristic is often the legal relationship or grievance in controversy." The onslaught on class actions has been more successful than that upon standing, and has concentrated on abstract legal and procedural technicalities.[64] Chayes concludes:

> "In standing cases . . . affluent or middle class plaintiffs seeking to vindicate environmental values seem to do pretty well . . . The losers (in class actions) are unwed mothers looking for child support, blacks, other minorities and the poor challenging patterns of police brutality or demanding access to adequate housing or medical services."

American courts have a far wider range of remedial devices at their disposal to give effect to their decisions in litigation of a public as opposed to a private nature. A declaration or court order upholding constitutional or legal rights in such litigation has been well described as merely the starting point of the realisation of those rights in practice.[65] The development of particular forms of

---

[60] Chayes, "Public Law Litigation and the Warren Court" (1982) 96 Harv. L.R. 4.
[61] *Sierra Club* v. *Morton* 405 U.S. 727 (1972); *Valley Forge Christian College* v. *Americans United for Separation of Church and State* 102 S. Ct. 752 (1982); *Simon* v. *Eastern Kentucky Welfare Rights Org.* 426 U.S. 26 (1976).
[62] *e.g.* on Clean Air and Clean Water Acts.
[63] Chayes, *op.cit.* n. 60, *supra.*
[64] *Zahn* v. *Int. Paper Co.* 414 U.S. 156 (1973); *Eisen Carlisle and Jaquelin* 417 U.S. 156 (1974); *General Telephone Co.* v. *Falcon* 102 S. Ct. 2364 (1982).
[65] Scheingold, *The Politics of Rights* (1974).

relief against public bodies to ensure that judicial decisions are implemented by large defendant bureaucracies has been a persistent theme in litigation since the 1960s. The special forms of relief owe their origin to judgments addressing segregated education and housing systems and reform of state penitentiary systems. Courts employed "special masters" who are administrative assistants to the court and who in prison cases aided "in implementing decrees in suits challenging conditions of confinement." Through "masters" the court will be supplied with "feed-back" of how its judgment is being implemented throughout a particular system. Their duties include fact-finding, investigating and reporting to the court after its decisions.[66] Stewart and Sunstein[67] describe the reaction of the courts in the United States to the "administrative state" with the creation of remedies "designed to increase public participation in agency decision-making." These they describe as rights of defence against unlawful action; rights of action and initiation whereby the courts have enjoined public bodies to make a decision conferring rights or benefits upon those seeking relief and which are very wide-ranging in impact as it seems the courts have been shaping the substantive outcome of the eventual decision of the body; lastly the "new property" hearing right concerned with legislative entitlement and the protection of interests by procedural fairness. Recent years have seen a judicial retrenchment in respect of the wide nature of judicial intervention in the provision of remedies against public bodies.[68] Nevertheless, commentators appear generally sanguine that the surrogate political process provided by courts in the United States, has still left a powerful apparatus through which alternative votes may be registered. It remains to be seen how successively it can survive assaults by the Executive and Supreme Court.[69]

Enough has been said to suggest that I am doubtful of the ability of our courts to develop a public law framework for litigation comparable with the United States. Attempts at creating such should be viewed with scepticism given that English law in its structure,

---

[66] (1979) 88 *Yale L.J.* 1062.

[67] Stewart and Sunstein, "Public Programs and Private Rights" (1982) 95 Harv.L.R. 1193. Injunctions are far more widely used against public bodies in the U.S.A. than they are in Britain.

[68] Chayes *op.cit.* n. 63, *supra* (1982); Lewis and Harden, "Law and the Local State" (1982) 5 *Urban Law and Policy* 65.

[69] On the executive side, see Executive Order 12,291,46 *Federal Register* 13193—placing limits on future rule-making; on the judicial side *Vermont Yankee* 98 S. Ct. 1197 (1978) limiting the contribution of "hybrid procedures" in rule-making; and *Industrial Union Dept. AFL C 10* v. *American Petroleum Institute* 448 U.S. 607 (1980). See n. 41, *supra*.

thought and culture is individualistic. At various stages, the common law has shown a remarkable strength and resilience when defending individuals against public excesses. But its philosophy has been the protection of property and proprietary interests, and not all can rest content that such a philosophy is appropriate to form a basis of protection for the range of needs and interests of citizens in a changing state structure. The point can be made by examining some of the technicalities involved in obtaining remedies against the state.

It seems that public law has been restricted to judicial review, statutory applications to quash and certain appeals.[70] The power to award damages on review under Order 53, r. 7 will seem now to have little application in practice.[71] To obtain damages, a citizen is best advised to sue in an action begun by writ or originating summons to vindicate a *private* right against a public body. When a party sues a public body in a cause of action,[72] one asserts rights of an individual nature which the common law or statute provides.[73] Although expressed to be common law, the State has many effective immunities from a liability in common with its citizens. This derives partly from legal quirks and accidents and partly from the privileged position of the Crown and public bodies which operate not as persons with a natural and private capacity, but with a

---

[70] To which objection will be taken that our constitutional law transcends these matters. Most of the corpus of constitutional law deals with the rules and conventions governing relationships between the various organs of the State and are not justiciable at the suit of individuals before the courts.

[71] See the arguments in the text, *supra*, and note Lord Scarman in *I.R.C.* v. *Rossminster* [1980] 1 All E.R. 80 at 105. There is a likelihood that a judge from the "Crown Office List" will try a private action involving a public body.

[72] Raising an estoppel against a public authority—that an official has made a representation to you which you have acted upon to your detriment or that it would be unfair for the authority to ignore—can be *enforced* by Order 53: *R.* v. *Liverpool Corporation ex.p. Liverpool Taxi Fleet Operators' Association* [1972] 2 Q.B. 299; *Att.-Gen. of Hong Kong* v. *Ng Yuen Shiu* [1983] 2 All E.R. 346 (P.C.); *R.* v. *I.R.C. ex.p. Preston* [1983] 2 All E.R. 300, as well as by raising a defence to enforcement proceedings, etc. More of a sword than a shield? *Preston* was reversed on appeal [1984] 3 All E.R. 625. *N.B. Ex p. Khan* [1985] 1 All E.R. 40, C.A.

[73] For the liability of the Crown, see Crown Proceedings Act 1947 and Hogg *Liability of the Crown in Australia, New Zealand and the U.K.* (1971). For breaches of statutory duty and when such breaches constitute a cause of action, see *Winfield and Jolowicz on Tort* (Rogers ed., 1979) Chap. 8. The Crown it appears cannot be sued for breach of a statutory duty unless the duty binds others apart from the Crown. For public corporations many of the statutory duties are so vague as to be virtually non-justiciable at the suit of an individual. The Crown is not bound by a statute unless the statute states that it is; and the Crown can take the benefit of a statute though not bound by it: *Town Investments* v. *Department of the Environment* [1977] 2 W.L.R. 450, H.L.

capacity framed in statutory and, for the Crown, prerogative powers.[73a] So for instance, governments cannot be estopped from developing or changing policy by pleas that they have acted or conducted themselves in a manner which an individual has relied upon or that they have made contracts or representations to which they must be bound if this prevents them from exercising their statutory or prerogative powers.[74] Likewise, public bodies cannot be held to representations made by themselves or servants which would result in them increasing their *vires*.[75] To allow this would be to encourage *ultra vires* activity—even though a perfectly innocent victim may suffer.[76] Recent decisions have attempted to allow representees to insist that public bodies stand by their representations where this would have the effect not of abusing, exceeding, or not exercising statutory powers but of rendering performance of those powers fairer.[77] The creation of a nuisance under statutory authority will carry no liability when Parliament has authorised, expressly or impliedly, the nuisance.[78]

Succeeding in actions against public bodies where the essence of the claim is negligence in the exercise of a statutory power is unlikely to meet with success when one is attacking the policy element of the decision, unless one can show that the decision is *ultra vires and* that it constitutes a breach of duty owed to the plaintiff in law to exercise reasonable care and the breach has caused the plaintiff harm which was forseeable.[79] These points are well developed elsewhere.[80] Should liability be established, compensation is paid out of the public purse which has many other demands upon it. The end result is that it is very difficult to succeed in actions against public bodies in private law where there is the additional burden of establishing that the activity is *ultra vires*; and those without a proprietary interest in the matter will have no cause of action. The common law has thrown the risk or burden in

---

[73a] Officials possess an *individual* liability.

[74] *The Amphitrite* [1921] 3 K.B. 500; *Laker Airways* v. *Department of Trade* [1977] Q.B. 643.

[75] A recent helpful discussion is in *Western Fish Products* v. *Penwith D.C.* [1981] 2 All E.R. 204, C.A.

[76] The case law in such instances is obscure and has caused confusion, often to avoid injustice. The services of the P.C.A. and C.L.A. should be recalled in this context.

[77] See cases in n. 72, *supra*.

[78] *Allen* v. *Gulf. Oil Refining Co.* [1981] A.C. 101, H.L.

[79] *Dorset Yacht Co.* v. *Home Office* [1970] A.C. 1004; *Anns* v. *Merton London Borough Council* [1978] A.C. 728; *Department of Health and Social Security* v. *Kinnear* (1984) 134 New L.J. 886.

[80] Craig *Administrative Law* (1983) Chap. 15.

these relationships upon private parties, to the advantage of the State and public purse. There is no liability for *ultra vires* activity *per se* unless a public body or official acts negligently; or maliciously or knowingly outside his powers or jurisdiction,[81] although it would appear that magistrates are not so protected.[82] This is a heavy burden for plaintiffs to overcome. Statutory schemes to compensate individuals for decisions rendering them the victims of the collective welfare, as in planning decisions or compulsory purchase causing blight, have gone some way to redress some of the deficiencies caused by common law, though the impetus of these decisions has been to move from a liability in law to conferral of a benefit under an administrative discretion.[83]

When a challenge is made upon the legality of action or decision-making of public bodies, the presumption is *omnia praesumuntur rite esse acta* which the plaintiff must displace on a balance of probabilities.[84] To establish the details of a decision will invariably require discovery of documentation where all the necessary evidence is not present on the record of the proceedings as in "judicial" processes. We have witnessed considerable erosion of judicial deference to pleas of Public Interest Immunity by Ministers or senior civil servants, so that even Cabinet documents can be the subject of an order for discovery.[85] Papers concerned with the governmental process at Ministerial level have been the subject of recent applications for discovery and pleas of Immunity, and it seems clear that in appropriate circumstances and subject to

---

[81] *Dunlop* v. *Woollahra Municipal Council* [1981] 2 W.L.R. 693, P.C.; *Bourgoin S.A.* v. *Ministry of Agriculture, The Times*, October 4, 1984. For punitive damages and oppressive government action, see *Rookes* v. *Barnard* [1964] A.C. 1129.

[82] Justices of the Peace Act 1979, s.45 and *McC.* v. *Mullan* [1984] 3 All E.R. 908, H.L. doubting *Sirros* v. *Moore* [1975] Q.B. 118.

[83] *e.g.* Land Compensation Act 1973; Vaccine Damage Payment Act 1979.

[84] For a graphic illustration see: *Cannock Chase D.C.* v. *Kelly* [1978] 1 W.L.R. 1, C.A. See n. 29, however. In the absence of evidence to the contrary, public bodies are presumed to have acted properly.

[85] The erstwhile Crown Privilege developed into Public Interest Immunity as an immunity for state bodies other than the Crown: *D.* v. *NSPCC* [1978] A.C. 171 though *cf.* Lord Scarman in *S.R.C.* v. *Nassé* [1979] 3 All E.R. 673, H.L. Both bodies in the above cases were incorporated by royal charter and "private," though only in *Nassé* was the immunity said not to exist. Clearly bodies in the public sector other than those of central government may avail themselves of the plea, whether successfully or not, but a private body will have to show a public interest in non-disclosure beyond confidentiality, *e.g.* information from informers as in *D.* v. *NSPCC*. For the discovery of documents of the highest class—cabinet documents—see Lords Scarman and Keith in *Burmah Oil Co.* v. *Bank of England and Att.-Gen.* [1979] 3 All E.R. 700, H.L.; and Lord Fraser in *Air Canada* v. *Secretary of State for Trade (No. 2)* [1983] 2 A.C. 394, H.L. doubting *dicta* of Lord Reid in *Conway* v. *Rimmer* [1968] A.C. 910.

the interests of state security, etc., they can be inspected by the judge if the applicant can persuade the judge that there is a "reasonable probability" that the documentation is very likely to assist his case and that it is necessary to dispose fairly of the case. A mere "hunch" that they might assist is not sufficient to cause the judge to look at the papers himself before he decides where the interests of justice lie: in discovery to assist the litigant in his cause, or in non-discovery to protect the public interest of security, frankness and confidentiality in public administration. The test which has to be satisfied before a judge inspects is an onerous one.[86] Public Interest Immunity is not confined to organs of central government, but its exact parameters are unclear.[87] There has been judicial reluctance to protect sources of information where there have been leaks to the media by civil servants or employees of nationalised industries. In the former case, the legal argument turned on the extent of the immunity for "persons" not to disclose photocopied documents revealing the identity of the "leak" as against Ministerial claims that recovery was necessary on the grounds of "national security"; in the latter that the information was necessary if British Steel was to protect its rights as an employer under contract or tort.[88] In neither case was there a "public interest" in knowing what was really happening in a Government department or knowing the reality of relationships between a Secretary of State and the British Steel Corporation which was considered important enough to protect the source of information from identification.

[86] Lords Scarman and Templeman in *Air Canada* believed the test of the majority was too strict. The State was treated as an ordinary individual who should not be subjected to fishing inquiries by litigants who might find something to assist their case. The State is not an ordinary individual. It does possess special immunities and it is a collector of vast amounts of information. Pleas against the State invariably involve an allegation of *ultra vires* activity and at a functional level this is invariably impossible to prove without evidence in the State's possession. "The task of the court was to decide the case fairly between the parties on the evidence available, and not to ascertain some independent truth by seeking out evidence of its own accord." The individual has to have some evidence of his own before he can ask the court for more.

[87] See n. 85, *supra*.

[88] *Secretary of State for Defence* v. *Guardian Newspapers* [1984] 3 W.L.R. 986, H.L. A 3–2 judgment ruled that it was in the "interests of national security" under the Contempt of Court Act 1981, s.10 for photocopied documents of the Defence Ministry to be handed back to the Crown to identify the "leak." Two dissentients did not believe the Crown had displaced the onus of establishing "national security" grounds, and the court rejected a proprietary claim defeating s.10 if it did not come within an exception. It seems that *B.S.C.* v. *Granada T.V.* [1982] A.C. 1096 (the nationalised industry case) might be decided differently under s.10. See: *Commonwealth of Australia* v. *John Fairfax and Sons* (1980) 32 A.L.J. 485.

The nature of relief offered under judicial review in England is of a narrow and limited dimension. Relief under Order 53 is discretionary not as of right, and reference has been made to time limits and procedural points.[89] The prerogative orders operate so as to insist that public bodies exercise their powers or duties properly and this is usually satisfied by a reconsideration of the issue, even if the public body comes to the same conclusion as it initially did. The court is concerned with *process* not substance.[90] Mandamus is a difficult remedy to obtain as its award may well impose financial obligations upon a public body if it is instructed to perform a public duty[91] and mandatory injunctions are likewise difficult to obtain.[92] A declaration cannot be awarded on an interim basis.

Courts appear reluctant to enforce statutory obligations upon public bodies where to do so would cause significant public expenditure. In cases concerned with the control of housing conditions under the Public Health Act 1936, the Divisional Court has given clear guidelines to magistrates on the exercise of their discretion if asked to issue a nuisance order under section 94(2) against an authority. The end effect was to moderate significantly the power of the nuisance order and the expense upon the authority, and a subsequent House of Lords decision effectively endorsed the approach of the Divisional Court.[93] Statutory obligations are interpreted benevolently for the authority. Under the Housing (Homeless Persons) Act, Lord Denning said that the decision-making of authorities should be looked at "benevolently" *vis à vis* homeless applicants. Even when a tenant won in litigation against a public landlord which was found to be in breach of statutory covenants, the judgments were framed so as to give clear guidelines to authorities on how to circumscribe the apparent effects of the decision.[94] McAuslan argues that these cases should be compared with the frequent occasions when courts give succour to private landlords—often property companies—when local authorities claim the former are breaking their duties under Housing and Pub-

---

[89] See n. 25a, n. 34 and n. 35, *supra*.

[90] See r.9(4); and also *Shah* v. *Barnet B.C.* [1983] 1 All E.R. 226 at 239–240, *per* Lord Scarman on limitations of mandamus; *Chief Constable of North Wales Police* v. *Evans* [1982] 3 All E.R. 141, H.L.

[91] *R.* v. *Bristol Corporation ex.p. Hendy* [1974] 1 W.L.R. 498, C.A.

[92] See n. 34, *supra*. Even awards of habeas corpus have recently been held to be subject to public convenience: *R.* v. *Governor of Brixton Prison, ex.p. Walsh* [1984] 3 W.L.R. 205, H.L.

[93] *Nottingham City D.C.* v. *Newton* [1974] 1 W.L.R. 923, *Salford C.C.* v. *McNally* [1975] 2 All E.R. 860, H.L.

[94] *Liverpool C.C.* v. *Irwin* [1976] 2 All E.R. 39, H.L. See also McAuslan, *op.cit.*

lic Health Acts. The picture painted is often of a beleaguered individual beset by rapacious authority—a cameo which is often difficult to reconcile with the facts.[95]

Conclusion

I will conclude by arguing that there is a bias towards inertia in the British Constitution. Law is a special product of this inertia. The important biases operate at a systemic not a personal level. Law is presented as being beyond personal preferences and above political conflict. Yet its method is to transmute conflicts of political, economic and social moment into disputes between *individuals* based upon individual entitlement and duty. The techniques of law operate to conceal the biases inhering in its structure. A conflict, for instance, about the best way of producing a suitable transport policy for the urban environment becomes an issue concerned with the fiduciary duties owed by an authority to its beneficiaries as if the former were a private trust.[96]

The idea of law often conveys a basic set of moral imperatives or a belief that legal processes can provide an opportunity to establish what basic moral imperatives are and what they dictate in particular circumstances, or how they should inform the working of public institutions. If we expect something of this order from our courts, we will face disappointment. If judges attempt it, the results could be disastrous. Senior judges may look with expectation on the possibilities of "procedural public law," but it is doubtful whether the role of our courts, free from prior restraint, is going to alter significantly in resolving grievances or providing remedies against the State.

My own attitude is to look with favour on the creation of an independent and prestigious overseer of public administration, possibly developing the *Wass* model. The Council on Tribunals was deliberately starved of such potential and the Administrative Conference of the United States established in 1964 to "identify causes of inefficiency delay and unfairness in administration" may hold some useful lessons. Engaging a full-time chairman and staff, it sub-contracts its research to outside experts. It comprises nine

---

[95] McAuslan *op.cit.* Chap. 7, pp. 195–210.
[96] The "Fares Fair" *dispute* in *Bromley L.B.C.* v. *GLC*. Or the respective merits of alternative educational philosophies become an issue of abstruse and pettifogging statutory construction of terms such as "reasonable" on the presumption that such vague terms are susceptible to definitive objective analysis: *Tameside* and s.68 of the Education Act 1944.

standing committees dealing with specialised topics.[97] It is essential that such a body's membership is independent of Government and that its recommendations have bite.[98] I have made suggestions for administrative reforms in this chapter and throughout the book. I would add the necessity for a Freedom of Information Act. These are big hopes and it remains unlikely that our Governmental élites will meet them, though some of them have attracted the support of a former Permanent Secretary of the Treasury.

Just in case the judiciary prompt our public administration under Order 53 to engage in a re-examination of its values, then these concomitant contributions towards a greater openness and accountability would be desirable were judicial involvement to engender a movement towards "responsive"and "reflexive" law.[99] The former concentrates upon the purposive quality of law and its encouragement for affected communities to participate in government and administration. The latter sees law providing "regulated autonomy . . . which will redefine and redistribute property rights (and) create the structural premises for a decentralised integration of society by supporting integrative mechanisms within autonomous social systems . . . (relying) on procedural norms that regulate processes, organisations and distribution of rights and competencies."[1] It might sound a little like corporatism with a conscience, but has the time not been reached when the final death knell is given to the belief "if administration is to be beneficial and effective, it must be master of its own procedure"?[2]

---

[97] *e.g.* Regulation of Business; Public Access and Information; Grants, Benefits and Contracts; Judicial Review; Rule-Making, etc. The record of the Conference is mixed, and it has not convinced all that it is sufficiently independent of the Executive: see *Taming Leviathan* S.D.P. (1983).

[98] And here, of course, everything depends upon the Government. See: Wass, *Government and the Governed* (1984), *supra.*

[99] Nonet and Selznick, *Towards Responsive Law* (1978); Teubner, "Substantive and Reflexive Elements in Modern Law" (1983) 17 *Law and Society Review* 239.

[1] Teubner *op.cit.* pp. 254–255. Should it sound a little far-fetched, look at the recommendations of Professor Gower for reform of the institutions in the investor market, Cmnd. 9125 (1984).

[2] *Per* Lord Shaw, *Local Government Board* v. *Arlidge* [1915] A.C. 120.

INDEX